Catholicism and the Welfare State in Secular France

To my parents,
for loving and continuously encouraging me over the years

CATHOLICISM AND THE WELFARE STATE IN SECULAR FRANCE

FABIO
BOLZONAR

LEUVEN UNIVERSITY PRESS

This book appears in the peer-reviewed series
KADOC Studies on Religion, Culture & Society

ISBN 978 94 6270 388 9
eISBN 978 94 6166 533 1
D/2023/1869/34
https://doi.org/10.11116/9789461665331
NUR: 704

CONTENTS

PREFACE

This book, which is loosely based on my doctoral dissertation, is the outcome of a long intellectual journey that led me to meet different people in different countries and to benefit from the exchanges I had with them. In this sense, this book is the outcome of a collective enterprise.

I started to be intrigued by the relationships between religion and politics when I studied at the University of Milan, from where I first graduated in Philosophy and then in International Studies. My early interest in this broad field led me to study Part III and IV of *Leviathan*, in which Thomas Hobbes presented most of his theological doctrines. Even though that part of Hobbes' masterpiece is almost equally as long as Books I and II, it is overlooked by courses in Political Philosophy and Political Theory. What guided me was not a precise hypothesis on the linkages between religion and politics, but, rather, the vague idea that religious ideas can still leave a remarkable imprint on the public decisions in our secularized European societies.

I further developed my research interests at the University of Edinburgh. Its School of Social and Political Studies is a wonderful place to study. There, I met Stephen Kemp, Daniel Clegg, Allison Smith, and Ingela Naumann. The long discussions I had with them helped me refine my ideas and they became a proper research project that I developed at the University of Cambridge, under the supervision of Professor Göran Therborn. I owe immense gratitude to Professor Therborn. He is not only one of the most intellectually brilliant scholars I have ever met but also a caring person. Without his constant academic and personal support, I would never have completed my doctoral studies and this book would never have seen the light of day.

I am also greatly indebted to several scholars that I met in the universities where I studied and worked over the years. It is not possible to mention all of them. However, I would like to thank David Lehmann from Cambridge University, James Midgley, Peter Evans, Michael Austin, and Jonah Levy from the University of California, Berkeley, Denis Pelletier from École Pratique des Hautes Études in Paris, Luca Ozzano from the University of Turin, and Airo Hino from Waseda University. All of them gave me useful advice to improve my work, and some of them had also the patience to attentively read some sections of my manuscript.

The revision of the original manuscript of this book accompanied me for some years. The several projects in which I was involved over time led me to postpone it. In the meantime, important works have been published about the subjects covered by this book. After having struggled to engage with the most recent scholarship, I decided to leave the manuscript almost as it was. If I continued to keep pace with this scholarship, I think this book would have never been published. I would like to apologize for this limitation of my study and I would kindly ask the reader to consider this book as a reasonable state of the art in the mid and late 2010s.

This book has also been the result of personal experience that allows me to continue to believe in my work, despite some setbacks. However, it would not have been possible to go through difficult moments without the love of my parents and the support of several great friends, notably Andrea, Edoardo, Enrico, Fabio, Gianluca, Giulia, Laura, Marco, Osvaldo, Polina, and Silvia.

Finally, I wish to give a special thank you to Professor Patrick Pasture, who believed that my manuscript was worth developing into a book and encouraged me to publish it and Luc Vints of KADOC, who showed endless patience during the editorial process.

As always, all mistakes in this book are the responsibility of the author.

Bolzonar Fabio
Paris, 18 May 2023

PART I

1
INTRODUCTION

In the first paragraphs of *Sociology of Religion*, Max Weber pointed out that "the most elementary forms of behaviour motivated by religious or magical factors are oriented to this word [...] Thus, religious or magical behaviour or thinking must not be set apart from the range of everyday purposive conduct".[1] In Weber's opinion, social scientists should make an effort to study the changing characteristics of religiously motivated behaviours and the varying historical circumstances that allow ideas to shape social and economic activities.[2] This book takes Weber's idea seriously and it investigates the influence of Catholicism on the historical development of the French welfare state since the Second World War.

Even though the policy impact of religious values, notably Catholicism, has been increasingly acknowledged, the academic literature has overlooked their changing influence over a long time frame.[3] This lacuna can impede an adequate theorization of the impact of Catholicism in the social policy domain

1 Weber, *The Sociology of Religion*, 1.
2 Swidler, 'Foreword', ix.
3 Bäckström, et al., eds, *Welfare and Religion in 21st Century Europe. Volume 1*; Chamberlayne et al., eds, *Welfare and Culture in Europe*; Esping-Andersen, *The Three Worlds of Welfare Capitalism*; Flora and Heidenheimer, 'Introduction', 5-14; Huber and Stephens, *Development and Crisis of the Welfare State*; Jordan, 'Religion and inequality'; Manow, 'The "good, the bad and the ugly"; Manow and Palier, 'A Conservative Welfare State Regime without Christian Democracy?'; Palier, 'Les transformations du modèle social français hérité de l'après-guerre'; Van Kersbergen, *Social Capitalism*; Van Oorschot, Opielka and Pfau-Effinger, eds, *Culture and Welfare State*; Wilensky, 'Leftism, Catholicism and Democratic Comporatism'.

as the study of long periods of time enable a better assessment of the macro-structural changes in comparison with specific periods that may be subject to the influence of contingent factors.[4]

This book aims to contribute to a theory of the mobilization of Catholicism in shaping the development of social policies in contemporary Western European societies. This is done in three main ways. First, it focuses on values and how they influence social legislation. Second, it pays attention not only to the political decisions taken by Christian democratic parties, but also to the mobilization of other social and political actors inspired by Catholic values. Though Christian democracy played a crucial role in shaping some continental welfare states, social policies with a Catholic imprint were also supported by right-wing parties, voluntary organizations, and social movements. The influence on these actors should be considered in order to gain a more comprehensive understanding of the impact of Catholicism on social policies. Third, it extends the period that is usually taken into consideration by the scholarship on the influence of Catholicism on social protection by investigating the social policy changes introduced during the Occupation (Chapter 2) and from the mid 1990s to the mid 2010s (Chapters 6 and 7).

Although the welfare state literature is the main reference for this study, the various chapters are also indebted to the scholarship on secularization, pressure groups, and social movements. Working at the interstice between scholarly fields and cross-fertilizing them is a useful research strategy to study the complex and multi-level changing role of religion in current times.[5]

This book is based on the investigation of several social policy developments in France since the years of the Vichy regime. France was chosen because is a particularly difficult, but at the same time intriguing, case for the questions here under investigation. Catholicism has managed to leave its imprint on the French system of social protection despite the great effort to secularize the social domain during the Third Republic (1871-1940), the disappearance of the French Christian democratic party (Mouvement Républicain Populaire, MRP) in 1967, the deconfessionalization of the main Catholic labour union (Confédération Française des Travailleurs Chrétiens, CFTC) in 1964, the dramatic secularization of French society, and the assertive secularism of public authorities.[6] Even though the chapters of this book are focused on France, we hope that its conclusions can provide some insights into the impact of Catholicism in other Western European countries where Catholicism

4 Braudel, 'Histoire et sciences sociales', 13-15.

5 Davie, *The Sociology of Religion*, 130.

6 Kuru, 'Passive and assertive secularism'; Manow and Palier, 'A Conservative Welfare State Regime without Christian Democracy?', 159-171. At the congress of Paris on 6-7 November 1964, 70.1 per cent of the delegates approved the change of name of the CFTC to the Confédération Française Démocratique du Travail (CFDT), and they modified the statute whose preamble cancelled any reference to Christian social morality. See Adam, *La CFTC*, 89.

has shown stronger resilience to the process of secularization and in which there have been more favourable institutional conditions than in France for the penetration of religious values into the policy domain.

The remaining part of this introductory chapter is divided into three parts. The first one discusses some of the main works on the impact of Catholicism on contemporary welfare states that inspired the research undertaken for this book. The second part presents the methodological approach of our study. Finally, the third part provides an outline of the book.

Catholicism and the Welfare State: Beyond Christian Democracy

Catholic social thinking or Catholic social thought is the intellectual underpinning of the mobilizations of Catholic and Catholic-inspired actors to shape Western welfare states.[7] Four features distinguish this body of thought. First, Catholic social thought is "not static but dynamic in response to changing circumstances and needs". [8] In its almost 125 years of existence, Catholic social thought has been moulded by historical events and it has adapted to new contexts.[9] For example, post-war Christian democratic social reformers in France and Italy dismissed the corporatist ideas that inspired social Catholics in the first half of the twentieth century because they recalled memories of the corporatist experience of fascism in Italy and the Vichy regime in France.[10] In contrast, South American Christian democratic parties have generally been more keen to advocate corporatist arrangements because they did not have the inhibitions about corporatism that characterized European Christian democrats. Second, Catholic social thought has attempted to articulate a third way "between statist socialism and liberal capitalism and has insisted that the economy is to serve the needs of people".[11] Third, Catholic social thought draws its principles from scripture and natural law tradition.[12] However, as we will show in this book, in more recent times Catholic authorities and Catholic-inspired actors have increasingly abstained from using religious arguments derived from doctrinal documents to sustain their positions in public debates. Instead, Catholic authorities have relied more on common-sense statements, religious interpretations of humanistic values (e.g. human dignity and non-discrimination), and scientific or pseudo-scientific theories. In other words,

7 Boswell, McHugh and Verstraeten, *Catholic Social Thought*; Curran, *Catholic Social Teaching and Pope Benedict XVI*, 1.
8 Hornsby-Smith, *An Introduction to Catholic Social Thought*, 85.
9 Curran, *Catholic Social Teaching and Pope Benedict XVI*, 66.
10 Grew, 'Suspended Bridges to Democracy', 22.
11 Hornsby-Smith, *An Introduction to Catholic Social Thought*, 85.
12 Ibid., 85.

the Catholic discourse has undergone a kind of 'internal secularization' to broaden its resonance. Fourth, "Catholic social thinking flows from numerous sources".[13] Although the encyclical *Rerum Novarum* issued by Pope Leo XII in 1891 is a landmark document of social Catholicism, Catholic social thought is older than Leo XII's encyclical. It started to be elaborated and disseminated in the early decades of the nineteenth century through the publications by Catholic intellectuals and the experiences of Catholic social reformers who wished to apply Catholic values to tackling the problems of their times.[14] In France, for instance, the origins of social Catholicism can be traced back to the social engagement of reactionary, liberal, and conservative Catholics who rejected the social transformations of the industrial society and were concerned about the spread of socialist ideas among the working classes.[15] The heterogeneity of Catholic social thought should not be interpreted as a weakness. Instead, it is probably its strength. As pointed out by Catherine Audard in relation to liberalism, an ethical or a political doctrine can be strengthened by its internal pluralism as it enables the doctrine to widen its resonance among various social classes.[16] In consideration of the heterogeneity and internal pluralism of Catholicism, it is probably more appropriate to speak of multiple forms of Catholic social thought that vary over time and contexts. However, we can individuate some core themes of Catholic social teaching in the special concern for the poor, the promotion of social solidarity, the defence of the common good, and the advocacy of the principle of subsidiarity.[17] Through the defence of these ideals, the Catholic Church wished to indicate pragmatic ways to deal with social problems and maintain its prophetic integrity.[18]

The current scholarship started to acknowledge the impact of Catholic social teaching on welfare state arrangements only in the late 1970s. The recognition of the importance of Catholicism was mainly a consequence of the incapacity of the then dominant theoretical paradigms to explain the welfare developments in several European continental countries.[19] At that time, the existing academic literature was deeply influenced by the power resources approach, a paradigm that essentially argues that the decisive cleavage in Western countries is the opposition between capital and labour, bringing enduring conflicts between left-wing social and political actors (i.e. socialist or social democratic parties and labour unions) and employers over the redistribution

13 Ibid., 85-86.

14 Cahill, 'Catholic Social Teaching', 67.

15 Duroselle, *Les débuts du Catholicisme social en France.*

16 Audard, *Qu'est-ce que le libéralisme?* 12.

17 Benedict XVI, *Address of His Holiness Benedict XVI to the Participants in the 14th Session of the Pontifical Academy of Social Sciences*; Curran, *Catholic Social Teaching and Pope Benedict XVI*, 66; Kim, *An Introduction to Catholic Ethics since Vatican II.*

18 O'Brien and Shannon, *Catholic Social Thought*, 7.

19 Van Kersbergen, *Social Capitalism*, 15.

of national wealth.[20] The strength of left-wing parties and trade unions was positively correlated with the expansion of welfare states. To sustain this conclusion, several scholars took the case of Sweden as an example. In this country, the Swedish social democratic party had a pivotal role from the late 1940s to the mid 1970s and introduced generous social policies. Without entering a discussion on the weaknesses of the power resources approach, for the questions under investigation in this book two main criticisms can be made of this paradigm. First, the contraposition between left-wing parties and unions, on one side, and employers' organizations and the actors that supported them (e.g. liberal-oriented parties), on the other, is a simplistic perspective from which to study the development of welfare states. New social programmes have been introduced by conservative and right-wing governments too. The great expansion of the French system of social protection, for instance, happened between the middle of the 1940s and the late 1970s (the so-called 'Glorious Thirty'), which was a political period dominated by right-wing parties.[21] In this sense, empirical evidence suggests paying attention to not only the influence of left-wing parties to explain welfare state developments, but also the programmatic platforms of other parties, the dynamics of national politics, the capacity of social and political entrepreneurs to build up political coalitions to promote the expansion of social protection, and so on. Second, the opposition between labour and capital was not the only, nor always the most important, social cleavage. In some continental European countries, such as France, Germany, Italy, and the Netherlands, for instance, the religious cleavage provoked by state-church conflicts had a more important impact than the labour-capital cleavage on policy reforms and determined the timing and the evolution of welfare states.[22]

In some of the early studies on the influence of Catholicism on social policies, Harold Wilensky and John Stephens individuated some elements of Catholic ideology (e.g. the anti-capitalist positions of the Church, its positive attitudes toward the introduction of policies against poverty, and the notion of a just wage) that inspired the mobilization of Christian democratic parties.[23] Although Wilensky's and Stephens' works opened new research avenues for welfare state scholarship, their conclusions were jeopardized by the questionable reliability of the databases they used. Furthermore, their focus on aggregate social expenditure did not allow them to explore the complexity of the

20 Castles, *The Social Democratic Image of Society*; Esping-Andersen, *Politics against Markets*; Korpi, *Working Class in Welfare Capitalism*; Stephens, *The Transition from Capitalism to Socialism*.

21 Ambler, 'Ideas, Interests and the French Welfare State', 1.

22 Flora and Alber, 'Modernization, Democratization, and the Development of the Welfare State', 43.

23 Wilensky, 'Leftism, Catholicism and Democratic Comporatism'; Stephens, *The Transition from Capitalism to Socialism*, 100.

historical circumstances that made Catholicism an important causal factor in shaping welfare state arrangements.[24]

Gøsta Esping-Andersen's book *The Three Worlds of Welfare Capitalism* was a decisive step toward a more theoretically refined conceptualization of the role of religion in influencing Western welfare states. According to Esping-Andersen, the systems of social protection can be distinguished in accordance with their degree of de-commodification, the possibility of individuals or families upholding acceptable standards of living without relying on markets, and social stratification, the capacity of the welfare state in the ordering of social relations. On the basis of these two concepts, Esping-Andersen identifies three kinds of welfare regimes: liberal, conservative, and social democratic.[25] The conservative ideal type bears the historical imprint of Catholicism and the influence of the Church.[26] It clusters Austria, France, Germany, and Italy. In contrast with liberal regimes, conservative welfare states share the social democratic belief that the effects of the market economy should be corrected by policy interventions. However, the level of de-commodification of conservative welfare states is generally lower than in social democratic ones (i.e. Denmark, Finland, Norway, and Sweden). Furthermore, in conservative regimes, social rights are attached to status as they provide distinct programmes for different status groups, and social policies have a limited redistributive impact as they are aimed at preserving social differences rather than promoting equality. Finally, their legislation tends to favour large families and the preservation of the male breadwinner model.[27]

Esping-Andersen's theorization had the great merit of indicating the ideological and political foundations of distinct welfare state ideal types. However, its conclusions are flawed by several weaknesses that have been pointed out by subsequent scholarship. For the purposes of this book, three criticisms seem particularly relevant. First, Esping-Andersen overlooked several crucial questions, such as the ways social services are delivered and the impact of social policies on the changing role of women in the family and in the labour market. Second, he did not study how transformations in social values were related to the reforms of the institutional settings of welfare regimes. Third, he did not pay attention to less institutionalized actors, such as civil society associations or social movements. Voluntary groups have traditionally been important actors in delivering several social services in Germany and Italy, and the recent change in the public-private mix in welfare states has prompted religion-based voluntary organizations to take on greater responsibilities in

24 Therborn, 'Another way of taking religion seriously', 109.
25 Esping-Andersen, *The Three Worlds of Welfare Capitalism*, 26-29.
26 Ibid., 27, 40, 60.
27 Ibid., 24-27.

many European countries.[28] These theoretical and empirical lacunae prevented Esping-Andersen from providing a comprehensive picture of conservative welfare regimes.

Kees Van Kersbergen's *Social Capitalism* developed Esping-Andersen's theorization and overcame some of the shortcomings that affect it. In this work, the author recognized a distinctive type of welfare state that bears the imprint of Catholic values.[29] This kind of welfare state, which is the outcome of the mobilization of Christian democracy, is called by the author social capitalism.[30] The most salient characteristics of social capitalism are: social policies heavily oriented to cash transfers; passive employment policies that discourage female participation in the labour market; the aim of minimizing public authorities' control of the welfare state; the high level of fragmentation of social programmes; and the limited vertical redistributive impact of social policies. Moreover, social capitalism shows a preference for families rather than individuals as social rights tend to be granted to the (male) head of the family rather than to individuals.[31]

Van Kersbergen's observations are supported by accurate statistical analyses of social expenditure and the study of the political and electoral strategies of Christian democratic parties since the early years after the Liberation. The 'methodological promiscuity' of Van Kersbergen's study allowed him to reach several insightful conclusions on the characteristics of conservative welfare states that the current scholarship has also labelled Christian democratic, Continental European or Bismarckian welfare states. However, we can make two main observations about *Social Capitalism*. First, Van Kersbergen does not adequately consider how Catholic values mixed up with other ideals and interests in different periods and national contexts. In other words, we think that *Social Capitalism* should have paid closer attention to how and why Catholic social ideals were adapted to the different social capitalist countries over time and welfare policies were influenced by the power of political actors, previous institutional arrangements, and distinct political cultures. For example, among other continental welfare states, France stands out for its progressive gender and family policies. In this country, the "weakness of Christian democracy and the subordination of the voluntary sector to state power diminished the political strength of those espousing conservative views concerning gender roles and the family".[32] The Italian welfare state bears the strong imprint of the clientelism used by the Italian Christian democratic par-

28 Alber, 'A framework for the comparative study of social services'; Bäckström and Davie, 'A Preliminary Conclusion', 189.
29 Van Kersbergen, *Social Capitalism*, 4.
30 Ibid., 236.
31 Ibid., 4.
32 Morgan, 'The politics of mothers' employment', 289.

ty (Democrazia Cristiana, DC) to strengthen its political support through the distribution of economic favours.[33]

Second, Van Kersbergen's book devoted almost exclusive attention to political parties and labour unions and neglected the role played by the Catholic civil society associations that were a key component of Christian democracy.[34] In some countries, in the first half of the twentieth century, Catholic associations contributed to the political socialization of Christian democratic leaders, the majority of whom came from the different branches of Catholic Action.[35] In the late 1960s, in France and in several other Western countries, left-wing Catholic organizations were quite active in advocating the expansion of social protection.[36] A study of the impact of Catholicism on the welfare state would miss something important if it did not consider the social reforms advocated by Catholic and Catholic-inspired voluntary organizations and their involvement in the management of social programmes. This seems particularly relevant in the current times because the process of welfare retrenchment, budgetary constraints, and declining trust in public authorities have led several governments to devolve important policy competences to voluntary organizations.[37]

Since the mid 1990s, a burgeoning body of scholarship has investigated the influence of values and ideas on public policies.[38] Some studies have acknowledged the imprint of religious values on the roots of modern welfare states and the institutional settings of some core social policy areas, such as elderly care, family social legislation, and poverty policies.[39] The changes undergone by continental European welfare states have arguably been the question that has particularly attracted the attention of scholars.[40] Continental or Christian democratic welfare states were described as frozen landscapes, but they eventually began to change.[41] Although this conclusion is largely shared by the current scholarship, the causes and the patterns of the intervening transformations have been the object of debate. For example, Bruno Palier argued that social policy transformations that characterized continental European welfare systems happened through the gradual layering of policy in-

33 Ferrera, 'The 'southern model' of welfare in social Europe', 25.

34 Kalyvas, *The Rise of Christian Democracy in Europe*, 113.

35 Mayeur, *Des partis catholiques à la démocratie chrétienne*, 167.

36 Gerd-Rainer and Gerard, eds, *Left Catholicism.*

37 Bäckström et al, eds, *Welfare and Religion in 21st Century Europe. Volume 1.*

38 Béland and Cox, eds, *Ideas and Politics in Social Science Research*; Engeli, Green-Pedersen and Thorup Larsen, eds, *Morality Politics in Western Europe*; Knill, Adam and Hurka, eds, *On the Road to Permissiveness?*; Knill et al., 'Religious tides'; Van Oorschot, Opielka and Pfau-Effinger, eds, *Culture and Welfare State.*

39 Alber, 'A framework for the comparative study of social services', 145-146; Fix, *Religion und familienpolitik*; Manow, 'The "good, the bad and the ugly"', 8; Kahl, 'The religious roots of modern poverty policy', 92-95; Opielka, 'Christian Foundations of the Welfare State', 102-103.

40 Kalyvas and Van Kersbergen, 'Christian democracy', 198-200.

41 Esping-Andersen, 'Welfare State without Work', 24.

novations over existing institutional settings. Though policy developments have generally been introduced at the margins of social protection, their accumulation has produced remarkable changes.[42] These transformations did not completely erase the Christian democratic imprint of continental European welfare states also in those countries that experienced a dramatic process of secularization and Catholic-oriented parties disappeared or lost much of their previous influence. In France, for instance, the persistence of the Christian democracy imprint on the welfare state depended on the fact that the MRP shaped social protection in the early post-war years, which was a crucial period for its refoundation. This has allowed Catholicism to leave a long-standing imprint on French social security even after the decline and the final disbanding of the MRP.[43] According to Jonah Levy, Christian democratic welfare states of continental Western Europe attenuated some of their historic 'vices' or inequities (such as disability benefits for people who were not sick or disabled) to pursue 'virtuous' goals: "redistributing income toward the poor without increasing public spending; improving the functioning of the economy without reducing benefits to the truly needy; and facilitating (through side-payments) the negotiation of far-reaching, tripartite social pacts".[44]

In contrast to Palier, Martin Seeleib-Kaiser et al. noted that the policy changes implemented in Austria, Germany, and the Netherlands since 1975 did not follow any clear direction.[45] Their extent was also quite limited in comparison with those of the so-called Glorious Thirty. On the other hand, there has been a gradual convergence between the policies promoted by Christian democracy and social democracy. This process of convergence is defined by the authors as liberal communitarianism, meaning a modernized version of Christian democratic welfare states characterized by supply-side policies, withdrawal from the male breadwinner model, and promotion of the role of the market in addressing social problems. Furthermore, the political coalitions in power in Christian democratic welfare states showed their enduring support for family policies and the promotion of legislative measures aimed at strengthening social cohesion, which are two political goals that have been often promoted by Christian democratic parties.[46]

Unfortunately, the studies by Palier, Levy, and Seeleib-Kaiser overlooked the class coalitions that promoted the policy transformations that they describe. A book edited by Philip Manow and Kees Van Kersbergen has provided a penetrating explanation of this latter issue by investigating the relationship between social cleavages, electoral rules, and class coalitions in determining

42 Palier, 'Ordering Change', 89.
43 Manow and Palier, 'A Conservative Welfare State Regime without Christian Democracy?, 159-171.
44 Levy, 'Vice into virtue?', 240.
45 Seeleib-Kaiser, van Dyk and Roggenkamp, *Party Politics and Social Welfare*, 159.
46 Ibid., 159-163.

welfare state developments. In a nutshell, the authors claimed that proportional electoral systems allowed the institutionalization of the religious cleavage in those countries characterized by serious tension between religious hierarchies and public authorities. As a consequence, political parties in defence of religious values were established and these parties promoted the formation of social coalitions that supported the creation of Christian democratic welfare states.[47]

This analysis, which deemphasizes the influence of Catholic values, can be suitable to explain the complex origin of welfare states that bear the imprint of Catholicism, but it does not shed much light on the most recent transformations of Christian democratic welfare regimes. In this sense, Manow and Van Kersbergen's study seems to conclude that religious influence on welfare states is a phenomenon of the past. In so doing, the book dismisses the new role played by Catholic and Catholic-inspired actors in the social domain and their changing lobbying strategies in contemporary secularized societies.

To better approach these topics, we should consider the academic literature on secularization. Until the late 1970s the sociological scholarship was heavily influenced by the paradigm of secularization: those theories of religion elaborated in the 1960s and 1970s that claimed that modernization goes hand in hand with secularization, and thereby the more modern our societies become, the less religious they will be.[48] Several studies pointed out that the process of urbanization has disrupted the traditional social networks of rural communities instilled with religious beliefs and rituals, the increasing trust in scientific explanations of reality has replaced religious narratives, and the Roman Catholic Church's history of covering up child sexual abuse have further weakened the authority of Catholic hierarchies.[49] More recently, Ronald Inglehart, among others, has noted that secularization has accelerated in the twentieth century "largely because of rising existential security and a shift from pro-fertility norms to individual-choice norms". In other words, "pro-fertility norms are no longer needed for societal survival, and individual-choice norms are spreading rapidly in much of the world, undermining religiosity".[50] Can we say, following Charles Taylor, that we are living in a secular age and we "can engage fully in politics without ever encountering God"?[51]

47 Manow and Van Kersbergen, 'Religion and the Western Welfare State', 14-28.

48 Berger, *The Sacred Canopy*; Luckmann, *The Invisible Religion*; Martin, *A General Theory of Secularization*; Wilson, *Religion in Secular Society.*

49 Gill, 'Religion and comparative politics', 121; Inglehart, *Religion's Sudden Decline*, 2; Norris and Inglehart, *Sacred and Secular*; Stark and Finke, *Acts of Faith*, 61; Voicu, 'Religion and gender across Europe', 146.

50 Inglehart, *Religion's Sudden Decline*, 16.

51 Taylor, *A Secular Age*, 1.

It is challenging to provide a straightforward answer to this question. Since the late 1980s, scholars have become increasingly critical of the paradigm of secularization. Some historical studies have pointed out that the theories of secularization have never found adequate empirical confirmation.[52] Taylor's claims are probably an overstatement and his conclusions are partly flawed by the fact that he draws them mainly from the study of Western countries.[53] If we broaden our perspective, we can note that the world we live in is not becoming more secular, but more religious.[54] Arguably Western Europe is the only exception to the global trend of a return to religion. However, also in this part of the world the social influence of religion should be closely scrutinized because there is still much to understand about the changing role played by religious values in the public domain and the process of secularization does not necessarily imply the disappearance of religion from secular societies.[55] In several European countries diffused religious values, hollowed out of their confessional imprint, continue to be a symbolic reference for a large part of the population.[56] Religion still remains an important factor in shaping political alignment and voting behaviour.[57] For instance, the identity of the Union pour un Mouvement Populaire (UMP), France's largest right-wing party in the first decade of the twenty-first century, was based on an implicit reference to the Christian democratic legacy.[58] In a study of the French mainstream Right, Florence Haegel highlighted how the UMP tended to attract the largest number of votes from the Catholic electorate and how Catholic values constituted an enduring source of inspiration for a great majority of UMP militants.[59] As pointed out by Steve Bruce, one of the staunchest defenders of the thesis of secularization, today, no modern sociologist thinks that secularization is inevitable. The so-called paradigm of secularization "was an exercise in historical explanation" rather than a physics-like law.[60]

In consideration of the contrasting indicators about the role of religion in the public sphere, it would be more interesting to investigate how the social influence of religion has changed rather than discussing its stronger or declining influence. This would permit us to move beyond the debate on seculariza-

52 Gorski and Altınordu, 'After Secularization?', 55; Stark, 'Secularization, R.I.P.', 249.
53 Fox, *An Introduction to Religion and Politics*, 36-37.
54 Berger, 'Religious Transformations and the Future of Politics', 2-4; Ferrarotti, *La religione dissacrante*, 35.
55 Berger, 'Religious Transformations and the Future of Politics', 6; Pelletier, *La crise catholique*, 7.
56 Cipriani, *Diffused Religion*; Le Bras and Todd, *Le mystère français*, 8.
57 Bréchon, 'La religion, le facteur le plus explicatif du vote!', *Le Figaro*, 7 May 2012; Haegel, *Les droites en fusion*, 233.
58 In May 2015, this party was rebranded Les Républicains. Rémond, *Les droites aujourd'hui*, 237.
59 Haegel, *Les droites en fusion*, 229-231
60 Bruce, *Secularization*, 3-4.

tion in order to explore the current transformations of the religious field, the adaptation of religions to the modern world, and study the new discourses, identities, and strategies of religious and religious-inspired actors.[61]

Previous studies have noted that not only religion has never disappeared from the public sphere, but there has always been a return to religion.[62] This process is the result of the failure of the process of advanced modernization that has been unable to fulfil the expectations it created and this has renewed the attractiveness of religion and religious-inspired organizations.[63] Following the declining authorities of churches, civil society associations can be new channels through which religious values can enter the public arena. The task of investigating the new strategies of Catholic and Catholic-inspired associations to shape social policies is taken up in the second part of this book, in Chapters 5, 6, and 7 that venture to explore the impact of religious values on welfare policies from the mid 1990s to late 2010s. In this sense, the second part of the book is complementary to the first part from a chronological and empirical perspective. While Chapters 2, 3, and 4 study how Catholic values were promoted through engagement in the political arena from 1940 to mid 1995, Chapters 6 and 7 investigate how Catholic values have been more recently supported through the mobilization of the civil society actors. How could religious values influence the social policy domain in a society that had moved away from religion? Which are the new actors that bring religious values into the social policy sphere? What are the new forms of mobilization in defence of religious values? The second part of this book attempts to answer to these questions.

To approach them we can build on the conclusions of those scholars that argue that religion still permeates the cultural domain of secularized societies. This phenomenon can be also observed in secular France where the effort to secularize the public sphere was probably stronger than elsewhere. The French public discourse, the attitudes of political elites, and republican ideals (e.g. the conception of the state, the idea of *laïcité*, and social citizenship) bear the imprint of Catholicism.[64] As noted by John Madeley, in entering the secular era, religion has preserved, at least in part, some long-standing cultural and anthropological influences. In other words, in contemporary societies religion is less a set of doctrinal norms and more a sort of religiosity, cultural and anthropological principles bearing the imprint of religious values widespread in societies.[65] Similarly to Madeley, in a book entitled *Le mystère française* (The French mystery). Hervé Le Bras and Emmanuel Todd note the enduring social influence of religious values in France. By studying demographic trends,

61 Poulat, *Une Église ébranlée*, 10.
62 Gauchet, *Un monde désenchanté?*, 193.
63 Hervieu-Léger (in collaboration with Champion), *Vers un nouveau Christianisme?*, 224.
64 Hervieu-Léger, 'Sécularisation', 1149.
65 Madeley, 'Religion and the Welfare State', 43-49.

educational choices, family structures, female employment rates, patterns of urbanization, and voting behaviour between 1980 and 2010, Le Bras and Todd have claimed that the anthropological attitudes inspired by Catholicism that emphasize the importance of tradition, hierarchy, and religious ethical values are still largely in existence.[66] This phenomenon was summed up by them in the concept of zombie Catholicism, by which they mean the idea that Catholicism has survived its death as a dominant institutional religion and has taken up another life in which it is a kind of ethical set of principles inspired by Catholic anthropological and cultural norms.[67] What is happening in contemporary secular societies is not the drying up of faith, but its institutional deregulation. This is why religion is not absent from the public sphere, although religious authorities cannot shape the public life as they did in the past.[68]

We think that the enduring influence of religion in secularized societies is possible for three main reasons. First, the activism of religious groups is, at least implicitly, understood and approved by a consistent part of the population, even though only a minority of people are actively affiliated to religious associations. The social engagement of faith-based associations inspired by social Catholic values is respected by a large part of the population, and the involvement of these associations in social services enables them to instil their values in the policy processes. Second, modernization provokes a deeply distressing sense of symbolic insecurity because it puts under discussion long-lasting references.[69] Political entrepreneurs and religious-inspired movements can exploit this sense of insecurity to advocate forms of unsecular politics: "a political context in which religious ideas, symbols, and rituals are used as the primary (though not exclusive) instrument of mobilization by at least one major political party".[70] We believe that the collective mobilization against same-sex marriage described in Chapter 7 is an example of unsecular politics. The anti-gay marriage campaign was the result of the efforts of a vast social movement to create a political context in which the Catholic understanding of family and parenthood was employed to mobilize public opinion against the modernization of family legislation pursued by the Hollande presidency. Third, the persistent influence of religion in the public sphere is favoured by the process of secularization. In other words, secularization is not a threat, but an opportunity for religion.[71] This idea, which has some of its roots in the thesis elaborated by some Protestant theologians in the middle of the twentieth century, seems particularly suitable to describe the role

66 Le Bras and Todd, *Le mystère français*, 7.

67 Ibid., 72.

68 Gauchet, *Un monde désenchanté?*, 326.

69 Hervieu-Léger, 'Sécularisation', 1153.

70 Kalyvas, 'Unsecular Politics and Religion Mobilization', 293-294.

71 Beck, *Der eigene gott*, 40-46; Rémond, 'Un chapitre inachevé (1958-1990)', 401.

played by religion in contemporary societies.[72] The fading religious cleavage, the disbanding of some Catholic-minded political parties, the weakening affiliation of religious-inspired organizations to established churches, and the decreasing authority of the latter can persuade public powers that the religious organizations are not a threat to their authority and they let Catholics to contribute to policy decisions.[73] In this sense, the assertive secularism that led French authorities to take exclusionary attitudes towards religion is not any more necessary in a secularized society and decision makers are keener to let religious groups to be involved in the policy process.[74]

Although current transformations of the social and political fields can open up new windows of opportunity to Catholic organizations, the impact of religious values on the political sphere does not have a straightforward answer. It is challenging to envisage whether the advent of a post-secular era will favour mutual coexistence and dialogue between religious and secular worldviews[75] or whether it will provoke the re-emergence of ideological conflicts.[76] The study of the French case shows that both these outcomes are possible.

Studying the Role of Catholicism in Social Policy Developments

For our research, we adopted a case study approach. A case study design seems particularly suited to exploring a complex phenomenon that needs to be scrutinized in depth.[77] The influence of Catholicism on social policy developments in France is a difficult subject due to the complexity of French social legislation and the great pluralism of Catholicism. All religions are characterized by an irreducible internal diversity that makes them a kind of mosaic.[78] Furthermore, the idiosyncrasies of French politics,[79] with its distinct regime of *laïcité* that establishes a formal separation between the religious and the political field, make any generalization about the conclusions of this study subject to several conditions. However, France can be considered a decisive case study of the institutional influence of Catholicism, because of the difficult situations faced by Catholic groups in exercising their influence on the social policy sphere. In this sense, conclusions drawn from the study of France may be extended to other countries where the activism of Catholic organizations

72 Bonhoeffer, *Widerstand und* ergebung; Tillich, *The Courage to Be*.
73 Rémond, 'Un chapitre inachevé (1958-1990)', 400.
74 'Kuru, 'Passive and assertive secularism'.
75 Habermas, 'Notes on post-secular society'.
76 Berger, 'Religious Transformations and the Future of Politics', 141-142.
77 Sartori, 'Comparing and miscomparing', 252; Stake, 'Case Studies', 90-94; Yin, *Case Study Research*, 13.
78 Poulat, *Aux carrefours stratégiques de l'Église de France*, 213.
79 Boudon, 'Situation de la démocratie française', 590.

and the institutional constraints on their involvement in social policy affairs have been weaker.

This book does not intend to be an exhaustive study of French social security. Its main aim is to explore the historically changing influence of Catholicism on the welfare state. Therefore, it focuses on several key policy issues, areas, and debates that highlight the development of the mobilization of Catholic and Catholic-inspired actors to shape social policies in different historical periods.

We consider the policy decisions taken at the national political level. This choice was motivated by two main factors. First, in France, the most important social policy choices have generally been taken at the national level, even though the process of decentralization has promoted the development of local social policies.[80] Second, the study of local realities would have introduced excessive complexity, with the risk of overlooking macro-structural changes.

The book adopts an historical perspective to reveal the changing influence of Catholicism. Such an approach is suited to understanding the long-term evolution of Catholic mobilization, as the characteristics of Catholic activism have dramatically changed over time. The combined consideration of the findings of the various periods can thus furnish the reader with a comprehensive outlook on the evolving characteristics of the impact of Catholic actors and values in the social policy sphere.

Various sources provided the empirical material for our study: archival documents; legislative documents; administrative papers; material about political parties, associations, and social movements; semi-structured interviews; and descriptive statistics. The relative importance of these sources depended on the historical periods being taken into consideration and the questions under investigation. For instance, archival documents and official publications were the main sources of data for the early periods covered by the research, while semi-structured interviews were the prevailing sources of information for the more recent periods.

All written documentary sources were interpreted within their specific context. This consideration is crucially important in evaluating the authenticity, credibility, representativeness, and meaning of sources.[81] Though official documents and public declarations of political actors do not always convey the precise strategy followed by their authors, they should not be disregarded. There is certainly a gap between what is publicly claimed and what is actually done. However, final decisions are never completely inconsistent with public claims. Furthermore, official documents and statements can be considered an important source of information because they present social and political actors' positions, ideological orientations, and the justification for their actions.

80 Valasik, 'Church-State Relations in France in the Field of Welfare', 132-134.
81 Scott, *A Matter of Record*, 6.

More than twenty semi-structured interviews with people involved in the various policy processes, public debates, and social mobilizations on social policy issues were conducted.[82] To them should be added eight interviews with leading scholars and politicians specializing in the arguments considered by the book. Furthermore, around forty interviews with people who took part in the anti-gay marriage marches were conducted and fifteen interviews with those who attended a national rally in support of same-sex marriage. Although these interviews taken during the demonstrations did not have a scholarly rigour, because practical constraints (e.g. limited time, noisy places, and impossibility of recording all or part of the interviews) impeded the deepening of the discussion of the arguments raised during the interviews, they provided some precious insights into the reasons for collective actions. Several issues that emerged during these interviews were then explored during the interviews with key people involved in policy debates. A set of questions was always prepared before every interview. They provided a frame of reference without imposing any strict constraint on the flow of discussions with the interviewees as every conversation was made up of several follow-up questions that were inspired by the arguments that came out during the discussion. The answers from the interviews were always integrated and compared with the knowledge acquired from the study of other data in order to triangulate our findings. In addition to the other methods of data collection aforementioned, we also used non-participant observations. We attended, as an observer or sometimes as an accredited researcher, the major demonstrations, rallies, and meetings organized by the anti-gay marriage campaign. Taking part in these events provided first-hand impressions of the mobilizations and the opportunity to get in touch with mobilization leaders and grassroots activists.

A final important methodological point is related to the influence of the values of the author on the conclusions presented in the different chapters. Positionality is a problem that should be taken seriously, notably in studies that deal with value-laden issues. In a well-known address delivered in 1966, Howard Becker contended that sociologists studying problems that are relevant to the world we live in are caught in the crossfire between those who ask them to conduct value-free research and those telling them to commit to value positions. According to Becker, it is impossible to conduct research uncontaminated by personal and political sympathies. Instead, the crucial issue is to "use our theoretical and technical resources to avoid the distortions that [our ethical and political commitments] might introduce into our work".[83] This effort is so necessary because committing to distinct values can jeopardize the validity of studies and it is not a strategy worth pursuing.[84] To avoid possible

82 They were politicians, senior members of associations, and social movement leaders.

83 Becker, 'Whose side are we on?', 247.

84 Bruce, *Researching Religion*, 108.

biases due to our values, we performed a "phenomenological bracketing to eliminate every type of prejudice" and remain in control of the knowledge that "thereby dictates the rules for interpreting religious phenomena".[85] In practical terms, this was done by basing our conclusions on the in-depth reading of archival materials and original publications, carefully listening to the people who were interviewed to understand their points of view, and triangulating our findings. In other words, every effort was made to let the empirical material speak for itself, as far as possible. Though this methodological reflexivity is not completely satisfactory, it was probably the most effective strategy to prevent excessive biases.

Outline of the Book

The chapters of this book explore the impact of Catholicism in France from the Second World War to the mid 2010s, before the come to the power of Emmanuel Macron who impressed a profound change in French politics, whose outcomes on the relationship between religion and politics, as we write, are still difficult to evaluate. Each chapter tells a part of the story of the evolving institutional influence of Catholicism on the French welfare state. Chapter 2 considers some social policy innovations introduced by the Vichy regime, whose welfare reforms were of crucial importance for the foundations of the system of social protection built up after the Liberation.[86] Although Pétain proclaimed his intention to restore the influence of Catholicism in the public sphere, the chapter shows that he prioritized the need to establish a stronger state apparatus and exercise stricter social control over the promotion of Catholic values. In the end, Vichy's social legislation limited the role of Catholic organizations and it contributed to the secularization of the social policy domain. Chapter 3 explores some policy reforms enacted after the Liberation, most notably in the early post-war years, that laid down the foundations of a system of social security bearing the imprint of Catholicism.[87] The analysis presented in this chapter shows the limits of Catholic influence on the French welfare state. Furthermore, it points out the contradictory political actions of the MRP in shaping social legislation. We claim that this party not only promoted social policies that bore the imprint of social Catholicism, but it also disregarded Catholic ideals for political purposes. Chapter 4 studies the gradual erosion of the Catholic imprint on the French welfare state during the first three decades of the Fifth Republic and argues that the impact of Catholicism on social legis-

85 Cox, *A Guide to the Phenomenology of Religion*, 215.
86 Hesse and Le Crom, 'Conclusion', 355-364.
87 Manow and Palier, 'A Conservative Welfare State Regime without Christian Democracy?', 147.

lation was quite negligible, although the values of the Gaullist movement and the PS were partly inspired by Catholic values. The reasons for this apparent puzzle are discussed.

With Chapter 5 the second part of this book begins. Whereas Chapters 2, 3, and 4 study the influence of Catholicism through state authorities and political parties from 1940 until the early 1990s, Chapters 5, 6, and 7 investigate the impact of Catholic values on the French welfare state from the mid 1990s through civil society and social movements. However, before assessing the influence of Catholicism, it is necessary to map out its social presence in contemporary secular France. This is the task of Chapter 5. The chapter also claims that the new public role of religious-inspired organizations can lead to the establishment of closer forms of collaboration between public authorities and religious-inspired actors (see Chapter 6), or the resurgence of ideological conflicts (see Chapter 7). Chapter 6 studies the influence of voluntary organizations and in more detail of the Fondation Abbé Pierre (FAP), a non-profit organization with a Catholic background, on the housing legislation. We chose this policy field because it has generally been paradigmatically important for the Catholic movement, a vast network of Catholic associations have been working on housing-related issues, and housing legislation has undergone remarkable changes. The chapter delineates a trajectory in the development of French housing legislation from the mid 1990s to the early 2010s that has been characterized by the increasing activism of public authorities and the growing institutional influence of non-profit associations. Furthermore, Chapter 6 also argues that the crisis of legitimacy of public institutions and the integration of voluntary organizations in the policy sphere provide philanthropic organizations with the opportunities to promote their values. Whereas Chapter 6 describes an example of close collaboration between public authorities and Catholic-inspired associations, Chapter 7 investigates the confrontation between public powers and Catholic actors by looking at the social mobilization against same-sex marriage that occurred in France from late 2012 to mid 2013 and some reforms of abortion policies introduced by the Hollande presidency. Chapter 8 presents the main findings of the research study for this book, provides a comprehensive overview on the historical influence of Catholicism on French welfare state, and indicates some issues and areas that would deserve further investigation.

2
CATHOLICISM AND THE WELFARE STATE IN A REACTIONARY REGIME (1940-1944)

Military defeat in June 1940 inevitably led to the end of the Third Republic and opened the way for the foundation of a new state in that part of France that was not occupied by German and Italian troops. Senators and deputies reached the town of Vichy, where, in a casino hastily refurbished to resemble a parliament, an extraordinary session of the National Assembly was scheduled for 10 July.[1] That day they approved a single-article constitutional bill that gave full powers to Philippe Pétain, a marshal who had distinguished himself in the First World War, to promulgate a new constitution.[2] This was the beginning of the Vichy regime.[3] Even though this regime bears responsibility for hideous crimes, notably against the Jews, that have left an enduring imprint on French collective memory, it would be unfair to avoid considering its contribution to French social protection.

Inspired by a reactionary ideology, Pétain intended to realize a National Revolution, a political project aimed at restoring the supposedly traditional values of France that the propaganda summarized in the slogan 'Travail,

1 'Une repétition générale de l'Assemblée Nationale au Petit Casino de Vichy', *Le Figaro*, 9 July 1940.

2 Loi Constitutionnelle du 10 julliet 1940, *Journal Officiel de la République Française, Lois et Décrets*, 11 July 1940, 4513.

3 Bolzonar, 'Dealing with a difficult past'; Hesse and Le Crom, 'Conclusion', 355-364; Smith, 'The Two World Wars and Social Policy in France', 127–48; Joly, *L'état contre les Juifs: Vichy, les Nazis et la persécution anti-semite.*

Famille, Patrie' (Work, Family, Homeland).[4] The republican motto 'Liberté, Egalité, Fraternité' (Liberty, Equality, Fraternity) was replaced by a motto with a traditionalist and an apparent Catholic imprint.[5] Although Pétain had not been a devout Catholic during his life, he considered Christian morality the solid foundation of French civilization, as he declared at a press conference with American journalists in August 1940.[6] Besides Catholicism, the development of social legislation was part of Pétain's project to reform France.[7] The selective and discriminatory expansion of social benefits became an instrument used by the regime to strengthen its legitimacy, exercise stricter social control, and shape society, similar to what fascism and Nazism did in Italy and Germany. However, Vichy attributed greater importance to Catholicism than fascism and Nazism did. While Hitler was hostile to Catholic groups and Mussolini considered Catholicism as a force whose social and political influence should be taken into consideration, the regime established by Pétain was a believer.[8]

4 The influence of fascism on Vichy's political ideology is the subject of an ongoing debate. Wheras some historians have claimed that French society in the 1930s and 1940s was immune to fascism (See Berstein and Winock, eds, *Fascisme français*; Julliard, 'Sur un fascisme imaginaire'; Paxton, *La France de Vichy*; Rémond, *Les droites en France*; Slama, 'Vichy était-il fasciste?'), others have argued that fascist ideas were widespread in the French intellectual and political circles of the time (See Dobry, ed, *Le mythe de l'allergie française au fascisme*; Soucy, *French Fascism*; Sternhell, *Ni droit ni gauche*). Without entering a complex historiographical discussion, two main reasons lead us to consider Vichy France a reactionary rather than a fascist regime. First, Vichy's political ideology lacked the subversive attitude that characterized fascism. Pétain just wanted to restore the weakening values of an idealized traditional French society (e.g. agrarianism, clericalism, and patriarchalism) and to react to the liberalization of social norms that happened during the years of the *belle époque*. In other words, Vichy's political ideology did not have some of those crucial characteristics that the historian Emilio Gentile ascribed to fascism, notably a totalitarian vision of politics and a belligerent policy of conquest aimed at creating a new civilizational order. See Gentile, *Il fascismo in tre capitoli*, vi. Second, in contrast with fascism in Italy, the Vichy regime was unable to regiment the French as Mussolini did with the Italians. Pétain did not have the economic resources, the time, and a solid state apparatus to do that. For a long time, French historiography has also sustained the idea that Vichy's ideology owed much to the reactionary, anti-Semitic, and Catholic traditionalist philosophy of Charles Maurras. However, as noted by Jean-Louis Clément, the Maurrassisme of Vichy was more a myth used to discredit the regime than a reality. See Clément, 'The birth of a myth'.

5 Duquesne, *Les Catholiques français sous l'Occupation*, 51.

6 Pétain, 'Comme le géant de la fable, la France retrouvera ses forces en reprenant contact avec la terre', *Le Figaro*, 24 August 1940, 1-2.

7 Pétain 'La Révolution Nationale vise à restuarer les disciplines collective, fécondité de la famille, sens de la patrie qualité du travail', *Le Figaro*, 19 January 1941, 1; Kuisel, *Capitalism and the State in Modern France*, 128; Pétain, 'La politique sociale de l'avenir', 114.

8 Conway, *The Nazi Persecution of the Churches*; De Felice, *Mussolini il fascista*, 383-384; Paxton, *La France de Vichy*, 198.

The current scholarship on Vichy France has principally investigated the influence of Catholicism on the regime's ideology and the linkages between Vichy senior officials and the Catholic Church.[9] Although this historiography has provided invaluable conclusions, it has paid less attention to the influence of Catholicism on Vichy social legislation. Did the regime restore the influence of Catholic values in the social policy domain? What was the role assigned to Catholic groups? What was the impact of the Vichy years on post-war social reforms? This chapter addresses these questions. This is achieved by combining a legal perspective, interested in legislative changes, and a political perspective that is focused on the role of social and political actors.

This chapter shows that the social policies introduced by Vichy's governments were not only inconsistent with Catholic ideals but they clashed with Catholicism, even though the regime upheld Catholic values. Building on the thesis of Colette Bec, who argues that Pétain placed Vichy's social policies within the authoritarian project of the National Revolution,[10] this chapter claims that the regime used social laws to establish a stronger and authoritarian state, which was the paramount goal of the National Revolution, and, consequently, it disregarded the demands of Catholic organizations, limited their autonomy, and contributed to the secularization of the social domain to consolidate the political power of central state authorities.

This chapter focuses on three cases that, from different perspectives, substantiate with empirical evidence how Vichy's social policies clashed with Catholicism. The first case shows that expenditure on social insurance, family allocations, and maternity benefits was inconsistent with the Catholic pro-family rhetoric of the regime. The second case clarifies why the reform of public hospitals introduced by the *Charte de l'hopital* in 1941, and the related decrees on the employment laws of medical and paramedical personnel in 1943, promoted the secularization of the health care system. Finally, the third case considers some features of the corporatist reform enacted by the *Charte du travail* in 1941, and it discusses why the authoritarian imprint of this reform diverged from the view of corporatism prevailing among Catholic trade unionists.

Like Chapter 3, this chapter notes that favourable conditions for the impact of Catholic values on social legislation, notably political actors in power inspired by Catholic values, did not necessarily lead to the strong influence of Catholicism on welfare policies. Broadly speaking, this observation questions the compatibility between religion and politics that is a topic explored throughout this book. While this chapter investigates the relationship between Catholicism and social policy developments in an authoritarian political context, the next one will study this argument in a democratic political context.

9 Rathbone, 'Athletes for France or athletes for the Church', 89.
10 Bec, *La sécurité sociale*, 84-85.

The first part of this chapter presents some observations on Catholicism in Vichy France. The second part reports aggregate data on the expansion of social protection. Our analysis then discusses some crucial social policy reforms and the positioning of the main Catholic groups about them. Finally, the last part briefly summarizes the conclusions and outlines several political developments that matured during the years of the regime and that influenced the social policy changes introduced after the Liberation.

Catholicism and Politics in Vichy France

The current historiography has recognized the influence of Catholicism on the Vichy regime. Previous studies have noted that this regime was inspired by clericalism, supported the social doctrine of the Church and considered Catholicism one of the founding principles of the National Revolution.[11] The linkages between Catholicism and the regime were favoured by the fact that they shared several ideological principles: the rejection of individualism, egalitarianism, liberalism, and socialism, the concern for class struggle, the promotion of a corporatist social order, the idealization of traditional agrarian societies, and the consideration of the Catholic Church as a cornerstone of the national culture.[12] Pétain was eager to let the Church contribute to the national *redressement* of France. His benevolent attitude toward the Catholic authorities was enthusiastically reciprocated by French bishops, who helped the regime to bolster its legitimacy, even though the Church rejected an organic integration and subordination to the regime.[13] The linkages between Vichy and Catholicism were also extended to the policy level. The early ministers defended Catholic values, and an increasing number of Catholics were recruited by public administrations, although the most senior positions were taken by those civil servants hired during the republican period.[14] Catholic functionaries became so numerous, notably in the bodies dealing with social affairs, that the Church did not need to remind the government of its positions on family questions. In 1940 the Vichy regime resembled that kind of good, old French Catholic order and the type of state that most Catholics were looking for.[15]

11 Azéma and Wieviorka, *Vichy*, 176; Baruch, *Le régime de Vichy*, 34; Cabanel, *Le Protestantisme français*, 141; Fouilloux, *Les chrétiens français entre crise et libération*, 103; Rémond, *Les droites en France*, 236.

12 Atkin and Tallett, *Priests, Prelates and People*.

13 Clément, *Les évêques au temps de Vichy*, 71; Luft, 'Religion in Vichy France', 79-80.

14 The list of them included, for instance, the Minister of Education Jacques Chevalier, Georges Lamirand who became Secretary General for Youth, and Robert Garric who was appointed as the head of the Secours National.

15 Cointet, *Nouvelle histoire de Vichy*, 260. Vignaux, *Traditionalisme et syndicalisme: essai d'histoire sociale (1884–1941)*, 17.

The influence of Catholicism on Vichy's social policies demands careful consideration. Following the so-called Paxtonian revolution, the ground-breaking studies by Robert Paxton, historians have highlighted the complexity of the Vichy regime, which was not a unique and unchanging ideological bloc.[16] The National Revolution was also a mix of different ideological traditions. Conservative Catholicism and social Catholicism were only two of its components, along with conservative liberalism and fascism.[17]

Although political power was concentrated in the hands of Pétain, who sustained a Christian conception of the state, Vichy's governments included senior politicians who were indifferent to Catholicism, if not anti-clerical, like François Darlan and Pierre Laval.[18] Furthermore, Vichy political orientations shifted over time, with fascist tendencies acquiring a growing influence in the later years of the regime. Finally, the political impact of Catholic actors was also hindered by the crisis that had been affecting French Catholicism since the early 1930s. Even though the outbreak of the Second World War was accompanied by a revival of religious beliefs and was followed by the diffusion of new missionary initiatives, like the Mission de France and the Mission de Paris, in the early decades of the twentieth century France was experiencing a process of de-Christianization.[19]

With regard to family policies, scholars have noted that several social laws were inspired by Catholic moralism,[20] such as those that criminalized abortion,[21] prohibited divorce in the first three years after marriage,[22] and condemned homosexuality.[23] Some employment policies were intended to push mothers out of the labour market, as advocated by the Church.[24] However, it is arguable that the regime policies had a clerical character. Several reforms of family legislation seemed to have been motivated more by the intention to tighten social control than to defend Catholic morality. For example, the

16 Atkin, *The French at War*, 43; Deacon, *The Extreme Right in the French Resistance*, 10; Lee, *Pétain's Jewish Children.*

17 Jackson, 'Vichy and fascism'; Larkin, *Religion, Politics and Preferment in France since 1890.*

18 Berstein and Milza, *Histoire de la France au XXe siècle. Vol. III*, 313.

19 Duroselle and Mayeur, *Histoire du Catholicisme*,106; Le Bras, *Introduction à l'histoire de la pratique religieuse en France.*

20 Boninchi, *Vichy et l'ordre moral.*

21 Loi n° 300 du 15 février 1942, *Journal Officiel de l'État Français, Lois et Décrets*, 7 March 1942, 938.

22 Loi n° 1461 du 2 avril 1941, *Journal Officiel de l'État Français, Lois et Décrets*, 13 April 1941, 1587-1588.

23 Loi n° 744 du 6 août 1942 , *Journal Officiel de l'État Français, Lois et Décrets*, 27 August, 1942, 2922.

24 A bill approved in 1940 forbade the recruitment of married women by all public administrations. See Loi du 11 octobre 1940, *Journal Officiel de la République Française, Lois et Décrets*, 27 October 1940, 5447-5448. In *Rerum Novarum*, Leo XIII wrote that "a woman is by nature fitted for home-work, and it is that which is best adapted at once to preserve her modesty and to promote the good bringing up of children and the well-being of the family". See Leo XIII, *Rerum Novarum*, § 42.

Gounot Bill, which established closer institutional collaboration between family associations and public bureaucracies, had an authoritarian character as it curtailed the autonomy of these organizations by making them subject to pervasive control by the state authorities who could revoke most of their internal decisions, including the appointment of presidents.[25]

The influence of Catholic values on Vichy's social policies has not been the object of much debate, despite the fact that the social legislation of the regime has attracted increasing attention since the early 2000s. This is all the more striking given that the development of social protection was a goal of social Catholicism and the regime alike. Apart from the seminal book by Philippe-Jean Hesse and Jean-Pierre Le Crom, *La protection sociale sous le régime de Vichy* (Social protection under the Vichy regime) and the edited volume by Michel Dreyfus and colleagues, *Se protéger, être protégé. Une histoire des assurances sociales en France* (Protect yourself, be protected. A history of social insurance in France), most studies of Vichy's social protection have been related to specific policy areas, notably family,[26] and they have overlooked the normative imprint of the various fields of the regime's social legislation.

The social policy scholarship has paid scant attention to Vichy France. The pioneering book by Henri Galant, *Histoire politique de la securité sociale française* (Political history of French social security), dismisses the influence of the Vichy period on French social legislation. This prevents Galant from giving an adequate account of the institutional constraints on the decisions taken by post-war social reformers. A similar weakness affects the comprehensive study on French social security by Bruno Palier, *Gouverner la sécurité sociale* (Governing social security). A recent work by Philippe Manow and Bruno Palier pays specific attention to the influence of Catholicism on social policy developments from 1871 to 1960. However, the two scholars consider the Vichy period a mere parenthesis in the evolution of French social protection.[27] Their choice is arguable for two reasons. First, Vichy governments introduced several major institutional innovations in French social security (e.g. hospital reform, the establishment of the Fédération Nationale des Familles, and the generalization of family benefits). Second, Manow and Palier sustain the view that the process of institutional path dependency played an important role in the early evolution of the French welfare state. However, it seems reductive to consider path dependency an exhaustive explanation for the various and multi-faceted developments of social protection. Furthermore, if path dependency is considered an important causal variable for the development of social protection, Manow

25 Loi n° 1107 du 29 décembre 1942, *Journal Officiel de l'État Français, Lois et Décrets*, 31 December 1942, 4246-4247.

26 Capuano, *Vichy et la famille*; Ceccaldi, *Histoire des prestations familiales en France*; Pedersen, *Family, Dependence, and the Origins of the Welfare State*.

27 Manow and Palier, 'A Conservative Welfare State Regime without Christian Democracy?', 158.

and Palier should have investigated the social legislation of Vichy that introduced several important institutional changes. However, they do not do this.

A promising perspective from which to understand the influence of Catholicism on Vichy social policies is provided by Colette Bec, who notes that policy reforms are better evaluated when we consider their inspiring principles instead of the legislative framework that they establish. If we look at Vichy social legislation, we can have the impression that it was a continuation of that of the Third Republic. However, this thesis, which is widely accepted by the current scholarship, is misleading because it overlooks the fact that Pétain placed the regime's social reforms within the project of the National Revolution instead of the solidaristic values of the Republican period.[28] In other words, the policy paradigm of the regime was dramatically different from that of the Republican governments. Building on Bec's conclusions, this chapter claims that Pétain subordinated the regime's social reforms to the political authoritarian principles of the National Revolution. In this sense, the marshal principally used social policy to build an authoritarian state apparatus, tighten social control, and strengthen the regime's legitimacy. These politics clashed with the pluralism, universalism, and the idea of a limited state sustained by the great majority of socially engaged Catholics and Catholic organizations.

Social Policies during the Vichy Regime

At the risk of some oversimplification, we claim that the social legislation of the Vichy regime was inspired by three main aims: the expansion of social protection, the effort of reorganizing its highly fragmented institutional settings, and the use of social policies to tight social control. Though propaganda emphasized the activism of the government in the social policy domain, the 'reformist' effort of Vichy administrations should not be overestimated. While some measures expanded the policies introduced by the previous governments, others were enacted to compensate the material disruptions of the war.[29] Some social policies apparently met the long-standing demands and values of Catholic groups (e.g. promotion of collaboration between labour and capital, support for a male breadwinner model, and the stronger institutional recognition of family associations). However, the predominant aim of Vichy governments was to use these policies to strengthen the authoritarian politics of the regime. This purpose created some conflicts between the Vichy regime and most Catholics, who gradually distanced themselves from the 'Catholic' Pétain.

28 Bec, *La sécurité sociale*, 84-85.

29 Undated archival document on the social and economic conditions of France, Archives Nationales [AN], Fonds du Comité d'Histoire de la Deuxième Guerre Mondiale et Fonds Privés Relatifs à la Période 1939-1945, 72AJ/13.

The Expansion of Social Protection

The development of social protection in France happened at a later stage than in other Western European countries. In the early 1940s, France was still a welfare laggard. Religious issues were largely responsible for that. At the end of the nineteenth century, when Germany was introducing early social insurance schemes, French political debate was dominated by bitter conflicts between the state and the Catholic Church over the school question, which overshadowed all other social issues.[30] When the political elites in the early decades of the Third Republic started to pay greater attention to social protection, their initiatives had a secularist approach, which was only partly lessened in the late 1930s. In other words, they wished to expand the competences of public authorities by taking up several services previously managed by voluntary religious organizations.[31] The Vichy regime intended to establish a broader and administratively centralized welfare state. However, it had not enough time, legitimacy, and political stability to carry out a comprehensive plan of social policy reforms.[32]

The expansion of social protection during the years of the regime is shown in the increase in the numbers of workers enrolled in compulsory social insurance schemes and the growth of social expenditure, even though several new policies did not have adequate financial coverage.[33] The Vichy governments extended the typology of works and risks covered by insurance. Though the numbers of insured had already grown since the 1930s, with a step increase in 1937, their upward trend became more dramatic during the years of the regime. From the end of 1940 to the end of 1944, the figures of workers enrolled in social insurance schemes increased by 20 per cent, going from roughly 12 million to 15 million.[34]

Equally dramatic was the increase in social expenditure. Family issues should have been a priority according to the propaganda that depicted Vichy France as a pro-family state.[35] However, family legislation was affected by several problems that delayed and impeded the expansion of social benefits. Laws were often unclear, conflicts of competences among public authorities were frequent, and the secretary of state for family and health had only limited powers to coordinate the government initiatives in the family domain.[36] To overcome these problems, on 4 March 1941, Henri Moysset, Secretary General to the Vice-pres-

30 Manow and Palier, 'A Conservative Welfare State Regime without Christian Democracy?', 158.

31 Renard, 'Intervention de l'état et genèse de la protection sociale en France (1880–1940)'.

32 Smith, 'The Two World Wars and Social Policy in France', 139.

33 Report on the financial situation of social insurances drafted by Pierre Laroque, 28 October 1944, Archives du Centre d'histoire de Sciences Po, PA 17.

34 Ministère du Travail et de la Sécurité Sociale (1947), *Rapport sur l'application de la legislation sur les assurances sociales*, 4.

35 Bordeaux, *La victoire de la famille dans la France défaite*; Pétain, 'La politique sociale de l'avenir', 114-115.

36 Capuano, *Vichy et la famille*.

ident of the Council,[37] sent a letter to all ministers and secretaries of state to remind them that every proposal for a law regarding family questions should be forwarded to the secretary of state for family and health, who had often been unaware of them until they were discussed at the council of ministers.[38]

The effectiveness of the family legislation was also jeopardized by the limited resources at disposal. Family associations were disappointed by the government's family laws and complained that allowances did not provide adequate support to families, particularly large families.[39] To shed light on the economic aspect of the regime's family policy, we report some data on maternity and family benefits in Figure 1 and Table 1. In consideration of the dramatic rise in prices during the war period, we prefer to present deflated figures to provide more reliable data than nominal values. After a decline in 1940, the real value of maternity benefits at 1939 constant prices began to grow in 1941 and reached a record in 1943, when it was 211 million francs. Thereaf-

FIGURE 1
TOTAL SOCIAL INSURANCE AND MATERNITY BENEFITS EXPENDITURE FROM 1939 TO 1945 (MILLION FRANCS ADJUSTED FOR INFLATION – CONSTANT PRICES BASE 1939)*

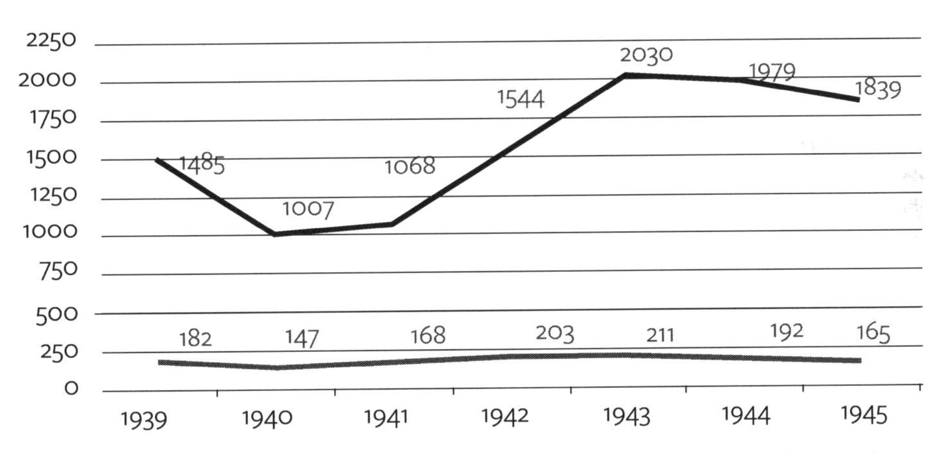

* Ministère du Travail et de la Sécurité Sociale (1947), *Rapport sur l'application de la legislation sur les assurances sociales*, 17.
Total social insurance
Maternit benefits

37 The National Council was a consultative body, composed of roughly 200 persons appointed by the government, that was established in January 1941 to replace the Parliament. Its aim was to help Pétain to revise the Constitution and advise him on political reforms. See Cointet, *Le Conseil national de Vichy*, 2.

38 Letter sent by Henri Moysset to all ministers and secretaries of state, 4 March 1941, AN, Fonds État Français (1940-1944), 2AG 605.

39 Note by the Secretariat General of the Head of State, 13 January 1941, AN 2 AG 605.

TABLE 1
EVOLUTION OF FAMILY BENEFITS BETWEEN 1940 AND 1944 FOR THE SEINE DEPARTMENT*

		Rate of the benefits based on average department salary (% figures)							
		Number of Dependent Children							
		Family Allocations				Unique Salary Allowance			
Period of Application	Average Salary	1	2	3	Every other child	1 (< 5 years)	1 (> 5 years)	2	3 or more
1/4/1939 > 31/3/1940	1,500	5	15	30	+ 15	–	–	–	–
1/4/1940 > 31/3/1941	1,500	–	10	30	+ 20	–	–	–	–
1/4/1941 > 31/12/1941	1,500	–	10	30	+ 30	20	10	25	30
1 /1/1942 > 31/12/1943	1,700	–	10	30	+ 30	20	10	25	30
1/1/1944 > 31 /8/1944	2,250	–	10	30	+ 30	20	10	25	30
1/9/1944 > 31/7/1945	2,250	–	18	54	+ 45	30	15	37,5	45

* Comité Central des Allocations Familiales, *Statistiques*, 3.

ter, the real value of these benefits started to decline, and in 1944 they were roughly 192 million francs. The weakness of the financial support provided by maternity benefits appears more evident when we compare their trend with that of social insurance. After a sharp decline in 1940, the real value of social insurance at 1939 constant prices started to rise in 1941, and particularly increased in the following two years, to become 2,030 million francs in 1943. Following this peak, social insurance slightly declined in real terms to reach 1,979 million francs in 1944, which was nonetheless roughly 30 per cent higher than the real value that they had in 1939.[40]

Controversial conclusions about the regime's commitment to providing adequate economic support to French families can be also derived from consideration of the trend in family benefits. The total amount of these allowances was determined in relation to the estimated average department salary and a rate based on the number of dependent children. To compensate for higher living costs in urban areas, the law divided the territory into rural and urban municipalities, and established a higher estimated salary for the latter, even though rural family associations harshly criticized this criterion as they considered it discriminato-

40 Ministère du Travail et de la Sécurité Sociale (1947), *Rapport sur l'application de la legislation sur les assurances sociales*, 17.

ry.[41] Table 1 presents the evolution of the average salary and the rates for family allocations and the unique salary allowance for the Seine department.[42]

The estimated average department salary remained at the pre-war level until the end of 1941 even though the inflation rate rose by roughly 40 per cent in the biennium 1940–1941. In January 1942 the average department salary grew by 13 per cent (200 francs), from 1,500 francs to 1,700 francs. This augmentation did not result much in a positive return for welfare recipients because the inflation rate was 20 per cent in 1942 and its cumulative value was roughly 50 per cent in the biennium 1942–1943. A more substantial re-evaluation of the average salary was implemented in 1944. Its estimated value was augmented by 32 per cent (550 francs), from 1,700 francs to 2,250 francs. However, this re-evaluation was largely eroded by inflation, which grew by 22 per cent in 1944. Overall, the estimated average salary increased by 50 per cent (750 francs) between January 1940 and January 1945, but in the same period, the cumulative inflation was roughly 150 per cent. In this sense, welfare recipients were affected by the decline of the real value of the average salary, despite this salary being increased in real terms. Family allowances could have maintained their real values if the rates of benefits, the other criteria used to calculate them, had been substantially increased. However, this did not happen.[43] Before the rises introduced by post-war social reformers and apart from the slight increase of the family allocation rates for a household with more than three children in April 1941, family benefits rates were not raised.

Senior members of the government were aware of the weakness of the regime's family policies and the criticisms that it drew from family associations. On 13 January 1941, Pétain's office sent a report for urgent discussion to the ministry of the interior that included a series of proposals to ameliorate family legislation. Among them was the idea of re-establishing a ministry of family, devoting greater financial resources to family benefits, and increasing the budget of the secretary of state for family and health, which was far lower than for other central administrative bodies.[44] After Maxime Weygand,

41 Annexe X, 12 December 1940, AN, Fonds État Français (1940-1944), 2AG 605.

42 The unique salary allowance was supposed to provide more coherent support to those households, notably rural families, that could not benefit from the stay-at-home mother allowance. Established by Art. 23 of the Code de la Famille, the stay-at-home mother allowance was given to those households with at least one dependent child, which relied on only one professional income and lived in villages or towns with at least 2,000 residents. It amounted to 10 per cent of the average department salary and could not be cumulated with the unique salary allowance. *Journal Officiel de l'État Français, Lois et Décrets*, 11 April 1941, 1555. Ceccaldi noted that this new allocation acquired a prominent role in the government family policy because the great majority of the household of the time were single income. In 1943, the single income allowance represented 52.5 per cent of the benefits paid to French families. See Ceccaldi, *Histoire des prestations familiales en France*, 90.

43 Piketty and Zucman, 'Capital is back'. See database <http://pikkety.pse.ens.fr/fr/capitalisback>.

44 Ministerial notes on family policy, 13 January 1941, AN, Fonds État Français (1940-1944), 2AG 605.

Paul Baudouin, and Raphaël Alibert left the government in 1940, one of the remaining defenders of family interests was the Catholic philosopher Jacques Chevalier, who was appointed Secretary of State for Family and Health on 23 February 1941. Chevalier expressed his complaints about the government's family policy in a letter dated 27 May 1941 that he sent to Yves Bouthillier, Minister of National Economy and Finance. Even though Chevalier claimed that he understood the reasons why the executive could not expand family benefits, he also noted that the government decisions contradicted the promises for more generous allowances that were made to family associations, and he suggested organizing some propaganda initiatives to convince the population that the government was engaged in supporting French families.[45]

The effectiveness of Vichy family legislation was also undermined by the negligible resources of the administrative bodies dealing with it that were quite limited. In an administrative memo written on 8 July 1941 and addressed to Chevalier, the Director of the Cabinet of the Secretary of State for Family and Health, Paul Haury, pointed out that the resources of his department were only 58 per cent of those of the ministry of foreign affairs, 46 per cent of those of the ministry of education, and 12 per cent of those of the ministry of the national economy and finance. According to Haury, there was a blatant disparity between the important tasks that the secretary of state for family and health was asked to perform and the means at its disposal, which were derisory in comparison with those of other central administrative authorities.[46]

Consideration of the aggregate data on social benefits presented above shows that Vichy family policies were inconsistent with the demands for stronger support for families advocated by family organizations and Catholic authorities. However, more accurate conclusions on the inspiring principles of the regime's social policies can be drawn from the investigation of some key institutional social reforms.

The Reorganization of Public Hospitals

A second distinguishing feature of Vichy social legislation was the attempt to reorganize the institutional structures of social protection by strengthening the power of central state authorities. The reform of public hospitals paradig-

45 Letter sent by Jacques Chevalier to Yves Bouthillier, 27 May 1941, AN, Fonds État Français (1940-1944), 2AG 605. A similar dramatic disparity can be seen with regard to the subventions paid for the social initiatives managed by the Secretariat for Family and Health Care Affairs. While the subventions for family questions in January 1941 amounted to 4 million francs, those for youth affairs were 50 million francs, and for sport were 78 million francs. See Ministerial notes on family policy, undated, AN, Fonds État Français (1940-1944), 2AG 605.

46 Administrative memo by Paul Haury, 8 July 1941, AN, Fonds État Français (1940-1944), 2AG 605.

matically illustrates this effort. Even though in 1940 French hospitals were no longer social assistance centres only for poor and deprived people, as they were in the previous century, they still lacked an organic legislative framework to further their modernization.[47] The interest of Vichy governments in public hospitals was motivated not only by the fact that these institutions are a cornerstone of every system of social protection but also by the reason that public hospitals are powerful instruments for monitoring the population and tightening social control. By taking care of suffering bodies, a domain that in the past had traditionally been left to religious organizations, a state can exert a pervasive control over various aspects of the personal lives of patients and families. However, to reach this goal, the regime needed to reform the governance of public hospitals, extend their clientele, and strengthen the prerogatives of public authorities. With these aims in mind, the regime introduced the institutional reorganization of public hospitals with a bill issued on 21 December 1941[48], the so-called *Charte de l'hôpital*, which was integrated with the decree of 17 April 1943, regarding the employment rules of medical and paramedical personnel.[49]

The reform of public hospitals was based on the idea that these institutions had to be managed more professionally, dispense their services to the whole population, and be subjected to stricter control by the public authorities. First of all, the *Charte de l'hôpital* introduced a dramatic change in the governance of hospitals. The responsibilities of the director of the hospital and of its administrative commission, which was headed by the local mayor and was composed of six other members appointed by the prefect a government delegate, were strengthened. However, the secretary of state for family and health could repeal any deliberation of this commission, if it violated the law, administrative regulations, and the general interest. In this sense, the secretary of state for family and health and his delegates had considerable discretionary powers to repeal the decisions of hospital commissions.

The new law imposed professionalization of the competences of medical and paramedical personnel and a requirement that they should not be coopted at the local level, as had been the case before, but selected by a panel of people who would evaluate the candidates according to their qualifications.[50] This measure indirectly provoked the withdrawal of many senior religious people who did not have any certified qualifications.

The reform was also supposed to change the employment laws for the members of religious congregations who worked in public hospitals. The em-

47 Smith, *Creating the Welfare State in France*, 125-156.

48 Loi n° 5060 du 21 décembre 1941 relative aux hôpitaux et hospices publics, *Journal Officiel de l'État Français, Lois et Décrets*, 29-30 December 1941, 5574-5577.

49 Décret n° 891 du 17 avril 1943, *Journal Officiel de l'État Français, Lois et Décrets*, 26-27 April 1943, 1156-1171.

50 Chevandier, *L'hôpital dans la France du XXe siècle*, 213.

ployment conditions of these people were regulated by a bill dating back to 1851 partly changed by a law on 9 February 1927, which established that the members of religious congregations were not part of the hospital personnel, and the superior general was the only person who could appoint, transfer and replace them. Although the political elites of the Third Republic made a great effort to secularize France, they did not pay much attention to public hospitals, and in 1940 religious people still played a prominent role in the hospitals in rural districts, where they provided a cheap or free labour force.[51] The revision of the employment laws relating to the congregational personnel was immediately seen as a controversial issue. To avoid possible clashes with religious authorities, the *Charte de l'hôpital* did not introduce any change in this matter. It only established that an administrative regulation would be issued to redefine the tasks of the congregational personnel working in public hospitals. However, this was not enough to overcome the concerns of the superiors general of congregations, who immediately expressed their disagreement when they were informed that the new rules for the medical and paramedical personnel were likely to impose that all religious people working in public hospitals would be subordinated to the director of the hospital, who could appoint and dismiss them. The superiors general contested this proposal. According to them, religious people employed by public hospitals should be not assimilated as civil servants because they were serving the poor and not public administrations. Following a meeting in Lyon on 26-28 May 1942 (for non-occupied France) and in Paris on 23-25 June 1942 (for occupied France), Catholic congregations asked for the intervention of cardinals and bishops.[52] To support the demands of the superiors general, on 25 July 1942, Mgr Henri Alexandre Chappoulie, Delegate of French Cardinal and Bishops to the Government, wrote a letter to Raymond Grasset, Secretary of State for Family and Health, in which he pointed out that the new rules regarding the congregational personnel were ignoring the authority of the superiors general and would make it impossible to keep religious people working in hospitals.[53] The decree on the employment rules for medical and paramedical personnel was a compromise between the demands of congregations and the proposal of the government, even though it was more favourable to the latter. The law did not assimilate the congregational staff to the paramedical personnel working in hospitals and established that the hospital commissions could appoint and dismiss the members of the congregations only with the agreement of the superior general. On the other hand, Art. 67 of the decree gave these commissions the faculty to terminate any existing contract signed with a congregation

51 Imbert, *Les hôpitaux en France*, 100.

52 Letter sent by Mgr Henri Alexandre Chappoulie, 25 July 1942, AN, Fonds Ministère de l'Intérieur (Bureau des Cultes), F19 20316.

53 Letter sent by Mgr Henri Alexandre Chappoulie, 25 July 1942, AN, Fonds Ministère de l'Intérieur (Bureau des Cultes) F19 20316.

and replace its members working in a public hospital with religious people from other congregations or with non-religious personnel. In light of that, it was doubtful the capacity of the superiors general to oppose any decision of the hospital commissions over the congregational personnel. Furthermore, the decree established that the tasks of the members of congregations were determined by a decree drafted by the secretary of state to health.

The new legislation on public hospitals highlighted that the Vichy regime preferred to establish a more modern health care system rather than support the demands of congregations. Although this decision was justified on humanitarian grounds, given the poor health conditions of the French population during the war years, it was also motivated by political goals as it strengthened the control of public powers in the health care system.[54] While the reorganization of public hospitals furthered the process of secularization of social action, with the *Charte du travail* the Vichy governments introduced an authoritarian corporatist social order that clashed with the corporatist principles upheld by the great majority of French Catholic trade unionists.

An Authoritarian Corporatist Reform

Corporatism was a cornerstone of the new social order to be established by the National Revolution whose social design appeared in the *Charte du travail*.[55] Corporatism was also a central theme of the social doctrine of the Church. In the encyclical *Quadragesimo Anno* Pius XI claimed that the advantages of corporations were apparent to "anyone who gives even slight attention to the matter". Among them, the Pope mentioned peaceful collaboration between social classes and the repression of socialist organizations.[56]

The linkages between corporatism and Catholicism were particularly strong in France in the early decades of the twentieth century.[57] The intellectual efforts of René de La Tour du Pin, Frédéric Le Play, Albert de Mun, and Léon Harmel, corporatist doctrines become popular among French Catholic intellectuals and the establishment of a corporatist social order was a recurring object of debate among social Catholics.[58] For many of them, corporatism was the kind of third way between individualistic capitalism and totalitarian socialism that would allow solving the socio-economic problems of their time. However, the opinions of Catholics on this topic varied, notably on the

54 Undated archival document on the social and economic conditions of France, AN, Fonds Papiers du Comité d'Histoire de la Deuxième Guerre Mondiale, 72AJ/13.
55 Kuisel, *Capitalism and the State in Modern France* (Cambridge, 1981), 144. Leclerc, ed, *La sécurité sociale, son histoire à travers les textes*, 752.
56 Pius XI, *Quadragesimo Anno*, § 95.
57 Dard, 'Le corporatisme en France à l'époque contemporaine', 49.
58 The XXVII session of the *Semaines Sociales de France* held in 1935 was dedicated to corporatism.

relationships between corporatist organizations and state authorities, toward which most Catholics showed great distrust.[59] The ambiguous position of Pius XI, who praised the authoritarian state corporatism introduced by Dollfuss in Austria in 1934 but also emphasized the importance of the freedom of unionism, further contributed to the diffusion of different positions on corporatism in Catholic circles.

The major Catholic trade union, the CFTC, was suspicious of corporatism. The drastic limitation of freedom of association in authoritarian regimes that implemented corporatist reforms, such as Italy, Austria and Portugal, gave CFTC's unionists good reason to be cautious on this matter. In a speech in Bordeaux on 18 December 1933, the CFTC's President, Jules Zirnheld, said that Christian unionism could not accept the principles of Italian fascist corporatism.[60] At the CFTC National Congress held in 1934, Zirnheld reaffirmed the union's criticisms of authoritarian corporatism and claimed that the corporatist reforms introduced in Italy, Germany and Austria, regardless of their differences, shared "the brutal suppression of existing trade unions and economic organizations and the taking of possession of their patrimony; the total violation of the freedom of association; [...] the compulsory adhesion to the principle of a totalitarian state"[61] These criticisms against the state-led corporatism were included in the CFTC Legislative Programme drafted by the 1934 National Congress and in the CFTC Plan issued in 1936.[62]

Despite the concerns of CFTC's unionists about corporatism, there were common aspects between Catholic and Vichy corporatism. Inspired by counter-revolutionary ideas, both of them were against liberal individualism and socialism, defended family values, and rejected class struggle. However, there were also crucial differences between Pétain's corporatism and the prevailing understanding of corporatism among French Catholics. Two of them deserve specific attention, as they help understand why a large number of Catholics eventually rejected Vichy corporatism. First, Pétain's corporatism had a much broader ambition than that envisaged by Catholics, because the regime wanted to regulate a large variety of socio-economic activities and drastically limit the autonomy of employers and workers. Second, Vichy corporatism was distrustful of intermediary organizations and it intended to assign to public authorities a pervasive role in the management of corporatist organizations. In other words, while Catholic corporatism was based on the idea of peaceful self-regulation of socio-economic affairs by professional groups, Vichy corporatism intended to create a hierarchical social order managed by state authorities with the subordinated collaboration of the delegates of professional groups.

59 Mayeur, *Catholicisme social et démocratie chrétienne*, 53.
60 Zirnheld, *Syndicalisme chrétien et corporatisme fasciste*, 12.
61 Zirnheld, 'Le rapport moral', 926, author's translation.
62 Adam, *La CFTC*, 26.

On 8 July 1940 Zirnheld wrote to Pétain, then President of the Council of Ministers, to inform him of the CFTC positions on family and labour questions. In a reply sent on 14 July Pétain said that his opinions were consistent with those of Zirnheld and that a fruitful collaboration would be established with the CFTC to give to France a new spiritual development.[63]

The government's decisions contradicted Pétain's words. A bill approved on 16 August 1940, which was finalized with a decree issued on 9 November, announced the disbanding of all national professional organizations.[64] The fruitful collaboration with unions that Pétain had in mind did not imply an autonomous role for these organizations. This bill made it impossible for local unions to organize.[65] The dissolution of the CFTC was a shock for Catholic unionists who did not expect this decision, given the good relationship between their union and the government.[66] The bill of 16 August 1940 also imposed that every economic branch had to be regulated by a committee. These bodies were supposed to be temporary organizations for the coordination of economic activities that would function until the full implementation of the corporatist reform. Although they were composed of delegates from both employers and workers state authorities oversaw their decisions. As the law pointed out, in the current circumstances, employers and workers could not have full freedom to manage the new bodies. These committees became instruments that the government used to regulate national economic life and control professional organizations instead of promoting peaceful collaboration between social classes. In this sense, since its early steps, Vichy corporatism showed a strong distrust for intermediary organizations and it intended to create a hierarchical social order managed by state authorities with the subordinated collaboration of professional groups.

The disbanding of labour unions further strengthened the already widespread distrust of corporatism within the ranks of the CFTC. For this union, every kind of corporatism should have been based on the de la Tour du Pin's principle of "the free union in the organized body of the state". Even though this idea was quite vague, it became the intellectual paradigm through which most CFTC's unionists evaluated Vichy corporatist reform. The importance of this principle was highlighted by the General Secretary of the CFTC, Gaston Tessier, in an article published in January 1941 in the review *Droit Social*. According to Tessier, a corporatist order required the dynamism and autonomy of workers' unionism, which was not guaranteed by the new law introduced by the government that demonstrated a

63 Zirnheld quoted by Tessier, 'Le syndicalisme chrétien devant les récents événements', 37-38.
64 Loi du 16 août 1940 concernant l'organisation provisoire de la production industrielle, *Journal Officiel de la République Française, Lois et Décrets*, 18 August 1940, 4731-4733.
65 Launay, *Le syndicalisme chrétien en France*, 51.
66 Saudejaud, *Le syndicalisme chrétien sous l'Occupation*, 31-36.

centralizing aim.[67] Given the mounting opposition to the *Charte du travail* within the CFTC, some leaders of this union approached the Confédération Générale du Travail (CGT), which was critical of corporatism. The result of this rapprochement was the *Manifeste des Douze* (Manifesto of the Twelve), signed on 15 November 1941 by twelve unionists, three from CFTC and nine from the CGT, that affirmed the opposition to the corporatist reform introduced by Vichy and sketched the basic principles on which French unionism should have been based.[68]

The corporatist reorganization of industrial relations was introduced on 4 October 1941 in a bill called the *Charte du travail.*[69] The new legislation imposed the creation of a unique union for employers and workers who belonged to the same professional branch. Social committees, made up of the aggregation of the existing professional unions, had to be established at the firm-based, regional and national levels, to regulate the various problems related to professional life (e.g. salaries, working hours, security standards, unemployment issues, social assistance, and family benefits). However, these committees had more of a capitalist and authoritarian inspiration than a corporatist imprint because workers were not entitled to discuss any questions related to the management of companies but all the issues related to working conditions had to be regulated by mutual agreements between employers and workers' delegates. The *Charte* also forbade lockouts and strikes, and it included a series of norms that gave public authorities the power to dismantle every professional organization that they considered to be against the national interest. Although the *Charte du travail* did not fully subordinate unions to the government, it certainly depoliticized them and restrict their autonomy.[70]As noted by the Catholic philosopher and CFTC's unionist Paul Vignaux, the independence of workers and their autonomy from the tutelage of the state, two crucial principles for Christian unionism, were completely neglected by Vichy corporatism.[71]

The government made a great effort to demonstrate the consistency of the ideals of the *Charte* with the principles of social Catholicism and to downplay its authoritarian character that found favour with the German occupier.[72] For example, the *Pariser Zeitung*, the newspaper published in France during the war to express the views of the German authorities, expressed its satisfaction for the new law and wrote that "the Charte du Travail can be considered as the synthesis of the fascist corporatist system and the 'German Labour Front'".[73]

67 Tessier 'Le syndicalisme chrétien devant les récents événements', 35-40.

68 Manifeste des Douze, 15 November 1940, Archives CFDT, CH3 1.

69 Loi n° 4260 du 4 octobre 1941 relative à l'organisation sociale des professions, *Journal Officiel de l'État Français, Lois et Décrets*, 26 October 1941, 4650-4656.

70 Le Crom, 'Trade Unions and Labour Law in France during the Second World War', 118-120.

71 Vignaux, *Traditionalisme et syndicalisme*, 173-174.

72 Propaganda material, AN, Fonds Charte du Travail (1940-1944), F22/1774.

73 'La clef de voûte de l'organisation sociale', *Pariser Zeitung*, 31 October 1941, 10, author's translation.

The publication of the *Charte* opened a highly divisive debate among French Catholics. Although some of them were strongly critical, others enthusiastically welcomed the corporatist reform. Eugène Duthoit, President of the Semaines Sociales de France, wrote that the similarities between the pontifical sources and the *Charte* were striking and its "inspiration from spiritual power bursts forth with the force of evidence".[74] A similar opinion was expressed by Mgr Feltin, Archbishop of Bordeaux, who was one of the most fervent supporters of the *Charte du travail* among senior prelates. In a pastoral letter dated 2 October 1942 Mgr Feltin said that the *Charte du travail* "broadly speaking, gives an orientation in harmony with the social doctrine of the Church". On the controversial aspect of the unique union, he added that "if the Church recommended the formation of Christian unions under a liberal capitalist social regime, and penetrated, in its popular classes, by an intensive Marxist propaganda, it is because It saw in the association an effective mean for combating the tragic errors of this regime". Given that the socio-political conditions in Vichy France had changed and was more consistent with Catholicism, Mgr Feltin considered it a duty to invite all Catholics to cooperate in the professional organizations to be established by the corporatist reform.[75] Mgr Feltin's opinions were not shared by all French bishops. For instance, Mgr Liénart, Bishop of Lille, and Mgr Salièges, Bishop of Toulouse, repeatedly expressed their discontent with the reform and they claimed that it conflicted with Christian principles.[76]

To assist cardinal and bishops to understand the government corporatist reform, in October 1941 the Cardinal of Paris, Mgr Suhard, asked *Action Populaire* to study the *Charte*.[77] This task was given to Father Jean Villain, who was already familiar with the doctrine of the Vichy regime as he had summarized it in a civil manual to be distributed in schools.[78] On 22 October 1942, cardinals and bishops of occupied France held a meeting to decide what position to take on the *Charte du travail*. Following that meeting, they released a document in which they invited all Catholic employers and employees to contribute to the

74 The Semaines Sociales de France is an umbrella organisation that gathers together socially engaged Catholics. Duthoit, 'Préface', 2, AN, Fonds Charte du Travail (1940-1944), F/22/1778, author's translation.

75 Mgr Feltin, *Les syndicats et la Charte du travail. Lettre pastorale de Monseigneur Maurice Feltin*, 6-12, AN, Fonds Charte du Travail (1940-1944), F/22/1778, author's translation, 12.

76 Adam, *La CFTC*, 23-29.

77 Clément, *Les évêques au temps de Vichy*, 121.

78 Papers and documents on religious activities, 1941, AN, Fonds État Français (1940-1944), 2AG 27. Father Villain was the author of a pamphlet in which he had summarized the regime's corporatist doctrine. In this document, published in 1942, he wrote that the social committees were in perfect harmony with Christian social doctrine and added that "it is with great joy, with immense hope that we are waiting for the implementation of the provisions of the Charte" See Villain, *La Charte du travail et l'organisation* économique *et sociale de la profession*, 62, author's translation.

new professional order.[79] However, the attitudes of French Catholics was more diversified and critical than those of cardinals and bishops, notably among unionists.

The opposition of the CFTC and the Ligue Ouvrière Chrétienne (rebranded Mouvement Populaire des Familles, MPF, in November 1941) became stronger in late 1942, when the promulgation of all the regulations that accompanied the main text made the authoritarian nature of the government reform more evident. At the MPF National Council held in Lyon in September 1942, the rapporteur pointed out that the *Charte du travail* strengthened the state warship, it was a new attempt at social paternalism, and it could lead to totalitarianism.[80] The CFTC was more cautious than the MPF because it was internally divided and it was concerned that a refusal to integrate into the social committees would jeopardize its relationship with the Catholic hierarchies. However, Tessier and the other CFTC's unionists who rejected the *Charte* pushed their union to take a firm position against the corporatist reform. This happened at the national meeting held on 27 June 1943, in which, after a heated debate, the majority of the delegates voted against participation in the social committees. This decision confirmed the final rupture between the government and the CFTC.

The complexity of the *Charte du travail*, the delays in its application, and the resistance from the workers and several employers prevented the establishment of a comprehensive corporatist order. The *Charte* remained an ambitious project. However, in the few professional branches in which corporatist organizations were established, such as in the agriculture sector, the distance of these bodies from those envisaged by social Catholicism was quite evident. From its early stages, the clashes between the minister for agriculture and the corporations became constant. Disagreements and mutual suspicions came from both sides. While the Minister of Agriculture and Food Supply, Pierre Caziot, complained in March 1942 that the delegates of the Corporation paysanne, the new institution that gathered the major organizations dealing with agricultural affairs, intended to establish a second ministry of agriculture,[81] these delegates lamented the intention of the public authorities to control them. For example, in a pamphlet published in 1943, Louis Salleron, a leading theorist on agrarian corporatism, wrote that the minister of agriculture was used to violate the rules of corporations and to subject them to meticulous control.[82]

Instead of promoting the participation of workers in the life of their companies, corporatist organizations led a shift in the power relationship between labour and capital that allowed the introduction of more intense forms of ex-

79 Assemblée des Cardinaux et Archevêques, quoted in Duquesne, *Les Catholiques français sous l'Occupation*, 249.

80 Nizey with the collaboration of Chauvière, 'Le MPF à Vichy à travers les Conseils Nationaux 1940-1943', 27-69.

81 Boussard, *Vichy & la Corporation paysanne*, 165-182.

82 Salleron, *La Charte paysanne*, 15-17.

ploitation and stricter controls on the workforce.[83] In the end, Vichy corporatism was an authoritarian project that met the wishes of the more conservative entrepreneurs and the German occupier rather than realizing the peaceful collaboration between classes that was demanded by social Catholics.

A Legacy for Post-War Reformers

This chapter shows that key social policy reforms introduced by the Vichy regime were in conflict with Catholic values and interests, even though the regime publicly supported Catholic social values and Pétain was fascinated by the idea of establishing a Christian state.[84] Maternity and family benefits were expanded, as requested by the Catholic Church, but their trend was less dynamic and less resilient to inflation than social insurance. Through the modernization of the hospital system Vichy governments limited the influence of Catholic congregations on public hospitals. The attempt to establish a corporatist social order led the regime to disband all labour unions and integrate their organizations within the administrative state apparatus to drastically curtail their autonomy. Pétain embedded Vichy social policy reforms within the project of the National Revolution and used them in an attempt to establish a strong, authoritarian, and hierarchically organized state apparatus.[85] In doing so, he prioritized the political goals of the National Revolution putting aside Catholic values and constrasting the interests of Catholic organizations.

These conclusions allow us to answer the three questions regarding the impact of Catholicism on Vichy social policies posed in the introduction to this chapter. In relation to the first question that asked whether Vichy restored the influence of Catholicism on the social policy domain, this chapter provides a negative reply. Although Catholic ethical values left some imprint on Vichy social laws, the regime's social legislation was principally inspired by authoritarian attitudes.

The second question presented in the introduction wondered about the role assigned by Pétain to Catholic organizations in the system of social protection. This chapter points out that Vichy showed a clear intention to subordinate and control Catholic intermediary organization.

The remaining part of this section will answer the third question posed in the introduction, which asked what the political impact of the Vichy regime was on post-war social reforms. Vichy had a remarkable influence on post-war social reformism. To a large extent, this influence was the unintended outcome of the politics of the regime and the consequence of political changes that

83 Paxton, *La France de Vichy*, 269.
84 Ferro (with the participation of de Sampigny), *Pétain*, 117.
85 Bec, *La sécurité sociale*, 85-87.

Pétain had not planned, but that, nonetheless, occurred. Four of them deserve specific attention: the closer collaboration between the main forces that comprised the opposition to the regime, the disqualification of the Right, the delegitimation of clericalism, and the greater political engagement of Catholics.

The common opposition to Pétain favoured the collaboration between Catholics, socialists, and communists. This contributed to forging a sense of solidarity between them that helped in sharing ideas and developing common proposals for the future of France. The refoundation of the welfare state and the consolidation of French democratic institutions after the war would have been almost impossible without the cooperation established during the years of the Resistance.

The Vichy regime disqualified the Right. For several years after the Liberation, apart from marginal Pétainist groups, the French Right almost disappeared. Between 1944 and 1946, in that crucial period for the reorganization of the French system of social protection, the right-wing spectrum of the political arena was principally occupied by the MRP, whose political platform was in favour of socio-economic reforms.[86] The temporary weakness of conservative and liberal right-wing parties gave stronger political leverage to those forces that supported Keynesian policies and the expansion of social protection.

The early post-war years were characterized by the delegitimation of clericalism. This was mainly the consequence of the support given to Pétain by the Catholic Church up until the last months of his power. The indirect impact of these strict relationships between the Catholic hierarchies and Vichy was the decline of the Church's influence on French society and Catholic associations after the fall of the regime. The weakening moral authority of the bishops caused the beginning of the declericalization of Catholic civil society. The greater autonomy of Catholic social groups and the discrediting of the Church led social Catholics to place greater importance on their solidaristic, popular, and labourist values than on their denominational affiliation. Furthermore, the demise of clericalism and the greater relevance of solidaristic values contributed to closer cooperation between the Catholic unions and other labour unions to achieve the expansion of a comprehensive system of social protection.

The repressive authority of the Vichy regime provoked the evolution of the political attitudes of Catholics. The great majority of them became aware of a moral duty to have more direct political involvement. They started to believe that their engagement in civil society organizations, which had generally been a privileged field of Catholic mobilization, was not enough. This intellectual change in the Catholic milieu favoured the more stable integration of Catholic forces in the Republic and it was the premise for the foundation of the MRP, which played a crucial role in the foundation of French social security after the Liberation.

86 Irving, *Christian Democracy in France*, 70-73; Letamendia, *Le Mouvement républicain populaire*, 59-66.

3
FOUNDATION AND CONSOLIDATION OF A CHRISTIAN DEMOCRATIC WELFARE STATE (1944-1959)

The end of the Second World War inaugurated a rich period of social policy reforms. In most Western European countries, governments promoted a refoundation or dramatic restructuring of the national systems of social protection.[1] The poor laws, providing minimum benefits against extreme poverty, which characterized the social legislation of the late nineteenth and early twentieth centuries, were replaced with a broad range of income transfer programmes financed through progressive taxation.[2] In France, the governments in power after the Liberation implemented several structural social reforms. In these executives, Christian democrats held senior political positions that allowed them to play a key political role. This chapter investigates the impact of Catholicism on the French welfare state in the early post-war years and during the Fourth Republic, when the foundations of social security were laid down.

Comparative social policy scholarship has generally classified French social protection in the late 1940s as an example of a conservative or Christian democratic welfare state. The fragmentation of the system along occupational lines, wage-related benefits, welfare policies with weak redistributive impact, the prevalence of cash transfer allowances, passive labour market policies that discouraged female employment, and the prominent role of social part-

1 Guadagno, 'Theories of the welfare state', 111.
2 Esping-Andersen and Korpi, 'From poor relief to institutional welfare states'; Heclo, *Modern Social Politics in Britain and Sweden*, 10-16; Hemerijck, 'Two or Three Waves of Welfare State Transformation?', 35; Rimlinger, *Welfare Policy and Industrialization in Europe, America and Russia.*

ners (e.g. labour unions and employers) in the management of social funds were some of the most salient characteristics that permitted France to be considered a conservative or Christian democratic welfare state.[3] Though this chapter does not reject this classification, it would like to present some critical remarks on the Christian democratic character of French social security aimed at pointing out the limits of the influence of Catholicism on the French system of social protection.

Strong criticisms of the social policies introduced by the early post-war executives were recurring arguments in the speeches of the delegates at the MRP's National Congresses.[4] In a book of memories entitled *Les démocrates d'inspiration chrétienne à l'épreuve du pouvoir* (The democrats of Christian inspiration put to the test of power), the former leader and founder of the MRP, Francisque Gay, criticized the political action of the MRP and asked for a deep renewal of his party.[5] Likewise, in an article published in *Esprit* in June 1945, the Catholic philosopher Jean Lacroix pointed out that Catholics did not do the transition from the Resistance to politics. In other words, their governmental actions betrayed the ideals that they had developed during the Resistance.[6] At the general political elections in 1951, the MRP almost halved its share of the votes, dropping from 25.9 per cent in 1946 to 12.5 per cent.[7] Since the early 1950s Catholic electors increasingly started to prefer a Gaullist movement "that absorbed much of the MRP electorate".[8] The question is, why was dissatisfaction with Christian democracy so widespread in the French Catholic milieu in the period during which this party was building up a system of social security that, according to the current scholarship, bore the imprint of Catholic values?

The political discontent of French Catholics with the MRP is a complex problem whose exhaustive treatment is beyond the scope of this book. However, the study of several key welfare reforms enacted after the Liberation provides some answers to the question. This chapter claims that although the French system of social protection established in the late 1940s can be considered a conservative or Christian democratic welfare regime, it was also characterized by the strong role of central public authorities, high levels of bureaucratization of social security, limited autonomy of family associations

3 Esping-Andersen, *The Three Worlds of Welfare Capitalism*, 27.
4 Speeches given at the MRP National Congresses, several years, AN, Fonds Mouvement Républicain Populaire, 350AP/12-62.
5 Gay, *Les démocrates d'inspiration chrétienne à l'épreuve du pouvoir*, 28, 107-119
6 Lacroix, 'Les Catholiques et la politique', 70.
7 Letamendia, *Le Mouvement républicain populaire*, 152.
8 Berger, 'Religious Transformations and the Future of Politics', 119.

and intermediary organizations, and marginal investment in housing policies. These features were in contrast to the ideals supported by social Catholicism.[9]

This chapter continues the critical reading of the impact of Catholic values on the historical development of the French welfare state that has been undertaken in the previous chapter. More specifically, it argues that the presence of a mass Christian democratic party does not necessarily lead to the actualization of Catholic values in the social policy domain. The empirical investigation carried out for this chapter highlights that Christian democratic leaders not only promoted Catholic values, but they also disregarded them in order to consolidate their governmental positions and strengthen their electoral support. Some institutional features of social protection were also the consequence of a process of political bargaining that had little or nothing to do with religion. In this sense, we should be cautious about considering Christian democratic welfare states to be the outcome of the influence of political Catholicism. The presence of strong Christian democratic parties and Catholic unions can be a necessary but not sufficient condition for the projection of Catholicism into the public sphere.

The following pages pay specific attention to the MRP. Even though this party was short-lived, it had a decisive and long-lasting influence on social security.[10] In addition, in 1944-1945, Christian democracy was the principal political reference of French Catholicism. In France, as in Belgium and Italy, the Church asked Catholics to avoid dispersing their votes among different parties.[11] Although the MRP was unable to establish stable links with Catholic associations,[12] the majority of MRP's deputies elected in 1945-1946 came from Catholic associations, which contributed to their political socialization, and senior members of the CFTC were elected in the list of the MRP.[13] In view of their common ethical background, we should not be surprised that the main Catholic union sustained the MRP in the early post-war years. For example, circular n° 54 of the National Bureau of the CFTC, dated 25 July 1945, urged local confederations to ask their militants to support the candidates of the CFTC

9 To them may also be added limited public funding and the absence of a stable legislative framing for the recognition of the role of private schools until the introduction of the reform of the national educational system by the Gaullist government of Michel Debré in 1959. See Mayeur, *Catholicisme social et démocratie chrétienne*, 104.

10 Manow and Palier, 'A Conservative Welfare State Regime without Christian Democracy?', 149.

11 Vaussard, *Histoire de la démocratie chrétienne*, 176.

12 Pasture, 'Multi-faceted Relations between Christian Trade Unions and Left Catholics in Europe', 243.

13 Georges Bidault, André Colin, François de Menthon, and Albert Gortais were members of Catholic Action, Marcel Poimboeuf, Gaston Tessier, and Charles Viatte of the CFTC. See Letamendia, *Le Mouvement républicain populaire*, 63; Mayeur, *Des partis catholiques à la démocratie chrétienne*, 167; Mayeur, 'Les démocrates d'inspiration chrétienne', 118.

in the impending elections for the Constituent Assembly.[14] Given that Catholic unionists were present only in the lists of the MRP, this decision was an indirect political endorsement of the Christian democratic party. In 1945-1946 the links between the CFTC and MRP were also extended at the institutional level through the establishment of the intergroup of the *Syndicalisme Chrétien*, which was headed by the CFTC's unionist Henri Meck, who was elected President of Labour and Social Security Commission in 1946.[15]

This chapter is divided into three main parts. The first one presents the key ideas that inspired the Christian democratic social reformism at the Liberation. Then, the second part discusses some welfare reforms introduced by the early post-war governments. Three policy questions that were particularly important for the projection of Catholic ideals in the social policy sphere are here studied in more detail: the reforms of the institutional settings of social security, family policies, and housing policies. Finally, the third part provides some observations that evaluate the influence of Catholic values on the early developments of French social security.

The Roots of Christian Democratic Social Reformism

Political Catholicism is characterized by vague principles.[16] In consideration of that, this chapter starts by clarifying some central tenets of the political ideas that inspired the MRP's social reformism.

At the Liberation, like other European Christian democratic parties, the political platform of the MRP was inspired by reformist ideas. In 1944-1945 Christian democracy was not a conservative movement. The MRP was democratic, Catholic, and progressive.[17] The early post-war Catholic activists wanted to engage in politics, conceived as a dialogue with other democratic cultures as believers but without neglecting the *laïcité* of the French Republic.

The MRP had probably a stronger reformist agenda than other Western European Christian democratic parties because this movement considered itself a revolutionary force that intended to impress a profound transformation on France. A slogan that had been used at the party's first National Congress in 1944 was the request for *A revolution par la loi*. A motion adopted by the

14 Document of the 1945 CFTC National Bureau, Archives CFDT, Fonds Secrétariat Général (1944-1953), 4 H 7.

15 However, within the ranks of the CFTC the close links between this union and the MRP soon started to attract strong criticism and the CFTC National congress held in 1946 established that union leaders could not hold political positions. See Bethouart, 'Le ministère du travail et de la sécurité sociale', 91; Branciard, *Syndicats et partis*, 189-194; Portier, *Un siècle de construction sociale*.

16 Almond, 'The political ideas of Christian democracy', 742; Irving, *Christian democracy in France*, 22.

17 Goguel, 'Christian Democracy in France', 132.

aforementioned Congress pointed out that the MRP wished for

> a Revolution that will allow above all the moral and spiritual elevation of all men [...] a Revolution that will guarantee to everybody the right to live in security and dignity [...] a Revolution that will make the social and political democracy a full reality.[18]

The MRP's reformism was an exception in the political history of French Catholicism that has generally assumed conservative, if not reactionary positions. The MRP's progressive attitudes were the outcome of some historically specific circumstances in the second half of the 1940s, notably the demise of liberalism, the discrediting of clericalism, and the disarray of a large number of conservative Catholic groups because of their support for the Vichy regime. Even though social Catholicism was a common inspiring principle of the reformist agendas of Christian democratic parties, every national Catholic movement was shaped by different intellectual traditions. This is why it would be appropriate to speak of multiple kinds of Catholic social reformism. In relation to France, we can individuate three main ideological roots of the MRP's reformist agenda: social Catholicism; personalism; the ideas of the Resistance.

The MRP was a political outcome of social Catholicism and its quest for social reforms in contemporary societies.[19] The principles that characterized the origins of the MRP can be traced back to the political project for a Christian democratic party elaborated in 1943 by Gilbert Dru, a Lyonnais student executed by the Gestapo on 27 July 1944. Dru intended to match Catholic mysticism with the ideas of helping the poor, introducing social reforms to eradicate economic deprivation, and establishing a just economic order. The heritage of Dru's ideas had an enduring impact on the early Christian democratic leaders and theorists, and it led them to adopt a reformist political agenda.[20] Though Catholic social principles were shared by other European

18 Motion adopted by the 1944 MRP National Congress, AN, Fonds Mouvement Républicain Populaire, 350AP/12, author's translation.

19 The close resemblance between the political programme of the MRP and the social doctrine of the Church led the Catholic newspaper *La Croix* to define the MRP as a young party inspired by the social doctrine of encyclicals that was committed to the struggle for the triumph of spiritual values and the respect for the human person. *La Croix* also praised the political programme of the MRP, notably its social policies. See 'Le Programme du M.R.P.', *La Croix*, 30 August 1945, 4.

20 For example, Étienne Borne, one of the most respected theorists of the MRP, wrote that 'an act of faith [...] has no meaning unless it leads to action. Faith must generate thought and political engagement'. See Irving, *Christian Democracy in France*, 30. Albert Gortais, Deputy Secretary General of the MRP in 1947, claimed that political mobilization should be inspired by the values of Christian civilization. Speech by Gortais at the 1947 MRP National Congress. AN, Fonds Mouvement Républicain Populaire, 350AP/15.

Christian democratic parties, the MRP gave greater emphasis to republican ideals (e.g. freedom, justice, fraternity, and respect for human beings) and combined them with the rejection of clericalism.[21] The respect for the *laïcité* of the state, and the assumption that the Catholic hierarchy did not adequately understand the working classes suggested to the leaders of the MRP that they should avoid emphasizing the teaching of the Church in the MRP's programmatic platforms.

A second intellectual root of French Catholic reformism was the personalism of Emmanuel Mounier, which contributed to the distancing of the French Christian democratic movement from confessionalism and renovating its ideological baggage. As Mounier explained in an article published in *Esprit* in 1948, personalism was a complex philosophical doctrine with several origins derived from the existentialism of Søren Kierkegaard, the humanism of Karl Marx and Friedrich Nietzsche, and the spiritualism of Henri Bergson. Personalism was not a system, but a set of attitudes that placed at its centre the human person and the dialectic effort to make reality more consistent with human needs.[22] However, in the 1930s, the young Mounier conceived of personalism and politics as two distinct fields. Influenced by the anti-political views of Charles Péguy, Mounier considered politics as a domain in which ideals deteriorate through factionalism and the competition for power. However, personalism is a historically-grounded philosophy and the dramatic events that occurred after the late 1930s convinced Mounier that spiritual dimension and political engagement ought to go hand in hand to instil a spiritual dimension in our societies.[23]

The post-war writings of Mounier also stressed the importance of social reforms. According to the French philosopher, public authorities had to abolish the social and economic causes that alienated human beings, sustain trade unionism, promote the primacy of personal responsibility in the conduct of socio-economic affairs, and socialize economic production without establishing any strict state control.[24] Echoes of personalism can be found in the MRP's political platforms. For example, at the 3rd National Congress in 1947, the Deputy Secretary General, Albert Gortais summarized the long-term political trajectory of his party by saying that the MRP was committed to:

21 According to Robert Lecourt, the President of the parliamentary group of the MRP at the Consultative Assembly, "the MRP is a lay party that will never conceive the State other than lay". See, Lecourt, 'Notre laïcité', 1, author's translation. The rejection of confessionalism was also shared by senior members of the CFTC. In a letter written in 1944, Gaston Tessier, the General Secretary of the CFTC from 1919 to 1940 and from 1944 to 1948, wrote that the doctrine of the CFTC was based on Christian morality, but this union did not ask its members any act of faith. See Letter written by Tessier in 1944, Archives CFDT, Fonds Secrétariat Général (1944-1953), 4 H 112. Durand, *L'Europe de la démocratie chrétienne*, 114.

22 Mounier, 'Tâches actuelles d'une pensée d'inspiration personnaliste', 679-708.

23 Domenach, *Emmanuel Mounier*, 111-115.

24 Mounier, *Le personnalisme*, 120-121.

- establishing a system of social security aimed at reducing the social risks that individuals could not overcome by themselves;
- giving maximum freedom to private enterprises within the limits defined by the state;
- promoting the reorganization of companies to integrate workers into their management so that they had greater responsibility in taking managerial decisions;
- limiting the role of the state to avoid bureaucratic apparatuses that could threaten human freedom;
- defending social pluralism.[25]

The third root of the MRP's social reformism was the Programme of the National Council of the Resistance. The Resistance was a breeding ground for the MRP. The participation of French Catholics in the Resistance nourished their reformist attitudes in two main ways. First, it enriched their political background by opening it up to the influence of the ideas of the socialist and communist subcultures.[26] Second, through their collaboration with other forces, French Catholics developed a sense of national solidarity and the willingness to cooperate with other actors to introduce the social and economic reforms that inspired the Programme of the Resistance.[27]

Though these various intellectual sources of post-war Catholic reformism did not provide a detailed political programme, they nonetheless proposed some normative references. The following sections will illustrate and discuss several key policy reforms advocated by the MRP. This will allow an exploration of the MRP's reformism in action.

25 Speech by Gortais at the 1947 MRP National Congress, AN, Fonds Mouvement Républicain Populaire, 350AP/15.
26 Conway, *Catholic Politics in Europe*, 56-69.
27 Michel, *Les courants de pensée de la Résistance*, 392-403.

Foundation and Development of a Christian Democratic Welfare State

Four main laws are commonly considered to be the foundation of French social security: the decrees of 4 October 1945 (on the institutional organization of social security)[28] and 19 October 1945 (on social insurance)[29], the law of 22 August 1946 (on family benefits)[30], and the law of 30 October 1946 (on industrial accidents).[31] Given the breadth of the topic, this section considers only the debates and inspiring principles of the laws for the reorganization of the institutional settings of social security. It would also discuss some developments in two policy fields of great importance for contemporary Catholicism: family allowances and housing policies. These three policy areas can illustrate from different perspectives the successes and failures of politically engaged Catholics in shaping the early developments of French social security.

The New Institutional Organization of Social Security

The project for the establishment of social security started to be conceived at the end of 1944. On 9 September, the socialist Alexandre Parodi was appointed Minister of Labour and Social Security. Parodi asked Pierre Laroque to become director general of social insurance. Laroque was a former civil servant who joined Charles de Gaulle in London in April 1943 to come back to France after the Liberation. Laroque accepted on the condition to enact a comprehensive plan of social security.[32] His aspirations were not immune from utopian ambitions that animated not only post-war intellectual circles but also the political elites of the time.[33] After having received Parodi's reassurance that the introduction of such a plan was also his intention, Laroque accepted the proposed position and was formally appointed general director of social insurance on 5 October.

On 9 June 1945, Parodi also appointed a consultative commission headed by the State Counsellor, Maurice Delépine, to draft a comprehensive plan of institutional reforms. The debate in this commission revolved around two main aspects: the establishment of a unique territorial fund and the rules for the nomination of their administrators.

28 Ordonnance n° 45-2250 du 4 octobre 1945, *Journal Officiel de la République Française, Lois et Décrets*, 6 October 1945, 6280-6286.

29 Ordonnance n° 45-2454 du 19 octobre 1945, *Journal Officiel de la République Française, Lois et Décrets*, 20 October 1945, 6721-6731.

30 Loi n° 46-1835 du 22 août 1946, *Journal Officiel de la République Française, Lois et Décrets*, 23 August 1946, 7350-7352.

31 Loi n° 46-2426 du 30 octobre 1946, *Journal Officiel de la République Française, Lois et Décrets*, 31 August 1946.

32 Laroque, *Au service de l'homme et du droit*, 191-192.

33 Jabbari, *Pierre Laroque and the Welfare State in Post-War France*, 108, 131.

The government project intended to create a single territorial fund that managed the resources for all social risks instead of the existing highly fragmented system composed of a myriad of funds administered by a large variety of actors. For left-wing actors, the single fund was supposed to be a preliminary step toward the universalization of social security for all French people that was a leading idea of the programme of the Resistance adopted on 15 March 1944.[34] The project provoked strong opposition from the delegates of the mutualistic movement, the CFTC, and the representatives of family funds: an informal front that gathered together Christian democrats, self-employed workers, and upper and middle classes. The MRP supported the claims of these actors that were sceptical about the universalistic aims and were concerned for the possible redistributive impact of the reform. Their arguments mixed up vested interests and Catholic ethical principles. Three main criticisms were made about the establishment of a single territorial fund. First, this fund was a too powerful bureaucratic institution that undermined social pluralism. Second, the establishment of a single fund deprived workers of the freedom to choose a fund. Third, the interests of families did not receive the attention that they deserved because on the boards of the unique fund the delegates of family associations would have been a minority. Therefore, the interests of families were necessarily subordinated to those of other social categories.[35]

The rules for the nomination of the administrators of social funds were another controversial point in the early debates on social security. Whereas the CFTC wanted administrators to be elected by a proportional electoral system, the Confédération Générale du Travail (CGT) preferred that they were appointed. As the CGT was the largest union, the system of appointments would have guaranteed that it had the majority of positions on the boards of the social security funds.

The Commission Delépine rejected the project for the reform of social security by nine votes to eight. In the final report the Rapporteur of the Commission, François Mottin, pointed out that numerous members of the commission manifested their strong opposition to the totalitarian character of the project.[36] To overcome the opposition to the original project, Alexandre Parodi engaged in intense mediation during the weeks that preceded the parliamentary debate on the reform. However, the minister did not change his opinion about the need to establish a unique territorial fund. According to him, the preservation of a plurality of social funds preserved the mutualistic, unionist, and patronal paternalism over workers.[37] In preparation for the parliamentary

34 Conseil National de la Résistance, *Le programme d'action de la Résistance*, 5.
35 Report Mottin, AN, Fonds Assemblées Nationales, C//15293.
36 Report Mottin, AN, Fonds Assemblées Nationales, C//15293.
37 Speech by Alexandre Parodi, Archives d'Histoire Contemporain, Centre d'Histoire de Sciences Po, PA 18.

debate, the lobbying of mutualistic associations and Catholic groups against a single fund was intensified. The Confédération Générale des Cadres (CGC) also opposed the government project and it asked for a delay in the enactment of the reform. Strong opposition was also declared by the National Congress of the Fédération Nationale de la Mutualité Française, which would lose its autonomy in providing health care services.[38]

The reform of social security started to be discussed at the Consultative Assembly on 31 July 1945.[39] The arguments expressed by the various parliamentary groups substantially reflected the contrasting ideas, values, and interests that characterized the debate at the Commission Delépine.[40] In introducing the discussion, the rapporteur of the Labour Commission, Georges Buisson, who was a CGT delegate, pointed out that French social security had to achieve three main aims: the gradual generalization of social protection, greater redistribution of national income, and the establishment of a unique social fund. Although the first goal was also shared by the Catholic camp, the other two were more controversial. Gaston Tessier, the General Secretary of the CFTC, intervened during the parliamentary debate by declaring:

> I do not believe in the virtue of a system of unification imposed by force [...] I believe in democracy. I think that the sovereign nation can and has to organize itself, especially in and through freedom of association.[41]

The opposition by Christian democratic deputies was unsuccessful, even though it was resolutely supported by the CFTC whose 23rd Congress held in Paris in September 1945 pledged mobilization against the establishment of a unique territorial fund.[42] The decree of 4 October 1945 created the new institutional setting for social security that established primary, regional, and national funds in charge of the administration of social benefits.[43] The primary funds also included the existing mutualistic funds. Two-thirds of the members of the boards of social funds were appointed by workers and the remaining

38 Barjot, *La sécurite sociale, son histoire a travers les textes. Tome III*, 127.

39 Organisation de la securité sociale (Discussion d'une demande d'avis et d'une proposition de resolution. *Journal Officiel de la République Française, Débats de l'Assemblée Consultative Provisoire*, 1 August 1946.

40 Galant, *Histoire politique de la sécurité sociale française*, 53.

41 *Journal Officiel de la République Française, Débats Parlamentaires*, 1 August 1945, 1689, author's translation.

42 1945 CFTC Congress documents, Archives CFDT, Fonds Secrétariat Général (1944-1953), 4 H 7. On 21 September 1945 Gaston Tessier sent a letter to the then head of provisional government, Charles de Gaulle, to remind him that the Congress of the CFTC had rejected the establishment of a unique territorial fund. See Letter written by Gaston Tessier in 1945, Archives CFDT, Fonds Secrétariat Général (1944-1953), 4 H 112.

43 Ordonnance n° 45-2250 du 4 octobre 1945, *Journal Officiel de la République Française*, Lois et Décrets, 6 October 1945, 6280-6286.

one-third by delegates of employers. To mitigate the opposition of Catholic groups, it was decided that family allocation funds would benefit from a special, but temporary, autonomy from the rest of social security.

The promulgation of the decree of 4 October 1945 did not stop the lobbying of Catholic deputies and unionists and the mobilization of well-off and self-employed workers in support of a revision of the law.[44] The requests from these professional categories were supported by the MRP, which intended to rely on those electoral constituencies to consolidate its precarious position in the French partisan system. The MRP National Congress held on 13-16 December 1945 unanimously adopted a resolution in which it asked its parliamentary group to promote a major reform of the decree of 4 October, taking into consideration the demands of the mutualist movement and giving greater power to the delegates of workers in the management of social funds.[45]

The decree of 4 October 1945 also met with opposition from Catholic unionists, who were concerned for the autonomy of the mutualist movement and the role of the state in the management of social funds. The congress of mutualist funds held in Lourdes on 3-4 May 1946 asked for the abrogation of the decree of 4 October 1945, which the delegates considered "against the fundamental rules of freedom of association and unable to grant the necessary progress". This Congress also decided to undertake a broad campaign to promote the creation of mutualist funds inspired by Christian ideals and it asked for the support of the CFTC.[46] This union was equally critical of the institutional reform of social security introduced in October 1945. In a document published on 24 April 1946, Tessier pointed out that the public engagement taken on by the Minister of Labour and Social Security, Ambroise Croizat, to hold a

44 In a report presented to the Labour and Social Security Commission on 20 February 1947, the MRP deputy, Charles Viatte, supported the idea of a plurality of social security funds as advocated by the self-employed, the complete and definitive autonomy of family allocation funds, and the introduction of a new electoral mechanism that provided stronger representation for large families. See Documents of the Commission du Travail et de la Sécurité Sociale, AN, Fonds Assemblées Nationales, C//15409. See also Baldwin, *The Politics of Social Solidarity*, 168; Barjot, ed, *La sécurité sociale, son histoire a travers les textes. Tome III*, 45. At a meeting of the Labour and Social Security Commission on 6 March 1947, the delegate of small and medium-sized enterprises contested the unification of social security by complaining about the excessive financial burden imposed on self-employed workers who had to pay all social contributions themselves. He argued that different professional categories were subjected to different risks and had different needs. In accordance with that, the law should have given to every professional category the faculty to organize its own social security. See Documents of the Commission du Travail et de la Sécurité Sociale, AN, Fonds Assemblées Nationales, C//15409..

45 Quotation taken from a document written by Tessier in 1946 entitled 'La sécurité sociale: Une échange' (Social security: A discusssion), Archives CFDT, Fonds Gaston Tessier, 1 P 11.

46 Quotations taken from a document written in 1946 by Tessier and entitled 'La Confédération Française des Travailleurs Chrétiens et le plan actuel de sécurité sociale' (The Confédération Française des Travailleurs Chrétiens and the current social security plan), Archives CFDT, Fonds Gaston Tessier, 1 P 11, author's translation.

public discussion about the reform of social security was ignored by the government when it introduced the "liberticide measures" that reminded those of Vichy governments.[47] For the general secretary of the CFTC the establishment of social security was compatible with the plurality of social funds, as pointed out in a resolution adopted on 18 September 1945 by the 21st CFTC Congress, and the government should have allowed a broader parliamentary discussion of the reform to better understand its impact. In other words, for Tessier the government did not respect the commitments it had taken on and the method leading to the approval of the decree of 4 October 1945 was unacceptable.[48]

The demands of the MRP and Catholic unionists about the institutional settings of social security had to wait until 1946 to be fulfilled and they received greater consideration after 1947, following the breakdown of *tripartisme*.[49] On 3 October 1946, the election of the delegates in charge of social funds was introduced. This measure, demanded by Catholic unionists, showed that the balance of power between Catholics and leftist groups was changing in the direction favoured by the former.[50] A law approved on 21 February 1949 also granted the permanent autonomy of the family allocations funds.[51] Finally, the government headed by the MRP's Georges Bidault decided that the plurality of social insurance funds was not under discussion any more.

The final institutional settings of social security were a compromise between the demands from political actors and those from business groups. While the representatives of workers were largely responsible for the administration of social security, at the same time the labour unions did not contest the capitalist system. However, these arrangements implied the renunciation of one of the main long-standing demands of social Catholicism: the strengthening of the role of work councils. The history of French work councils, as in Belgium, was the story of a great failure.[52] The ultimate aim of the 'young theorists' of the MRP was to transform all larger enterprises into work com-

47 Quotation taken from a document written by Tessier in 1946 entitled 'La sécurité sociale: Une échange' (Social security: A discusssion), Archives CFDT, Fonds Gaston Tessier, 1 P 11, author's translation.

48 Document written by Tessier in 1946 and entitled 'La Confédération Française des Travailleurs Chrétiens et le plan actuel de sécurité sociale' (The Confédération Française des Travailleurs Chrétiens and the current social security plan), Archives CFDT, Fonds Gaston Tessier, 1 P 11.

49 As a consequence of the Cold War, the PCF was ousted from the government. This allowed the MRP to acquire stronger political leverage because no political majority could be achieved without the support of Christian democratic deputies.

50 Undated document written by Tessier and entitled 'Pour une vrai sécurité sociale: Efficacité dans la libérté' (For a real social security: Efficiency in freedom), Archives CFDT, Fonds Gaston Tessier, 1 P 11.

51 Loi n°49-229 du 21 février 1949, *Journal Officiel de la République Française, Lois et Décrets*, 21-22 February 1949, 1943-1944.

52 Pasture, 'The April 1944 *social pact* in Belgium and its significance for the post-war welfare state', 705.

munities, in which labour would share in ownership and policy making with the managers and technicians.[53] The enlargement of the competences of work councils would have been a necessary step toward this goal. According to social Catholicism, these firm-based bodies composed of delegates from employers and workers would have assured peaceful collaboration between contrasting interests and eventually they would have prevented the class struggle.[54] Even though work councils managed some social assistance programmes in the early years after the Liberation, their tasks were gradually substituted by those undertaken by social security bodies. In the end, work councils became just consultative bodies with no or limited influence on the decisions taken by the management.[55] The quasi-corporatist collaboration between employers and employees envisaged by social Catholicism, personalism, and the political platform of the MRP was sacrificed for the defence of the fragmentation of social security.

A close look at the institutional settings of social security would suggest three further factors that demonstrate the inability or unwillingness of Christian democracy to promote the ethical values of its social reformism. First, the fragmentation of social protection allowed a great disparity of treatment between workers. Though Catholics have always been in favour of the preservation of status difference, they have never justified the widening of social inequality. The fragmentation of social protection, defended by the MRP in its attempt to secure the support of the middle and upper classes, self-employed workers, and the mutualist movement, created new inequalities because the workers affiliated to the special regimes received more generous benefits than those affiliated to the general regime, and the chronic financial imbalance of the latter funds had to be periodically levelled by resources from the state budget. In other words, the workers of the general regime carried part of the financial burden of special regimes and of the privileges of their members. During a period of strong economic growth, like that that followed the Liberation, this inequality would not attract much attention. However, from the early 1970s, when budgetary constraints led governments to introduce some welfare cutbacks, the status of special regimes began to attract increasing criticism, even from Catholic-inspired unions. For example, in an article published in *Syndi-*

53 Almond, 'The political ideas of Christian democracy', 757.

54 The participation of workers in the direct management of companies was a central demand of the CGT that required the enlargement of the rights of work councils. For example, in the Rapport d'Orientation of the 26th Congress held in Paris in April 1946, this labour union asked for an extension of the role of the work councils that had become an instrument for the democratization of the economy. 1946 Federal Congress documents, Archive Institute CGT d'Histoire Sociale, Fonds des Congrès, 22 CFD 1. In contrast with Catholic groups, the CGT had a more political conception of work councils and it regarded them as a means that workers could use to control companies instead of establishing collaborative relationships between employers and workers.

55 Irving, *Christian democracy in France*, 87; Le Crom, *Syndicats, nous voilà!*, 60.

calisme CFTC in 1974, Pierre Boisard, a senior figure of the CFTC, wrote, "TO EQUAL INCOME, EQUAL CONTRIBUTIONS [...] The employees do not have to bear the deficit of the regimes whose beneficiaries can enjoy higher incomes and do not accept improving their contributory effort."[56]

Second, the system of social security became a highly bureaucratized apparatus. Following approval of the decree of 4 October 1945, the MRP often complained about excessive state control of social security. However, it did not do much to overcome this situation. The various primary funds were part of a hierarchical administrative system and their actual autonomy was limited. The final decision on social policies depended on the choices of governments, even though social partners had the majority of seats on the boards of social funds.[57]

Family Policies

Family policy is a prominent field of social intervention for every welfare state, as family allowances generally have a strong impact on households' living conditions.[58] Family benefits are also a policy area that has arguably attracted the greatest attention from social Catholicism. As Gortais pointed out at the MRP's National Congress held in 1946, for Catholic politicians the family was a fundamental unit of society, a small and natural community that had to receive economic support, social recognition, and political representation.[59]

While the institutional reorganization of social security opened heated debates between political parties, the discussions on the need to expand family benefits were characterized by almost unanimous agreement. This was related to the fact that familism was largely prevalent in the French political society of the time, though the MRP was the only major party whose political platform gave explicit emphasis to family values.[60] Therefore, it would be inaccurate to ascribe the development of family policies and the generosity of family allowances to the exclusive influence of the MRP.[61]

The early governments in power after the Liberation showed great commitment to expanding family policies.[62] An *ordonnance* of 17 October 1944 in-

56 Boisard, 'Sécurité sociale et solidarité', 16, author's translation.

57 Palier, *Gouverner la sécurité sociale*, 134.

58 Kaufmann, 'Les états providence européens dans leur rapport avec la famille', 121-122.

59 Speech of Gortais at the MRP's 1947 National Congress, AN, Fonds Mouvement Républicain Populaire, 350AP/15..

60 Lenoir, 'Family Policy in France since 1938', 151-152.

61 Bell, *Parties and Democracy in France*, 108; Letamendia, *Le Mouvement républicain populaire*, 364.

62 In a speech at the National Assembly on 6 August 1946 Ambroise Croizat affirmed that familistic and demographic concerns dominated not only the legislation on family allowances, but also that of social security. See *Journal Officiel de la République Française, Débats Parlamentaires*, 7 August 1946, 2989.

creased family allowances by 80 per cent for two-three children households and 50 per cent for more than three-child households.[63] However, the generosity of the allocations should not be overestimated, because several allowances that were grouped in the family branch of social security had other destinations apart from families. In this sense, they were used as a sort of compensation for other social risks. In addition, the nominal increase of allowances was partly eroded by the high inflation rates of the post-war years.

The various family benefits were not equally distributed because a natalist bias characterized the legislation of the time. This is noticeable when comparing the figures for family allowances by household type, shown in Table 2. The benefits for larger families were more generous than for smaller families. However, between 1944 and 1948 the allowances for two-child families grew more sharply than for other households. Whereas the allocation for two-child households and three-child households grew by 418.5 per cent and 332.1 per cent respectively, those for five-child households increased by 280.2. From late 1944, the rise in family benefits was mainly due to the re-evaluation of the salary that was used as a reference to calculate them. To prevent the devaluation of benefits in real terms, it was also decided to link this salary to the inflation rate. However, the strong expansionary trend of family allowances came to an early end in the late 1940s when the growth in fertility rates in the post-war years weakened political concerns about the demographic situation of the country. Social expenditure on family benefits continued to grow in nominal terms, but its real value started to decrease. This process of gradual retrenchment was mostly carried out by not linking them to the variation in prices and salaries. This led to a decline in the purchasing power of family allowances.[64]

TABLE 2
FAMILY ALLOCATIONS FROM 1944 TO 1948, BY HOUSEHOLD TYPE
(IN FRANCS PER MONTH)*

	Two Children	Three Children	Five Children
1 Sept 1944	405	1,215	3,038
1 Aug 1945	540	1,620	4,320
1 July 1946	1,130	2,825	6,215
1 Aug 1947	1,400	3,500	7,700
1 Jan 1948	2,100	5,250	11,550
Change from 1944 to 1948	+ 418.5%	+332.1%	+280.2%

* INSEE, *Les indices et séries chronologiques*. See <https://www.insee.fr/fr/information/2411675>.

63 *Journal Officiel de la République Française, Ordonnances et Décrets*, 18 October 1944, 976-977.
64 Chesnais, 'La politique de la population française depuis 1914', 220.

Post-war social reforms also implemented a broad institutional reorganization of the family branch of social security. A law approved on 22 August 1946[65] established the same level of contributions all over the country and the provision of benefits to all families.[66] The universalistic principle of the new reform made French family policies more similar to those of social democratic welfare states than conservative or Christian democratic regimes.[67] The benefits created by the law were family allowances, maternity allowances, prenatal allowances, and single-income allowances. Family allowances were given to parents from the birth of their second child. Maternity allowances were the prolongation of prenatal allowances. The single-income allowance was given to those households whose income depended only on the salary of one of their members.[68]

The new family legislation was motivated by different policy goals and not all of them were inspired by Catholic values. For example, maternity and prenatal allowances had an evident natalist purpose as they imposed age limits on which mothers could access these benefits. The origin of French natalism can be traced back to not only the Catholic subculture, but also the nationalistic circles that during the pre-war years organized some campaigns to raise political awareness of the poor demographic situation of France that, they claimed, was undermining the military strength of the army and making France increasingly dependent on colonial troops. Family allowances were also intended to give greater economic support to families and to keep women out of the labour market. The growing female employment rates were a cause for concern for the Church that denounced the negative consequences for the quality of family life provoked by women working outside their households. For example, in a speech given to the members of various Catholic women's associations on 21 October 1945, Pius XII asked for restoring "woman as soon as possible to her place of honor in the home as housewife and mother!".[69]

Though the expansion of family benefits could be considered a success for Catholic groups, a comprehensive analysis of the new legislation shows the limits of this apparent victory. Apart from its generosity (at least until the late 1940s), French family legislation was distinguished by a proliferation of laws and regulatory frameworks that strengthened state control of families. The stronger protection provided by the family legislation increased the ca-

65 Loi n° 46-1835 du 22 août 1946, *Journal Officiel de la République Française, Lois et Décrets*, 23 August 1946, 7350-7352.

66 Barjot, ed., *La sécurite sociale, son histoire a travers les textes Tome III*, 61.

67 Morgan, 'The Religious Foundations of Work-Family Policies in Western Europe'.

68 In the 1950s, family allowances were further extended to other categories of workers apart from those in the industrial and commercial sectors, but the basic institutional settings of family allowances remained substantially the same. See Lenoir, 'Family Policy in France since 1938', 159-164.

69 Pius XII, *Questa grande vostra adunata*.

pacity of the state authorities to monitor and condition family life. The involvement of public powers in the family sphere was institutionalized through the reorganization and the establishment of new specialized administrative bodies, like the Caisses d'Allocations Familiales (CAF), the Institut National d'Études Démographiques (INED), the Haut Comité Consultatif de la Population et de la Famille, and a myriad of working committees attached to the ministerial departments and parliamentary commissions. Although these institutional bodies deepened the understanding of family problems, they made the family a domain of scrupulous political and administrative control.[70] As a consequence, the institutions in charge of family matters became competitors of the Catholic Church, which had traditionally advocated for itself the role of interpreting the problems and needs of families.

Furthermore, a system of juridical and medical control over families allowed public powers to monitor the lives of those families that received benefits. For example, prenatal allowances were given to future mothers only if they agreed to attend some periodical medical appointments. It is doubtful that these forms of state intervention were consistent with Catholic teaching that claimed that the contention "that the civil government should at its option intrude into and exercise intimate control over the family and the household is a great and pernicious error", unless "a family finds itself in exceeding distress".[71]

The governments in which Christian democrats hold senior position promoted the expansion of family benefits. However, this 'victory of the family' was not probably a 'victory of Catholicism'. The strong role of public authorities, the high legislative density that scrupulously regulated family life, and the establishment of several public institutions that studied, interpreted, and promoted family policies gave to the state normative supremacy and a power of orientation on family questions that were in competition, if not in contrast, with the authority of the Church.

Housing Policies

After the Liberation, housing was a major social question in France, notably in the largest cities that were undergoing rapid expansion.[72] Housing problems were the consequences of four factors: the shortage of houses due to the material destruction of the war, the deterioration of the existing buildings, the

70 Lenoir, *Généalogie de la morale familiale*, 371.
71 Leo XIII, *Rerum Novarum*, §, 14.
72 Fahey and Norris, 'Housing', 479.

dramatic growth in population, and massive immigration from rural areas.[73] The precarious housing conditions of France attracted the attention of those social reformers that had collaborated with the Resistance. A document entitled 'Ensemble des travaux d'étude de la Résistance' (The complete studies of the Resistance) recommended a reform of the housing legislation and suggested that future governments should urgently prioritize the construction of new dwellings.[74]

Christian democracy was probably the party family that dedicated more attention to housing problems than any other. This depended not only on the electoral return of the question, but also on the ethical principles that inspired political Catholicism. Rural families were generally one of the strongest constituencies of Catholic parties, the MRP included.[75] The new urban working classes were experiencing a rapid process of dechristianization and their political preferences shifted toward the leftist parties, especially the Parti Communiste Française (PCF).[76] The new process of urbanization thus eroded the social foundations of Catholicism and the electoral strength of the MRP. However, the interest of this party in housing questions was also motivated by ethical principles. The full development of the human person envisaged by the social doctrine of the Church and personalism required liberation from material constraints. Home ownership, or at least a decent house, was a necessary condition for a good life, represented direct encouragement for the creation of new families by young couples, and made people less keener to support the redistributive policies promoted by leftist parties.

The balance of the housing politics of the MRP was a series of remarkable public declarations, but fairly limited successful reforms. The MRP started to pay attention to housing questions in 1944. One of the early references to housing problems appeared in the party manifesto approved by the 1st National Congress held in Paris on 24-25 November 1944.[77] A more elaborated document was presented at the National Council on 25-26 August 1945. The motion from Les Equipes Ouvrieres, an MRP specialist group that was used to discuss workers' questions, stated that the housing situation was a major problem for workers and young families. It then demanded the introduction of laws that would redistribute vacant houses to needy families.[78] These measures seemed too radical for most of the MRP delegates. The conservative and

73 In 1945, the average age of French houses was over 100 years. See Conseil Économique et Social, *Le bilan et les perspectives d'évolution du logement en France*, 21. From 1946 to 1955, the French population increased from 40,125 to 43,627 million. See INSEE, *Population*. See <http://www.insee.fr/fr/themes/theme.asp?theme=2>.

74 Works and studies drafted during the Resistance, AN, Fonds Raoul Dautry, 307AP/160.

75 Goguel, 'Christian Democracy in France', 109-219, 175.

76 Dansette, *Destin du Catholicisme français*, 44-46.

77 MRP 1944 National Congress, AN, Fonds Mouvement Républicain Populaire, 350AP/12.

78 MRP 1945 National Council, AN, Fonds Mouvement Républicain Populaire, 350AP/56.

bourgeois constituencies of the MRP electorate would have probably rejected a large-scale programme of requisition and redistribution of private houses. Similarly to what happened during the debate on the reform of social funds, the MRP decided to back the interests of upper- and middle-income constituencies instead of those of the lower classes and the final declaration approved by the National Council only asked for the creation of generous housing allowances.[79]

As a prominent organization representing the working classes, the CFTC was also concerned about the housing conditions of the French popular classes. This major Catholic union reputedly demanded the introduction of generous housing allowances. This policy also had an apparent moralistic imprint because housing allowances should be primarily targeted at large families so that women could stay at home to look after their children.[80]

An early policy intervention in the housing domain was the decree issued on 11 October 1945 that authorized public powers to requisition vacant houses and to allocate them to homeless families.[81] The law had a strong symbolic impact, but it was almost never applied by local authorities, if we exclude the requisitions of a very few buildings in Paris and other major cities. Another reform of the housing sector that deserves some attention is Grimaud Bill on 1 September 1948.[82] This law, which was intended to change the relationship between landlords and tenants, allowed a moderate increase of rents, frozen since 1914, on the condition that the owner renovated the house. Yet, the financial incentive provided to landlords was so limited that most of them avoided making any improvements to their properties. The new bill also introduced a housing allowance that was funded from the budget of the family branch of social security, and, particularly, from the abolition of the single-income benefits for families with only one child aged above 10.[83]

Despite the enactment of the Grimaud Bill and the introduction of new housing benefits, the promotion of access to private ownership through tax breaks was the preferred policy strategy adopted by early post-war governments. In contrast, limited resources were devoted to the construction of Hab-

79 MRP 1945 National Council, AN, Fonds Mouvement Républicain Populaire, 350AP/56.

80 'Avant d'augmenter les loyers IL FAUT INSTITUER l'Allocation-logement', *Syndicalisme CFTC*, 11-17 September 1947; 'Y a-t-il des remèdes à la crise du logement?', *Syndicalisme CFTC*, 06-11 May 1948.

81 Ordonnance n° 45-2394 du 11 octobre 1945, *Journal Officiel de la République Française, Lois et Décrets*, 19 October 1945, 6646-6651.

82 The new law took its name from the MRP deputy Henri-Louis Grimaud, who was largely responsible for drafting it. Loi n° 48-1360 du 1er septembre 1948, *Journal Officiel de la République Française, Lois et Décrets*, 2 September 1948, 8659-8668.

83 Ministère du Travail et de la Sécurité Sociale (1949), *Rapport sur l'application de la legislation sur les assurances sociales*, 11.

itation à Loyer Modéré (HLM, Housing at Moderate Rent).[84] In this sense, the policy paradigm of the housing legislation in the early post-war years showed more a liberal imprint than social Catholic inspiration. This conclusion is further corroborated by the policies introduced since the early 1950s. For example, in a law passed on 21 July 1950 the state guaranteed loans for the construction of individual or collective houses through the Crédit Foncier de France.[85] However, the financial aid was provided only on the condition that the beneficiary already had enough savings to cover at least 40 per cent of the construction costs. As a consequence, the most needy families could not receive any economic support from the new law.

Given the aforementioned interventions in the housing sector, it is not surprising that the policies introduced after the Liberation had marginal or no effects in overcoming the housing problems of France. Furthermore, the governments of the time continued to disregard housing questions to prioritize the reconstruction of the industrial apparatus of the country.[86] They also avoided introducing stricter administrative rules to regulate the housing market. Having had a pivotal role in French politics in the early post-war years, the MRP bears a heavy responsibility for the inefficacy of housing legislation. The lack of political voluntarism of French Christian democrats led the MRP to dismiss a policy field that social Catholicism has considered of great importance for the projection of Catholic values in the public sphere.[87]

However, the failure the post-war housing legislation did not discourage the activism of French Catholics. One of the early initiatives to ameliorate the precarious housing conditions of poor families and the homeless came from a former MRP's deputy, Henri Grouès, better known by the name of Abbé Pierre. In 1949 he founded the Emmaüs movement. This organization aimed to provide basic shelter for those who were living in the streets or facing major housing problems, particularly in the largest cities. Emmaüs was not only a charity organization with a Catholic background, but also a life experience. Most of the early members of this organization lived together in communities, managed common economic activities to raise money for the association, and shared an evangelic life style.

The Emmaüs movement demonstrated great capacity for initiatives aimed to raise the political awareness of housing problems. The most well-known example was the appeal called 'L'Insurrection de la Bonté' (The Insurrection of Kindness) made by Abbé Pierre on 1 February 1954 on Radio Luxembourg, to

84 Effosse, *L'invention du logement aidé en France*, 269.

85 Loi n° 50-854 du 21 juillet 1950, *Journal Officiel de la République Française, Lois et Décrets*, 23 July 1950, 7866-7869. The *Credit Foncier de France* was a public institute that lent money at low interest rates for construction work.

86 Conseil Économique et Social, *Le bilan et les perspectives d'évolution du logement en France*, 21.

87 Letamendia, *Mouvement républicain populaire*, 87-94.

remind French people of the miserable conditions of the homeless who were living and dying in the streets of Paris. To give greater resonance to his radio message, the Abbé asked the conservative-leaning newspaper *Le Figaro* (read by the powerful, according to the Abbé) to publish his appeal. The public message on 1 February had a terrific and unexpected success. Around 500 million francs (roughly 11.5 million euros in 2021) in donations were collected in a few weeks.[88] The employees of some companies even worked overtime to make a donation to Emmaüs. The radio message also had a remarkable policy impact. On 4 February the Parliament, with a unanimous vote, decided to allocate 10 billion francs (231 million euros in 2021) for the construction of affordable dwellings for people in need.[89] This outcome was surprising because just a month before, the same Parliament had rejected a proposal to allocate only 1 billion francs (roughly 23 million euros in 2021) for building emergency housing. The example of the Emmaüs movement and the successful appeal of its founder shows how an unintended consequence of the failure of political Catholicism to address social problems was the emergence of new forms of social engagement. What had changed was the focus of the mobilization of Catholicism, which moved from the political domain to the social sphere.

A Christian Democratic Welfare State?

This chapter proposed a critical reading of the influence of Catholicism on some key policy areas during the years of the foundation and consolidation of French social security. The research presented here does not pretend to offer an exhaustive historical treatment of the development of the French welfare state after the Liberation, but rather to highlight the contrasted, incomplete, and contradictory affirmation of Catholic values in the social policy domain. In this sense, the aim of the chapter was an attempt to integrate the existing studies of the role of Christian democracy in order to acquire a more fine-grained understanding of its historical role.

Although the academic literature tends to consider the French welfare state in the late 1940s as a conservative or Christian democratic regime, this chapter claims that we should be cautious about claiming that it had a Catholic imprint. The fragmentation of French social security was more the outcome of a strategy carried out by the MRP to consolidate its power position in the French political system than the influence of religious principles. The strong role of the state, the high bureaucratization of social security, and the margin-

88 Fondation Abbé Pierre, *L'Insurrection de la Bonté*. The conversion of 500 million francs into euros was done through the INSEE's Franc-euro converter. See INSEE, Convertisseur franc-euro.

89 Desmard, Étienne and Delahaye, *L'Abbé Pierre*, 46.

alization of intermediary organizations, notably work councils, diverged from the ideals of social Catholicism. The limited attention paid to housing problems and the liberal imprint of the housing legislation highlight that post-war governments neglected a policy area of great importance for Catholic social reformers. The chapter concludes that the French welfare state in the years of the Fourth Republic can be considered as an imperfect kind of conservative or Christian democratic welfare regime, a system of social protection that was far from showing a consistent influence of Catholic values.

4
CATHOLICISM IN THE YEARS OF GAULLISM AND MITTERRANDISM (1959-1995)

The establishment of the Fifth Republic in late 1958 was a major change in French political life. The semi-presidential system strengthened the powers of the president of the Republic, although his influence on political life should not be overstated. Paradoxically, the head of the state was burdened by his new powers that were counterbalanced by the increasing role played by the Parliament.[1] The two-round majority electoral system favoured the bipolarization of French politics and marginalized minor and centrist parties, including the MRP.[2] These dramatic political developments went hand in hand with the introduction of several welfare reforms aimed at reorganizing the institutional settings of social security and to adapt the social legislation to the dramatic social and economic transformations that were occurring in France.[3] This chapter investigates the influence of Catholicism on some crucial social policy developments during this epoch of remarkable changes by focusing on the years from the onset of the Fifth Republic to the end of the Mitterrand presidency.

The period considered here was characterized by a great expansion in social expenditure, which grew from 14.6 per cent of annual gross domestic product (GDP) in 1959 to 29 per cent in 1995.[4] Social benefits became the principal expense of the national budget and an increasing part of households'

1 Roussellier, 'Un pouvoir présidentiel encombré de sa force', 11, 21.
2 Letamendia, *Le Mouvement républicain populaire.*
3 Barjot, ed, *La sécurite sociale, son histoire a travers les textes. Tome III*, 329.
4 Palier, *Gouverner la sécurité sociale*, 32.

income.[5] Until the mid 1990s, the French welfare state maintained its conservative or Christian democratic imprint, even though the MRP had been experiencing an irreversible crisis since the early 1950s and was disbanded in 1967.[6] Philip Manow and Bruno Palier proposed an explanation of this intriguing puzzle.[7] According to these scholars, the French welfare state kept its conservative or Christian democratic imprint because the MRP was able to exercise a decisive impact in the years of the foundation of social security and, then, a process of institutional path dependency permitted the perpetuation of this influence.[8] This chapter does not completely agree with this conclusion for two reasons. First, Manow and Palier's argument overlooks the changing relationship between values and politics that had occurred since the early 1950s. In other words, they do not consider whether and to what extent some social Catholic values were sustained by leading political actors. Second, Manow and Palier's explanation inverts a dependent variable with an independent variable. In other words, the process of path dependency that preserved the conservative or Christian democratic imprint of the French welfare state should be considered the outcome to be explained, rather than the factor that justifies the long-standing influence of Catholicism on social security.

Instead of proposing an institutionally-centred analysis, this chapter advances a politically-oriented explanation of the persistent influence of Catholicism on the French welfare state. This chapter claims that the resilient conservative or Christian democratic imprint on social security was the unintended outcome of the limited political voluntarism of right-wing and left-wing governments that did not venture into introducing a far-reaching reform of social security.

The chapter also notes that social policy reforms introduced by the right-wing and left-wing governments between 1959 and 1995 did not follow a coherent trajectory. The works of Bruno Jobert and Pierre Muller are particularly useful in explaining this outcome. According to Jobert and Muller, policy reforms are motivated either by what they called the logic of dominion or by the logic of consensus.[9] While the logic of dominion leads to the introduction of liberal-oriented policies advocated by pro-business actors (e.g. employers' associations, liberal elites, and international economic organizations), the logic of consensus pushes politicians to implement laws that meet prevailing social demands because political authorities always fear the possibility of losing

5 Bichot, *Les politiques sociales en France au XXe siècle*, 91.
6 Pelletier, *La crise catholique*, 8.
7 Although Manow and Palier's study is aimed at illustrating the role of Catholicism up until 1960, it shows some intention of proposing an explanation for the long-standing Catholic imprint on French social security up until the early 1990s.
8 Manow and Palier, 'A Conservative Welfare State Regime without Christian Democracy?', 159-171.
9 Jobert and Muller, *L'état en action*, 24-33.

their legitimacy and power, when their decisions sharply diverge from the predominant demands of public opinion. Building on this theoretical framework, this chapter argues that the institutional reforms of social funds introduced in 1967 by a Gaullist government and the liberal turn of François Mitterrand in 1983 were examples of the logic of dominion. In contrast, most of the innovations to the family branch of social security introduced since the 1960s were examples of the logic of consensus. The evolution of collective values in the late 1960s undermined traditional Catholic familism, which was further weakened by the erosion of its social basis (e.g. patriarchal families, rural civilization, and authority of the Church).[10] Traditional Catholicism did not pay off electorally any more. In light of that, we can understand the liberalization of family legislation and the increasing support provided to working mothers and young couples without children instead of large families. However, for pragmatism, self-interest, and opportunism, the governments in power during the period considered in this chapter avoided implementing a comprehensive reform of French welfare that preserved its Christian democratic imprint.

This chapter is divided into three main parts. The first one discusses some key social policy changes introduced by Gaullist and conservative governments. Then, the second part studies some welfare reforms enacted by the socialist governments between 1981 and 1995. Finally, the concluding part summarizes the observations presented in the previous two parts.

The Social Reforms of Gaullist and Right-wing Governments

De Gaulle did not develop an original social thought. His inspiring ideas on social questions were derived from his family Catholic background, to which he always demonstrated great attachment.[11] Catholic ideals inspired the political platform of the Gaullist Rassemblement du Peuple Français (RPF) that a consistent part of Catholic electors considered a defender of their interests.[12] Furthermore, de Gaulle's thought showed some similarity of arguments, themes, and vocabulary with Roman Catholicism.[13] Gaullism and social Catholicism shared the opposition to liberalism and communism, the rejection of the class struggle, the effort of promoting a stable collaboration between capital and labour, attention to the conditions of the working classes, mistrust of industrialism, and nostalgia for an agrarian (and hierarchical) society. However, Gaullism and political Catholicism diverged on their understandings of the role of civil society and the separation of the state from religious organizations. In other

10 Lenoir, *Généalogie de la morale familiale*.
11 Rémond, 'Introduction', 7-8.
12 Goguel, *Chroniques électorales. 1*, 109.
13 Portier, 'Le général de Gaulle et le Catholicisme', 561.

words, de Gaulle distrusted intermediary organizations and he defended the *laïcité* of the state.[14] In light of that, we should not be surprised that Gaullist governments did not introduce social policy reforms inspired by Catholic values. The reform of social funds in 1967 and some of the developments in family legislation are two revealing examples that show the inspiring principles of the social legislation of Gaullism in the early decades of the Fifth Republic.

The Reform of 1967

In 1958, French Christian democrats welcomed the return to power of General Charles de Gaulle. Almost twenty years after Pétain, politically engaged Catholics were again supporting a former senior official who intended to save France during a difficult moment in its life.[15] However, their enthusiasm was short-lived. Discontent soon mounted within the ranks of the MRP. At the MRP National Congress in 1959, the intervention of the Minister of Labour and Social Security, Paul Bacon, was strongly criticized. The MRP's delegates considered that the measures introduced by the government were socially unjust and they blamed the Gaullist government for trying to impress a liberal turn on French social legislation.[16]

However, de Gaulle did not pay much attention to social legislation and the social policy reforms that he envisioned were quite vague. In a speech given at Oxford University on 25 November 1941, he envisaged a transformation of the social institutions of France, but he did not provide any clear detail about the policy changes he had in mind.[17] In a speech at the Royal Albert Hall on 18 June 1942, he declared: "the France that is fighting intends that victory be the benefit of all her children. Sheltered from regained national independence, security and greatness, She wants freedom, security and social dignity to be ensured and guaranteed to each Frenchman".[18] We had to await his return in 1958 to know the social reforms he wished to introduce. During a meeting with a delegation of the CFTC on 9 June 1958, a few days after he was appointed prime minister, de Gaulle presented a proposal for a constitutional reform that would have provided formal political representation for labour unions in the Senate.[19] Although de Gaulle's idea of transforming the Senate into a

14 Levillain, 'La pensée sociale du général de Gaulle face à l'héritage du Catholicisme social', 49; Petitfils, *Le gaullisme*, 39-40.

15 We are referring here to the crisis of May 1958 when there was an attempt at a military coup in Algeria, intended to prevent the formation of the government of Pierre Pflimlin in France and to impose a radical right-wing turn on French politics.

16 MRP 1949 National Congress, AN, Fonds Mouvement Républicain Populaire, 350AP/25.

17 De Gaulle, *Discours et messages*, 1, 146.

18 Ibid, 204.

19 Descamps, 'La CFTC-CFDT et la politique sociale du general de Gaulle et de ses gouvernments 1958-1968', 167.

quasi-corporatist body was not implemented, the debate on the reform of social institutions went on. In the first half of the 1960s, several study reports envisaged a transformation of social security.[20] The main topics around which the discussion revolved around were the control of the increase of social expenditure and the reform of the institutional bodies of social security. With these purposes in mind, in April 1964, Georges Pompidou appointed a commission aimed at proposing some solutions to the financial problems affecting social security and suggesting a reform of its institutional settings.[21] The Conseil National du Patronat Français (CNPF), the main employers' association in France, took part in this debate by publishing two programmatic documents. In the text issued in 1965, which reproposed several ideas already exposed in that published in 1961, French employers asked for stricter technical control of social security, saying that its expansion had to be monitored by independent technocratic bodies because the increase in social expenditure had negative consequences for the economic competitiveness of the country. Furthermore, the CNPF supported the idea that the administrations of the different social risks had to be separated from each other because their common management provoked financial confusion, and the boards of social insurance funds had to be composed of an equal number of delegates of employers and employees.[22] In this sense, the CNPF was demanding a radical transformation of the policy paradigm that inspired the social reforms introduced in the early post-war years. According to the main association of French employers, social benefits were not an investment, but an economic burden. The government seemed to have been quite sensitive to the arguments of the CNPF, as the reform of social security funds introduced in 1967 resembled the CNPF's proposals. The government elaborated this reform without consulting social partners, even though some of its principles were leaked in the spring and early summer of 1967.[23] The main innovations of the reform were as follows:

a. Introducing the separated administrative management of social risks. Four different branches of social security were created that administered sickness, industrial accidents, old-age pension, and family benefits. Three different funds in charge of their resources were established:

20 'Le rapport Friedel: décharger les caisses d'allocations familiales des dépenses indues notamment de l'allocation-logement', *Le Monde*, 28 March 1967; 'Le rapport Canivet: réduire les dépenses de santé les moins utiles, abaisser le coût des produits pharmaceutiques', *Le Monde*, 28 March 1967.

21 Barjot, ed, La sécurité sociale, 455; Valat and Laroque, 'La démocratie sociale dans la gestion de la Sécurité sociale de 1945 à 1994', 99.

22 Commissariat Général du Plan, *Commissariat général du plan d'équipement et de la productivité.*

23 Kocher-Marboeuf, *Le patricien et le général*, 59-72.

- Caisse Nationale de l'Assurance Maladie des Travailleurs Salariés (CNAMTS) for sickness, maternity, invalidity, and industrial accidents;
- Caisse Nationale d'Assurance Vieillesse (CNAV) for old-age pensions;
- Caisse Nationale des Allocations Familiales (CNAF) for family benefits.

b. The four branches of social security had to maintain their financial equilibrium, and in the case of deficit their administrators were allowed to increase social contributions or reduce social services;
c. Local social funds were strictly subordinated to national funds;
d. Workers and employers were represented by an equal number of delegates on all administrative boards;
e. The delegates of workers and employers were appointed (not elected, as before) from the most representative organizations of workers and employers.[24]

The administrative separation between the different social risks and the financial autonomy of funds further segmented French social security as workers received different treatment, not only in accordance with their professional category, but also because of the financial situation of the social fund to which they were affiliated. As pointed out by Laurent Lucas, a senior member of the National Bureau of the Confédération Française Démocratique du Travail (CFDT), the new statute of social funds created a compartmentalization of social security that seemed more inspired by the logic of private insurance than by social solidarity.[25] Additionally, the establishment of a rigid mechanism to keep the budgetary equilibrium of social funds further showed the liberal imprint of the reform.[26]

Although *Le Monde* wrote that the reactions of professional organizations showed a quasi-general hostility, the attitudes of the various social and political actors mainly reflected a left-right divide.[27] While the government defended the reform, the Left harshly criticized it. At the end of a meeting between a delegation of the Fédération de la Gauche Démocrate et Socialiste and the PCF on 3 August, the two organizations published a joint statement in which they claimed that "the government is engaged in the dismantling of social security as it was established in France in the aftermath of the Liberation" and they added that this politics was a deliberate attempt of social

24 Ordonnance n° 67-706 du 21 août 1967, ordonnance n° 67-707 du 21 août 1967, ordonnance n° 67-708 du 21 août, ordonnance n° 67-709 du 21 août 1967, 1967, *Journal Officiel de la République Française*, 21-22 August 1967, 8403-8414.

25 Lucas, 'Le comité pleins feux sur les ordonnances', 3.

26 Damamme and Jobert, 'Les paritarismes contre la démocratie sociale', 93.

27 'INTÉRESSEMENT DES SALARIÉS: réserve des organisations professionnelles', *Le Monde*, 3 August 1967.

regression".[28] In the same vein, on 10 August 1967 the National Bureau of Parti Socialiste Unifié (PSU) released a statement that claimed that the *ordonnances* of the government were "a socially unjust, economically untimely, and politically outrageous measure". According to the PSU, with the new reform "the social system of France will be subordinated only to the imperatives of the entrepreneurs".[29]

Some labour unions were equally critical. The CGT, whose influence on social funds was dramatically curtailed by the new system of appointment of the delegates, declared that the workers would not accept the reform and the CFDT defined the new legislation as a step back of twenty years.[30] However, smaller unions, such as Force Ouvrière (FO) and the new CFTC, composed of a minority of former CFTC's unionists who had not accepted the deconfessionalization of their union and its transformation into the CFDT, did not share the attitudes of the CGT and the CFDT. The reform could strengthen the influence of smaller unions on social funds because they could obtain the presidency of them with the votes of the employers' delegates. The reform of social funds did not provoke the outbreak of protest action. Although the trade unions announced a strong mobilization for the autumn of 1967, the rallies against the reorganization of social security were fairly small. As noted by *Le Monde*, these demonstrations appeared to be more the work of the militants than of the masses.[31]

As expected, the institutional reform of social funds increased the influence of the smaller unions. This was particularly the case for the CFTC. In 1967, with the votes of the CNPF the CFTC's unionist Pierre Boisard was elected President of CNAF and he maintained this post for 25 years, until his retirement in 1992. Similarly to what happened to the ministry of labour in the 1950s that became a stronghold of the MRP, the CNAF became a fief of the CFTC from the late 1960s to the early 1990s.[32] This case was an example that showed how the decline of political Catholicism in France was not matched by a reduction in the influence of Catholic actors in the administration of social security because socially and politically engaged Catholics could rely on their expertise and their strategic positioning to obtain substantial advantages.

The reform of 1967 changed the logic of social security by imposing a liberal-oriented turn on it. However, the legislator did not go so far as to im-

28 'La Fédération de la gauche et le parti communiste condamnent "une volonté délibérée de régression sociale"', *Le Monde*, 5 August 1967. The Fédération de la Gauche Démocrate et Socialiste was a coalition of left-wing groups founded in 1965 to sustain Mitterrand's candidacy for the presidential elections.

29 'Le P.S.U. dénonce «le mépris des droits des assurés sociaux»', *Le Monde*, 10 August 1967.

30 'INTÉRESSEMENT DES SALARIÉS: réserve des organisations professionnelles', *Le Monde*, 3 August 1967.

31 'Réformes sociales: l'histoire controversée des ordonnances', *Le Monde*, 2 September 2017.

32 Béthouart, 'Le ministère du travail et de la sécurité sociale', 67-105.

plement a more comprehensive transformation of the overall system of social protection. The gradual convergence between the CGT and the CFDT, the more politically-oriented opposition taken by these unions, the opposition of the PS and the PCF, and a social climate that forecast the protests of 1968 suggested to Gaullists that they should not implement other structural transformations of social security. Although in the second half of the 1960s the Gaullist movement was deeply influenced by liberal ideas, it was more attentive to the management of power.

Family Policies under the Right in Power

Until the 1960s French family laws were still shaped by Catholic traditionalist values. Despite the *laïcité* of the state, the Republic had delegated to the Church the regulation of the intimate.[33] The second half of the 1960s and most notably the 1970s represented a turning point. A series of legal reforms liberalized the family code and several developments in the family branch of social security weakened the Catholic imprint on the French welfare state. While the former shattered the legal-normative influence of Catholicism on French law, the latter undermined, at least in part, the socio-economic foundations of Catholic familism. Four main features characterized the policy developments in family legislation introduced by Gaullist and right-wing governments since the second half of the 1960s:

- moral liberalization of legislation;
- decline in family benefits;
- support for larger families;
- support for working mothers.

Moral Liberalization of Legislation

Since the second half of the 1960s, Gaullist and right-wing governments have enacted, with the political support of left-wing parties, a series of reforms that liberalized family legislation. In 1965, they changed the laws of the matrimonial regimes to allow women to undertake a professional activity without the prior authorization of their husbands.[34] In 1967, the Neuwirth Bill legalized the use of birth control pills for all women aged over eighteen.[35] In 1970, parental authority was reformed and in the family code the words "paternal power"

33 Portier, 'Norme démocratique et loi naturelle dans le Catholicisme contemporain', 39.

34 Loi n° 65-679 of 13 July 1965, *Journal Officiel de la République Française, Lois et Décrets*, 14 July 1965, 6044-6056.

35 Loi n° 67-1176 du 28 décembre 1967, *Journal Officiel de la République Française, Lois et Décrets*, 29 December 1967, 12861-12862.

were replaced by the more neutral expression "parental authority".[36] Finally, in 1975, the Veil Bill decriminalized abortion, which was authorized for therapeutic reasons and at the request of women in distress.[37]

These legislative developments significantly weakened the Catholic imprint on French family policies. The impact of the new laws promoted a reconsideration of the conception of the family.[38] They emancipated women and granted greater autonomy to children from the patriarchal authority of men. In other words, the family underwent a process of internal democratization. Furthermore, the new policies opened up the sphere of public intervention to new social risks (e.g. medical services related to family planning and abortion) and redefined the focus of social policies that became less centred on the family and more targeted on its members. This gradual shift of policy concern contributed to further distinguishing French family social legislation from that of other conservative or Christian democratic welfare states and to make it more similar to social democratic welfare regimes.

The aforementioned reforms met with firm opposition from the Catholic Church that under the pontificate of Paul VI took a conservative turn on morality issues. The reaction of the main family associations to the introduction of abortion was either hostile or prudent. The Confédération Nationale des Associations Familiales Catholiques (AFC) strongly rejected the new legislation. Throughout the 1960s and 1970s, the AFC continued to defend traditional Catholic familism, even though its intransigent positions were largely ineffective in preventing the liberalization of the family domain. In contrast, the Union Nationale des Associations Familiales (UNAF) abstained from opposing the Veil Bill. The close partnership that this organization established with public authorities probably contributed to moderating its positions.

The moral liberalization of family legislation was also contested by several politicians, who defended conservative moral views. Even though the party system of the Fifth Republic was not shaped by religious cleavages, religious values often re-emerged during political debates related to ethical issues.[39] In his speech at the National Assembly, the Gaullist deputy Albert Liogier described the Veil Bill as an example of moral degradation and he defined contraception and abortion as evil exercises of sexuality.[40] The well-known

36 Loi n° 70-459 du 4 juin 1970, *Journal Officiel de la République Française, Lois et Décrets*, 5 June 1970, 5227-5230.

37 Loi n° 75-17 du 17 janvier 1975, *Journal Officiel de la République Française, Lois et Décrets*, 18 January 1975, 739-741.

38 *Rerum Novarum* considered the family a small society whose rights are independent of the state and which is governed by the authority of fathers. See Leo XIII, *Rerum Novarum*, § 12-13. In the encyclical *Casti et Connubii* issued in 1930, Pius XI affirmed "the primacy of the husband with regard to the wife and children, the ready subjection of the wife and her willing obedience". See Pius XI, *Casti Connubii*, § 26.

39 Elgie, 'France', 127.

40 *Journal Officiel de la République Française, Débats Parlamentaires*, 28 November 1974, 7184.

jurist and Gaullist deputy Jean Foyer presented an amendment that asked for the rejection of the Veil Bill because he considered it against the European Convention of Human Rights. However, in contrast with Italy, in which the legalization of abortion had to face the opposition of the Right and the DC,[41] the political mobilization against abortion in France was weak and it principally came from single deputies.

Decline of Family Benefits

Until the Left came to power in 1981, family benefits decreased from 3.2 per cent of GDP in 1960 to 1.9 per cent in 1980.[42] This decline is more evident if per capita incidence is considered. As shown in Figure 2, family allowances per child based on per capita GDP followed a downward trend until 1976, when they reached their lowest level. Then, they started to increase after the re-evaluations introduced by Valéry Giscard d'Estaing and the early Mitterrand governments.

An increase in family allowances was a constant demand of trade unions and Catholic associations. The gradual erosion of these allowances negatively affected low-income households, particularly those living in urban areas where the living costs were generally higher than in the countryside. The growth of family benefits had also been far below the evolution of salaries.[43]

FIGURE 2
FAMILY ALLOCATIONS PER CHILD BASED ON PER CAPITA GDP FROM 1959 TO 1981 (% FIGURES)*

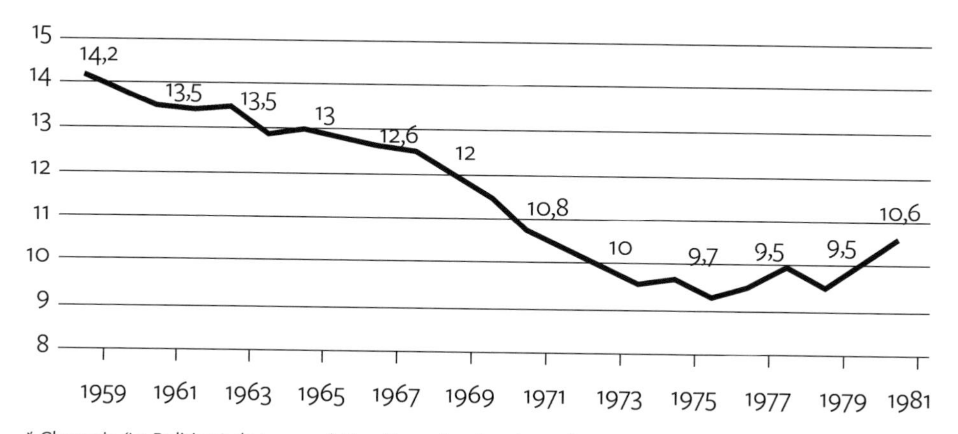

* Chesnais, 'La Politique de La population Française depuis 1914', 221.

41 Saresella, *Cattolici a sinistra*, 148-152.
42 CNAF, *Prestations familiales 2011*, 72.
43 On the other hand, the family allocations of non-salaried workers were ameliorated in the early 1950s. This was mainly due to their later development in comparison with salaried workers' allocations. See Ceccaldi, *Histoire des prestations familiales en France*, 159.

This resulted in a decline in the economic return on these allocations because a part of the household income had to be devoted to guaranteeing the same living standards for all members of the family.[44]

At least three main causes can explain the relative decline in family benefits. First, the weakening of the political influence of the MRP deprived the family camp of one of the strongest supporters of generous benefits. This role was partly assumed by Gaullists. However, the liberal wing of Gaullism, notably with Georges Pompidou, who wished to integrate Gaullist principles with liberalism, became the major component of the Gaullist movement and this political development did not make Gaullists as strong defenders of family interests as the MRP's deputies were.[45] Second, since the beginning of the 1960s, new social demands (e.g. more sophisticated medical services, high quality education, and decent old-age pensions) acquired greater importance than family benefits. The social constituencies that supported these new demands were more influential than family associations and the sense of pragmatism that characterized the Gaullist movement led it to disregard family interests. Third, the political and economic context of the 1950s was different from that of the late 1940s. Although France had undergone rapid industrial development in the early post-war years, the budgetary situation of the state was worsening. Public spending for the reconstruction of the country and several unproductive expenses, notably those related to colonial wars, required urgent intervention. When he came to power in 1958 de Gaulle appointed Antoine Pinay as Minister of Finances, a conservative-liberal politician who was popular among small savers, and asked a commission of experts chaired by the liberal economist Jacques Rueff to draft a report. Pinay and Rueff recommended the adoption of three key measures: fighting the rise of inflation through a reduction in public spending, sustaining the franc, and supporting exportation. These policy recommendations were fully accepted by de Gaulle who impressed a liberal turn on France that implied a subordination of social policies to economic needs.[46]

Support for Larger Families

The evolution of family benefits was not similar for all household types. As shown in Figure 3, between 1950 and 1970 the increase in family allocations for a household with two children was lower than the rise in inflation rate. In contrast, family allowances for a household with five children remained above the inflation.

44 Ibid., 160.
45 Petitfils, *Le gaullisme*, 103-104.
46 Berstein and Milza, *Histoire de la France au XXe siècle, Vol. III*, 132-133.

FIGURE 3
INCREASE IN FAMILY BENEFITS AND PRICES FROM 1950 TO 1970, BY HOUSEHOLD TYPE (INDEX NUMBERS BASE 1950=100)*

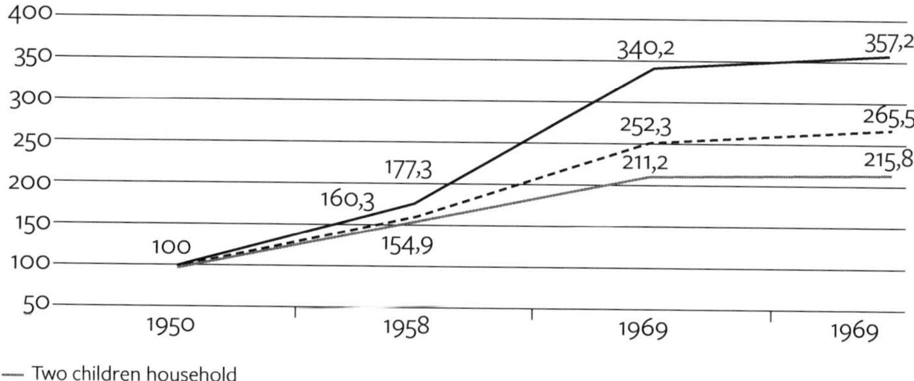

— Two children household
— Five children household
-- Prices
* Steck, 'Partie II', 335.

The greater financial support provided to larger families became more apparent in the late 1970s, when the declining fertility rate caused some public concern about the demographic situation of France. However, the governments of the time were not particularly active in this field, although they promised to implement some pro-natalist measures. A set of legislative innovations, targeted at larger families and with natalist purposes, was only introduced after 1977 and mainly for electoral reasons. Given the increasing consensus of the Left, guided by Mitterrand, who had lost the 1974 presidential election by a handful of votes, Pompidou wanted to secure the electoral support of larger families and Catholic constituencies. However, he did that without introducing structural reforms of the family branch of social security. In 1977, a complementary family allowance for families with three or more children was introduced. Between 1 January 1978 and 1 July 1979 family benefits for households with more than three children were substantially increased. Maternity leave for mothers with more than three children became 26 weeks instead of 16 weeks. A minimum income and special tax deductions were also guaranteed to larger families. Though the new laws seem to favour larger families and fulfil the demands of Catholic family organizations, they were mostly ad hoc measures that were ineffective in ameliorating the economic conditions of larger families.[47] In other words, they were examples of agenda marketing, an

47 Lenoir, 'Family Policy in France since 1938', 174-179.

attempt by the government to show its symbolic commitment to family interests rather than comprehensive policy reforms.[48]

Support for Working Mothers

In France, as in other Western European countries, female employment rates significantly increased after the end of the Second World War, notably in the early 1970s and among younger cohorts.[49] In light of that, we should not be surprised that the introduction of measures in support of female employment and working mothers obtain some relevance in the political agendas of the governments in power in the 1970s and 1980s. The participation of women in the labour market was not equally distributed among different occupational groups and social classes. The growth in female employment was higher among blue-collar families than among upper class families. In addition, the length of the working day varied according to the profession of husbands. While the wives of managers tended to work 6.9 hours per day on average, the length of the working day for blue-collar workers' wives was above 8 hours. Furthermore, the latter took more time to travel to their workplace than the more well-off women.[50] In other words, low-income mothers tended to work longer and they faced greater difficulty in reconciling family and professional life. The awareness of these problems started to mobilize not only feminist organizatons, but also Catholic associations. In 1975, the question of reconciling family duties and professional life was considered the topic of the year by the AFC. The motion on family policy at the AFC's 1977 General Assembly affirmed the importance of facilitating working mothers in the accomplishment of their educative mission.[51] The popularity of work-family reconciliation policies was so widespread that even Catholic groups backed them, and they gradually changed their traditionally critical attitudes toward working mothers, even though they continued to prefer that women remain at home.

The right-wing executives in power in the 1970s introduced some work-family reconciliation policies.[52] The government of Raymond Barre, for example, distinguished itself with its effort in promoting part-time employment, increasing financial aid for those families whose children needed to be looked after while the parents were at work, and supporting the establishment

48 Parsons, *Public Policy*, 121-125.

49 Afsa and Buffeteau, 'L'activité féminine en France', 85-91; INSEE, *Données sociales*, 26-32; Riboud, 'An analysis of women's labor force participation in France', S179-S183.

50 CNAF *Enquête 1971* on the needs and aspiration of families and young people, AN, Fonds Bureau de la Famille (Direction de l'Action Sociale), 19830667/5.

51 Assemblée Générale de la CNAFC, 'Motion sur la polique familiale', 33.

52 A study commission estimated that in 1977 more than half of births, around 380,000, were to professionally active women. Among them, 240,000 were employed in the private sector. See Ministère du Travail et de la Participation, *Maternité et travail*, 1.

of collective and family crèches.[53] Though these policies did not introduce a dramatic change of the family legislation, they weakened the traditional Catholic imprint on French family legislation that was then further undermined during the years of the Mitterrand presidency.[54]

The Mitterrand Years

Following the crisis of the MRP, Catholics looked not only to the Gaullist movement and to other right-wing parties, but also to the Left. The demise of a Christian democratic party can be followed by the widespread of its ideals and militants across the political spectrum, although there had always been militants and intellectuals engaged in left-wing organizations.[55] Some of them did not regret the final disbanding of the MRP. For instance, Georges Montaron, the director of the progressive Catholic journal *Témoignage Chrétien*, wrote that "the place of Christians of our spirit, in terms of civic action, is in the organizations of the left, in the clubs of the Federation, or in the P.S."[56] Since the Congress of Épinay in June 1971, the PS, under the leadership of François Mitterrand, opened itself to Christian activists who contributed to the dramatic increase in its membership.[57] Many socialist militants came from the ranks of the CFDT.[58] The deconfessionalization of the CFTC, however, did not represent a complete rejection of Catholicism. The new labour union integrated Christianity, socialism, and humanism by mixing Christian democratic values with the ideals of new social movements.[59] The CFDT gave a generation of militants to Mitterrand's PS and it helped to instil in this party some typical Catholic social ideals, notably the principle of subsidiarity, self-management, and recognition of the importance of the social role of families.

The election of François Mitterrand on 10 May 1981 ended a political anomaly in the history of the Fifth Republic. For the first time the Left had won a presidential election. The coming to power of a socialist president was accompanied by immense enthusiasm and by the impression that a new era was opening up, even though the PS's political platform was incoherent as it

53 Lenoir, 'Family Policy in France since 1938', 176.
54 Morgan, *Working Mothers and the Welfare State*, 106-135.
55 Bolzonar, 'A christian democratization of Italian politics'; Pelletier, 'Introduction', 7.
56 Montaron, 'Mort du parti catholique', 4.
57 Soulage, 'L'engagement politique des chrétiens de gauche, entre Parti socialiste, deuxième gauche et gauchisme', 439. The PS's effort to integrate Christian activists into its ranks also implied the organization of public events targeting them. For instance, in December 1972 the PS held a meeting entitled 'Opération porte ouverte. Le socialisme et les Chrétiens' (Operation open door. Socialism and christians). See Ferhat, 'Un chemin de Damas?'.
58 The CFDT became popularly called the 'Deuxiéme Gauche' (The Second Left). See Hamon and Rotman, *La deuxième gauche*.
59 Rosanvallon, 'L'identité CFDT', 9.

mixed different values, inspirations, and goals without any obvious priority among them.[60]

It is challenging to present a general overview of Mitterrand's social policy because of the several changes, if not dramatic turns, that characterized his long presidency. Its macro-economic and social measures can be broadly divided into two periods: from 1981 to early 1983 and from mid 1983 onwards. In the first phase, the socialist governments introduced some Keynesian economic policies (e.g. nationalizations, a sharp increase in public spending and social benefits, and higher taxation on highest incomes). The newly elected government intended to impress a social democratic turn on French politics and on the existing features of social security that had also attracted increasing criticism from Catholic organizations. Though the French welfare state of the time is generally classified in the category of conservative or Christian democratic regimes, the Catholic Church and Catholic-inspired unions were dissatisfied with it. In a document issued in 1980 and entitled 'La sécurité sociale et ses valeurs' (Social security and its values), the Commission Sociale de l'Épiscopat remarked the persistent inequalities among workers and the excessive bureaucratization of social security.[61] Throughout the 1960s and 1970s, the rise of social inequalities was also constantly criticized by the CFTC and the CFDT. The reform of social funds and the dramatic growth of social benefits introduced in the two years of the first Mitterrand presidency were supposed to meet these widespread demands for social justice from the ranks of the Left and social Catholicism.

However, from mid 1983, the Mitterrand presidency took a liberal turn. Socialists abandoned Keynesianism to embrace neoliberal and monetarist macro-economic policies. The proposal to change society proclaimed during the 1981 electoral campaign was replaced by a technocratic administration of power that favoured the opening up of France to financial capitalism. The development of social legislation suffered from this change to the macro-economic paradigm. Social benefits were partly frozen and some welfare cutbacks were introduced. However, the leftist governments also continued the moral liberalization of family legislation that had been started by the previous right-wing governments, and this contributed to the further weakening of the influence of traditional Catholicism on family policies. A more detailed study of the reform of social funds and the changing guidelines on the family legislation will illustrate the policy paradigm and the underpinning values of Mitterrand's social reforms.

60 The political economy of Mitterrand's 1981 presidential manifesto was contradictory. For example, it proposed the introduction of some typical Keynesian measures, such as a grand plan of public works (proposition n° 16) or the expansion of employment in the public sector (proposition n° 18), but at the same time, it also advanced the idea of reducing the social charges for companies (proposition n° 30). See Berstein, 'Le programme présidentiel', 77; Mitterrand, *110 propositions pour la France.*

61 Commission Sociale de l'Épiscopat Français, *La sécurité sociale et ses valeurs*, 3.

Renovating the Démocratie Sociale

The public policies enacted by the socialists during their first two years in power introduced some remarkable discontinuities with those of previous right-wing executives. Among the several reforms envisaged by Mitterrand's presidential manifesto, there was the intention to renovate the system of industrial relations and the so-called *démocratie sociale* by giving new rights to workers. The literal English translation of *démocratie sociale* may be misleading for a native-English-speaking reader because it does not precisely convey the meaning of the French concept. As summarized by Henri Rouilleaut, former advisor to the socialist Prime Minister Michel Rocard, *démocratie sociale* means a democratic approach to all forms of negotiation, collaboration, and exchange of information on social- and work-related issues between employers, representatives of workers, and public powers.[62]

Mitterrand's idea of strengthening the influence of workers in economic life was consistent with the demands of labour unions, notably with the proposals advanced by the CFDT throughout the 1960s and 1970s. In the columns of its bulletin *Syndicalisme CFDT*, this union often complained about the lack of democracy within companies and asked for the introduction of a system of self-management of business activities. The publication in 1981 of the papal encyclical *Laborem Exercens*, dedicated to work, contributed to reviving the debate on labour questions among Catholics and provided further doctrinal support for their demands to change the existing forms of workers' involvement in social and economic life of companies.

Two policy innovations enacted by socialist governments were particularly aimed at improving the *démocratie sociale*: the Auroux Bills and the reform of social security funds. Inspired by the ideals of the Popular Front, the short-lived leftist alliance that won the 1936 general political elections, the Auroux Bills intended to promote the firm-based negotiation of working conditions. [63] More precisely, these laws wanted to strengthen the rights of workers to express their opinions on the working conditions of their firms,[64] provide larger financial resources to work councils,[65] establish a system of collective bargaining at the company level,[66] and set up company committees in

62 Rouilleault, *Où va la démocratie sociale?*, 12.

63 Winock, *François Mitterrand*, 304. The Auroux Bills took their name from Jean Auroux who was Minister of Labour in the first Mauroy government from 22 May 1981 to 29 June 1982.

64 Loi n° 82-689 du 4 août 1982, *Journal Officiel de la République Française, Lois et Décrets*, 6 August 1982, 2518-2520.

65 Loi n° 82-915 du 28 octobre 1982, *Journal Officiel de la République Française, Lois et Décrets*, 29 October 1982, 3255-3268.

66 Loi n° 82-957 du 13 novembre 1982, *Journal Officiel de la République Française, Lois et Décrets*, 14 November 1982, 3414-3422.

charge of controlling the hygiene and safety conditions at work places.[67] Of these laws, only the establishment of firm-based bargaining procedures was applied. The other measures introduced by the Auroux Bills were put aside after the liberal turn of the Mitterrand presidency in 1983.

The reform of the social security funds was the other major governmental project that was intended to revive the *démocratie sociale*. The previous reform of these bodies introduced in 1967 dramatically curtailed the influence of the major labour unions. From 1967 to 1982, the CGT and the CFDT did not obtain the presidencies of any social security funds that were generally held by the members of employers' organizations or by the smaller unions. This marginalization of the CGT and the CFDT jeopardized the compromise that had inspired the system of social protection established at the Liberation because workers' interests were not adequately represented.

Though the Mitterrand presidential manifesto did not mention the introduction of any administrative reform of social security funds, the question was placed on the government agenda immediately after the election, given the strong pressure coming from the ranks of the CGT and the CFDT. The responsibility to elaborate a reform was assumed by Pierre Bérégovoy, who was Secretary General of the Presidency of the Republic and one of Mitterrand's closest collaborators. His appointment as the head of the Ministry of Social Affairs and National Solidarity just before the presentation of the proposal for the reform of social security funds was a symbolic act to show the commitment of the new President of the Republic to impose his political imprint on an important social reform. To highlight the government commitment to restore the *démocratie sociale*, in a speech given at the National Assembly in July 1982, Bérégovoy declared that the reform of social security funds was intended to abrogate the decrees of 1967 that were a mutilation of democracy.[68]

Bérégovoy's reform provoked strong protests from right-wing parties. Their arguments mixed liberal principles and technocratic arguments. For example, Jean Briane, deputy of the centrist Union pour la Démocratie Française (UDF), claimed that the new law would not guarantee the good management of social security, which could become the new instruments of the class struggle. The Gaullist deputy Étienne Pinte, deputy of Rassemblement pour la République (RPR), reminded the excessive responsibility given to unions before the reforms introduced in 1967 and their disastrous administration of social security.[69] In spite of parliamentary opposition, the administrative reform of

67 Loi n° 82-1097 du 23 décembre 1982, *Journal Officiel de la République Française, Lois et Décrets*, 26 December 1982, 3858-3861.

68 *Journal Officiel de la République Française, Débats Parlamentaires*, 7 July 1982, 4303.

69 *Journal Officiel de la République Française, Débats Parlamentaires*, 7 July 1982, 4308-4310.

social security funds was approved on 8 July and promulgated on 17 December 1982.[70] Its main innovations stated that:

a. Workers' representatives had the majority of seats in every local, regional, and national social security council (fifteen seats to delegates of workers, six to delegates of employers);
b. Workers' representatives were to be elected by a proportional voting system and selected from the lists presented by the most representative unions. Workers did not have the option of expressing their preference for someone who was not included in the lists of these unions;
c. Employers would continue to appoint their delegates instead of electing them;
d. The prime minister could designate a limited number of delegates to social security councils to represent the interests of family associations, the mutualistic movement, and the workers of social security funds.

Though its original intention was to promote the engagement of workers as advocated by democratic socialism and social Catholicism, the reform of social security funds met only in part these expectations. For instance, the government was in charge of deciding which were the most representative unions. Furthermore, the reforms did not allow the participation of new unions in the elections. The reform was aimed at democratizing social funds, but it eventually achieved the opposite result because the voting system imposed severe limits on the democratic choice of workers. Instead of democratizing social security, the government ended up to introducing a new balance of power between social partners. While the reform of 1967 strengthened the influence of employers and smaller unions, the new law restored the primacy of the CGT and CFDT, with which the Mitterrand presidency had established an informal alliance. In this sense, it is debatable that the new reform established an effective *démocratie sociale*. Mitterrand renounced the ambitious goal of reviving the *démocratie sociale* in favour of the pragmatic need to consolidate his power by supporting the CGT and the CFDT and limiting the influence of the employers' organizations and smaller unions. This was certainly not the last occasion on which the socialist president put aside social reformism. Particularly after 1983, the stabilization of internal consensus and the management of power became the paramount purpose of the Mitterrand presidency.[71] However, already in 1982, with the reform of social security funds, the PS showed a clear preference for the consolidation of power.

70 Loi n° 82-1061 du du 17 décembre 1982, *Journal Officiel de la République Française, Lois et Décrets*, 18 December 1982, 3779-3783.
71 Julliard, *Les gauches françaises*, 778.

Modernizing Family Policies

Although some kind of familism was widespread across the French political spectrum, the promotion of family values and interests has generally been the affair of conservative actors and Catholic organizations. Until the late 1960s, references to family problems had limited space in the political manifestos of the French Left. François Mitterrand intended to change this state of things. The reconciliation between the left-wing governments and the family (and family associations) started with a symbolic event. On 21 November 1981 Mitterrand presented the guidelines of his family policy at the UNAF National Congress in Paris. It was the first time that a socialist leader had spoken at a congress of the major family association of France. During his speech, Mitterrand announced his commitment to reducing inequalities between families and his intention to support all families. He also stresses his indignation about the fact that economic constraints deprived several couples of the right to have a child. As reported by *La Croix*, these proposals met with the almost unanimous and enthusiastic approval of the audience.[72]

However, the family policy of the socialist governments was not limited to the vague principles that Mitterrand outlined at the UNAF Congress. Four main goals distinguished it:

- moral liberalization of the legislation;
- increasing family benefits;
- supporting smaller families;
- strengthening work-family reconciliation policies.

The socialist governments modernized family legislation by bringing it more in line with the cultural, economic, and social transformations that were happening in France. In other words, the main aim of the socialist reformism was dismantling the most evident heritage of the moral conservatism of family legislation, supporting the increasingly numerous smaller families, and providing more generous financial benefits to the growing number of working mothers. By pursuing these aims, the social policy innovations introduced during the Mitterrand presidency contributed to further weakening the imprint of traditional Catholicism on French family legislation.

72 'La famille courtisée', *Le Monde*, 24 November 1981.

Moral Liberalization of Family Legislation

The eradication of the different kinds of social, economic, and gender discrimination was a crucial component of the socialist agenda in the early 1980s.[73] Several kinds of discrimination resulted from the traditional Catholic doctrines that still made a deep imprint on social legislation. However, it is worth pointing out that Mitterrand's effort at liberalizing family laws was not intended to be a crusade against the Church. The contraposition between public authorities and the Catholic Church that had long characterized French political history had lost much of its strength by the beginning of the 1980s. On the other hand, episodic clashes between the socialist governments and Catholic authorities happened under the Mitterand presidency. For example, the proposal of the socialist president to unify the national educational system provoked the biggest social mobilizations ever organized by Catholic organizations. However, the policy trajectory of the relationship between political authorities and Catholicism during the Fifth Republic was characterized by the appeasement of their mutual relationships. While the Church had increasingly accepted the *laïcité* of the state, political authorities had recognized the public role of religious organizations.[74] A paradigmatic example of the demise of the anti-clericalism of the Left was provided by Mitterrand's decision to include the delegates of religious organizations in the Comité Consultatif National d'Ethique.[75]

Mitterrand's liberalization of family legislation can be interpreted as a response to demands from a large part of the PS electorate, notably feminist organizations, young activists, LGBT (Lesbian, Gay, Bisexual, and Transgender) organizations, and some progressive Catholic groups. For example, the Catholic feminist Cécile de Corlieu, wrote a book in which she openly defended the right to abortion and Jeannette Laot was engaged in the Mouvement pour la Liberté de l'Avortement et de la Contraception. These Catholics did not consider their pro-choice positions on abortion and contraception to be a rejection of Catholicism, but, on the contrary, on the grounds of their personal and post-modern interpretation of Catholic doctrines, they demanded a reform of the existing social laws.[76] Though progressive Catholics were certainly a minority in the French Catholic milieu, their impact became stronger under

73 In commenting on the march in support of homosexual rights that occurred on 4 April, Pierre Bérégovoy, Mitterrand's spokesperson, pointed out that in the event of victory for François Mitterrand in the presidential election, the PS would propose a law to abrogate all kinds of discrimination. See 'Supprimer toutes les discriminationes', *Le Matin de Paris*, 4 April 1981.

74 Haarscher, *La laïcité*, 22.

75 Baubérot, *Histoire de la laïcité en France*, 110.

76 Crépin Annie, Historian and Deputy President of Femmes et Hommes, Égalité, Droits et Libertés dans les Églises et la Société (FHEDLES), 14 March 2014, personal interview.

the Mitterrand presidency because several Catholic feminist leaders became quite influential in the PS, and some of them, such as Renée Dufourt and Jeannette Laot, worked for the minister of women's rights.

Two leading principles guided the attempts of socialist governments to liberalize family legislation: removing the economic and social constraints that impeded the exercise of new rights and extending the moral liberalization of the family legislation to new fields. Two examples may illustrate this approach. Though in 1975 a conservative government legalized abortion, the social liberalism of the Right did not go so far as to take into account the economic constraints that did not allow women to access abortion services. For example, non-therapeutic abortion fees were not reimbursed by social security and economically deprived women could not afford to pay all the related medical expenses. Furthermore, in the early 1980s, public opinion was still poorly informed about the abortion law and medical personnel, particularly in the countryside, were not adequately trained.[77] To overcome the poor knowledge about abortion and contraception, on 18 November 1981 the government launched a national information campaign. Advertisements were broadcast in the mass media, despite the harsh criticism that they attracted from the Catholic Church and family associations. Special training programmes for teachers, social workers, and nurses were organized. However, these initiatives did not have much effect. A ministerial report in January 1982 entitled 'Les femmes en France dans une société d'inégalités' (Women in France in a society of inequalities) denounced the still limited information on abortion available to doctors, paramedic personnel, and most of the French population. This situation was worsened by the unequal territorial distribution of family planning centres.[78] To facilitate access to abortion for low-income women, on 10 December 1981 the Minister of Women's Rights, Yvette Roudy, announced a project of law for the reimbursement of all medical expenses for abortion by social security. This proposal immediately met strong opposition from the Senate, in which centrist and right-wing parties had the majority of seats, and the Catholic Church.[79] In contrast with the conciliatory attitudes of the Protestant Church, on 28 October 1982 the French bishops adopted by a large majority a document that strongly criticized the Roudy Bill.[80] Because of the obstruction-

77 Crépin Annie, Historian and Deputy President of FHEDLES, 14 March 2014, personal interview.

78 Ministère des Droits de la Femme, *Les femmes en France dans une société d'inégalités*, 76-85.

79 This French electoral system of the Senate tended to overrepresent countryside districts, which were generally more conservative than the urban areas. 'Sénatoriales: mauvais report des voix à gauche. P.C.-P.S.: rupture consommée', *Le Figaro*, 29 September, 1980; 'Le renouvellement triennal du Sénat: mauvais report des voix à gauche', *Le Figaro*, 29 September, 1980.

80 'Les évêques français condamnent très sévèrement l'avortement', *Le Monde*, 30 October 1982.

ism of the Right, the parliamentary procedure of the law lasted for more than a year. It was only after the personal intervention of Mitterrand, who imposed an urgency procedure for the final discussion of the law, that the Roudy Bill was approved at the end of December 1982.[81]

The abolition of sexual discrimination against homosexuals was another area of anti-discriminatory initiative promoted by governments. Though in the months before his electoral campaign Giscard d'Estaing declared his intention to revise the laws that criminalized homosexuality in France, the politics of the Right was quite contradictory on this subject.[82] Over LGBT rights, France was a laggard in the early 1980s. While homosexual acts were decriminalized in Sweden in 1944, the United Kingdom in 1967, and East Germany in 1968, in 1981 the French penal code still included the second paragraph of Article 331 that said that an indecent or against nature act committed with a minor of the same-sex could be punished with a period of imprisonment of between six months and two years and a fine of 60 to 20,000 francs (approximately 23 to 7,800 euros in 2021).[83] As soon as he came to power, Mitterrand not only showed a more tolerant attitude toward LGBT communities, but he also assumed a pioneering role in promoting social acceptance of homosexuality. On 11 June 1981 the minister of the interior sent a circular to all the prefectures of police asking them to end the patrols that they carried out in popular gay places. The brigade of the Paris prefecture that specialized in this task was disbanded. On 12 June 1982, the minister of health announced that France did not intend to consider homosexuality a mental illness any more. After some consultations with LGBT organizations, on 6 November 1981 the government proposed a law for the decriminalization of homosexuality. During the parliamentary debate, the rapporteur of the project, the socialist deputy Gisèle Halimi, declared that homosexuality was an individual choice and, as such, it should not be the object of any legal codification. She then added that religious morality should not define what a "good choice" in relation to sexuality should be.[84]

Like other reforms of family legislation, the new law was opposed by several centrist and right-wing deputies and it provoked some social discontent. The leadership of the protest was taken up by right-wing parties rather than by the Church or Catholic associations, as they preferred to avoid any

81 Loi n° 82-1172 du 31 décembre 1982, *Journal Officiel de la République Française, Lois et Décrets*, 1 January 1983, 15.

82 On 19 November 1980, for example, Parliament approved a norm that maintained the crime of homosexuality that had originally been established by the legislation of the Vichy regime.

83 The law had evident discriminatory purposes not only because it criminalized homosexual acts, but also because it established that the age of consent for homosexual persons was 18 (21 until 1974), whereas for heterosexual people it was 15.

84 *Journal Officiel de la République Française, Débats Parlamentaires*, 20 December 1981, 5367.

confrontation with public authorities. The RPR deputy and former Minister of Justice in the de Gaulle government, Jean Foyer, during his speech at the National Assembly declared that homosexual acts were against nature and their criminalization was aimed at protecting minors. He also added that socialists were rejecting not only Judeo-Christian morality, but also the secular morality of France[85]. The speech by Foyer showed how the French right-wing political elites were still attached to traditional religious views, even though France was a secular country. An implicit cultural Catholicism still permeated the French political Right and it conditioned its decisions on value-laden issues. This was further confirmed by the final vote on the law. All the major leaders of the Right, from Raymond Barre to Jacques Chirac, Jacques Chaban-Delmas, and the young François Fillon, voted against the bill. The Senate, composed of a right-wing majority, rejected the law on the decriminalization of homosexuality three times, but, given the asymmetry of power between the two Chambers, the bill was eventually approved by a vote of the National Assembly on 27 July 1982.[86]

Increasing Family Benefits

The family legislation of the Mitterrand presidency continued the modernization of this policy field pursued by the Giscard d'Estaing presidency. However, in contrast to his predecessor who considered social benefits to be a burden on the economic competitiveness of the country, Mitterrand, at least until 1983, believed that social allowances were a means to achieve a macro-economic policy aimed at stimulating internal demand.

One of the early measures introduced by the socialists was a sharp increase in family allowances. In July 1981, family allocations were re-evaluated by 25 per cent and again by another 25 per cent in February 1982.[87] However, apart from these increases, the government's family policy seemed to lack a coherent plan. On 5 May 1982, Yvette Roudy wrote a letter to the Prime Minister, Pierre Mauroy, to remind him that the rise in the female employment rate was an irreversible phenomenon and roughly 60 per cent of new births were to women who were working outside the home. Roudy also reminded Mauroy that the government should introduce adequate measures to support families, as Mitterrand had promised at the UNAF Conference in 1981. The minister of

85 *Journal Officiel de la République Française*, 20 December 1981, *Débats Parlementaires*, 5372-5373.

86 Loi n° 82-683 du 4 août 1982, *Journal Officiel de la République Française, Lois et Décrets*, 5 August 1982, 2502.

87 The Mitterrand presidency began with a dramatic increase in social expenditure and also expenditure in other policy domains. For instance, housing benefits rose by 25 per cent in July 1981 and by 20 per cent in December. The minimum old-age pension was raised by 62 per cent between 1981 and 1982. See Steck, 'Partie II. Histoire de 1967-2009', 139, 195.

women's rights added that on this question the moral and material interests of the family were consistent with those of the country.[88] However, the worsening of the national financial situation did not leave much room for manoeuvre to expand social benefits. In June 1982 the government introduced several austerity measures that targeted social benefits. Others followed in March 1983. Social security had to make its contribution to reducing the national deficit. The government intended to realize savings of 10 billion francs from social expenditure and 30 per cent of that sum was supposed to come from the family branch of social security.[89] Given the unpopularity of welfare retrenchment policies, politicians tend to pursue blame avoidance strategies that dissimulate welfare cutbacks.[90] The strategy used by socialist governments consisted of decreasing the re-evaluation rate of social benefits so that their increase became far lower than the inflation rate. On 1 July 1982, family benefits were augmented by just 6.2 per cent whereas the annual inflation rate for that year was around 14 per cent.[91] It was also decided that the base for the increase in family benefits had to be the expected evolution of prices calculated by the government instead of the actual inflation rate. Several reductions in welfare benefits were also introduced. For example, on 1 January 1983 the postnatal allowance for the third child was cut by 50 per cent and the ceiling for loans to young households was decreased by 25 per cent.[92] The austerity measures implemented after 1983 sanctioned the end of the Keynesian period of family policy of socialist governments. After 1983, like previous right-wing administrations, Mitterrand started to become more concerned about the possible negative economic impact of social benefits rather than about their role in stimulating internal demand.

Support for Smaller Families

The PS was not much in favour of the natalist principles and it wanted to provide greater economic support to smaller households. This orientation of family policies can be seen by comparing the evolution of family allowances between 1981 and 1983 for different household types, as shown in Table 3. Between these years, family benefits for households with two children increased almost by twice as much as for those with five children.[93] However, when reviewing the figures for the allocations for different households, it is

88 Letter written by Yvette Roudy to Pierre Mauroy, AN, Fonds Service des Affaires Sociales (Commissariat Général du Plan), 19920452/62.
89 Letter written by Yvette Roudy to Pierre Mauroy, AN, Fonds Service des Affaires Sociales (Commissariat Général du Plan), 19920452/62.
90 Pierson, "The new politics of the welfare state', 145.
91 INSEE, *Population.* See <http://www.insee.fr/fr/themes/theme.asp?theme=2>.
92 Steck 'Partie II. Histoire de 1967-2009', 197.
93 'Mitterrand aide le second enfant', *La Croix*, 24 November 1981.

still noticeable a natalist bias in the legislation. In February 1983, the total allowance for a family with four children was almost four times higher than that for a family with two children. The early socialist governments imposed a change on the trajectory of family legislation, but their reformism was not strong enough to impose a radical transformation that could reverse the familist imprint that characterized the legislation of the time.

After 1983, there was a revival in the influence of natalism on French family legislation, partly as a consequence of the growing political concern about declining fertility rates.[94] Under pressure from conservative groups and Catholic family associations, the government enacted several new policies that supported bigger families. In January 1985, for example, the parental education allowance was introduced. This benefit was a two-year period of paid leave allocated to every person who took care of a child younger than three years, and who interrupted or reduced her/his professional activities because of the birth, adoption, or hosting of the child. The natalist imprint of the new benefit was related to the fact that the allocation was provided only to households composed of two or more children. It was highly criticized by a part of the Left that considered it an indirect incentive for the withdrawal of women from the labour market. However, these criticisms were partly unjustified. The new law had not only natalist purposes, but it was also intended to oppose the permanent withdrawal of women from the labour market after the birth of their third child, because the bill guaranteed its beneficiaries the right to come back to their previous jobs.

TABLE 3
FIGURES FOR FAMILY ALLOCATIONS BETWEEN 1 MAY 1981 AND 1 FEBRUARY 1983, BY HOUSEHOLD TYPE (IN FRANCS PER MONTH)*

	Two Children	Three Children	Four Children	Five Children
1 May 1981	251.44	710.61	1,020.58	1,508.70
1 Feb 1983	455.04	1,023.84	1,599.75	2,161.40
Change from 1981 to 1983	+ 81.0%	+ 44.1%	+ 56.7%	+ 43.3%

* Documents on the family policy, AN, Fonds Service des Affaires Sociales (Commissariat Général du Plan), 19920452/62.

94 Lenoir, 'Family Policy in France since 1938', 183.

Promotion of Work-family Reconciliation Policies

During the 1980s, the introduction of work-family reconciliation policies became a prevalent paradigm of French family legislation. This was due to the change in social values and the increase in female employment rates.[95] Almost all social and political actors also shared the idea that policies had to promote part-time employment, provide extra financial support to families, and develop childcare facilities. In accordance with the widespread individualist attitudes of the time, the family measures introduced in the 1980s were intended to favour freedom of choice for families and mothers.[96] However, left-wing parties preferred policy interventions targeted at low-income families while right-wing groups showed some preference for universalistic policies.

Since the 1970s, Catholic associations had also started to advocate work-family reconciliation policies. At the CFTC Congress of Lyon in 1981, Jean Bornard, the CFTC President, recognized the need for childcare facilities to help working mothers, the extension of maternity leave, and an increase of the existing benefits to let working mothers combine work and family duties.[97] In the annex to the rapport d'orientatation presented at the National Conference held in Paris 1985, the AFC asked for the introduction of substantial financial aid to families to guarantee to mothers effective freedom of choice between working or staying at home, the promotion of part-time employment, and an increase in the number and variety of childcare facilities.[98] Though Catholic organizations still showed a clear preference for keeping mothers outside the labour market, and their attitudes were still affected by some moralism, their positions had started to change.

Two main policy instruments were used during the Mitterrand presidency to promote work-family reconciliation policies: the greater provision of childcare facilities and financial support for families, notably cash benefits or tax deductions.[99] Though it is not possible to provide here an exhaustive treatment of all the policy reforms introduced after the early 1980s, the illus-

95 Organisation for Economic Cooperation and Development, 'Social Expenditure: Detailed Data'. See <https://doi.org/10.1787/data-00167-en>.

96 Martin, 'Les politiques de la famille', 37.

97 Bornard, 'Special 41° Congrès', 10-11.

98 CNAFC, 'Annex au rapport d'orientation', 30-34.

99 It should be added that the promotion of part-time employment was another strategy used by the Mauroy government against unemployment. Part-time employment had large support among labour unions and Catholic associations. In contrast, it was viewed with some suspicion by feminist groups. A letter in 1981 to the Prime Minister Yvette Roudy, Minister of Women's Rights, harshly criticized the policy proposals in support of part-time employment. According to Roudy, part-time work meant a part-time salary, which implied part-time social promotion. However, part-time employment contributed to increase female participation in the labour market and women's return to work after the birth of a child. See Le van-Lemesle and Zancarini-Fournel, 'Moderniser le travail', 543.

tration of some key developments can illustrate the policy trajectory followed by leftist governments.

The Mitterrand 1981 presidential manifesto stated the commitment of the socialist candidate to create 300,000 new places in crèches.[100] This goal was linked to housing policies, as the vast programme of construction of social housing envisaged by Mitterrand was intended to provide the new residential areas with a large variety of social services, notable crèches. The PS's political programme was probably too ambitious, given the economic situation of France, and it was soon abandoned after the liberal turn in 1983. However, since the 1980s there has been a multiplication, a diversification, and a strong development of childcare facilities and services: collective crèches, micro-crèches, parental crèches, nursery assistance, and so on. Unable to develop a social democratic strategy that could promote a stronger role for public services, the socialist governments introduced a set of diversified measures and encouraged partnerships between public and private actors.

The number of private nursery assistants increased and their role was better regulated by legislation. The intervention of public authorities was more targeted at children aged above three and the introduction of a series of new laws meant that at the beginning of the 1990s almost all children aged between three and six had a place in a public pre-school institution.[101]

Financial transfers have generally been one of the main measures used to support French families, as in most other conservative or Christian democratic welfare regimes. In the 1980s cash transfers also had a relevant role in work-family reconciliation policies. In 1987, during the first government of cohabitation,[102] the home childcare allowance was introduced. The law, inspired by the liberal ideas of the right-wing government, established a tax break for those families that hired a person to look after their children.

The introduction of work-family reconciliation policies had a profound impact on the development of family legislation because they further weakened the cultural and social basis of Catholic traditional familism in two main ways. First, they promoted a shift in the orientation of employment legislation so that it was less exclusively committed to the preservation of full male employment, as in the immediate post-war period. However, the development

100 Mitterrand, *110 propositions pour la France*, Proposition nº 68.
101 Morgan, *Working Mothers and the Welfare State*, 106-120.
102 In relation to France, political scientists speak of a government of cohabitation when the President of the Republic and the Prime Minister belong to antagonistic political groups. This situation is the outcome of three interrelated factors: the fact that the French constitution prescribes that the Head of State and the Prime Minister have to share the executive power, the parliamentary and presidential elections do not happen at the same time, and the President of the Republic generally appoints as Prime Minister the leader of the largest political coalition in Parliament and that may be different from that to which the President of the Republic belongs.

of the employment legislation was not so dramatic as to change the overall setting of French social security. At the beginning of the 1990s the French employment regime was still a male breadwinner model. Moreover, the policy reforms introduced to reconcile professional and family duties indirectly encouraged further economic independence of women, even though they were not committed to gender equality as they were in Scandinavian countries.[103] Second, the increased role of public structures and private services in looking after children contributed to changing the process of socialization. The family environment certainly continued to have a great impact, but children were more in contact with social influences external to their family environment. By encouraging the introduction of work-family conciliation policies, Catholic associations were supporting the prevailing social demands of families, but, at the same time, they were indirectly weakening the social foundations of traditional Catholic familism, whose cornerstone was centred on the family as a principal, if not exclusive, socializing community.

Great Disillusions?

This chapter has discussed some social policy reforms introduced by the Gaullist, right-wing, and socialist governments between the return to power of de Gaulle and the end of the Mitterrand presidency. Like other parts of this book, the research presented here is not intended to provide an exhaustive treatment of the developments of social security, but rather it suggests an interpretation of the changing influence of Catholic values on the social policy domain during a period characterized by the deepening of the crisis of Catholicism and dramatic transformations in French society.

The principal conclusion reached in the chapter is the idea that the social reforms of Gaullist, right-wing, and socialist governments were mainly inspired by the logic of dominion or by the logic of consensus. In other words, sometimes they tried to meet the demands of pro-business actors, and, at other times, the prevailing social demands of French society. The reform of social security in 1967 and the austerity measures of the Mitterrand presidency are examples of the logic of dominion, while the modernization and moral liberalization of family policies are examples of the logic of consensus. The willingness to accept the demands of pro-business actors was a distinct characteristic of Gaullist and right-wing governments. It eventually had some impact on Mitterrand's politics, but only after the socialist president had to face a severe economic crisis that was threatening the financial stability of France.

In light of the declining social influence of Catholicism, the governments of the time largely disregarded or even opposed the demands of Catholic

103 Morgan, *Working Mothers and the Welfare State*, 106-134.

groups because they were not useful in strengthening their power, although Catholic values permeated the political ideologies of both Gaullism and Mitterrand's new PS. Gaullist and right-wing administrations on one side and socialist governments on the other pursued the moral liberalization of family legislation. Despite the several policy changes introduced during the early decades of the Fifth Republic, French social security kept its conservative or Christian democratic imprint because neither right-wing nor left-wing administrations intended to venture into the far-reaching reforms that would have challenged the structural foundations of the French welfare state.

The years of Gaullism and Mitterrandism ended up in great disillusionment for French Catholicism, which showed increasing signs of crisis. The policy reforms enacted during the period considered in this chapter demonstrated that political parties could not defend Catholic values. If Catholics wanted to support their ideals, they had to find new actors, new domains, and new strategies. Even though the Catholic subculture was in severe crisis, it was still lively and new forms of religious and social engagement in civil society had already emerged before Vatican II.[104] It was in the new social movements and voluntary organizations that French Catholics found the instruments to defend their values in an increasingly secular society, as the next chapters will show.

104 Berger, 'Religious Transformations and the Future of Politics', 107-108.

PART II

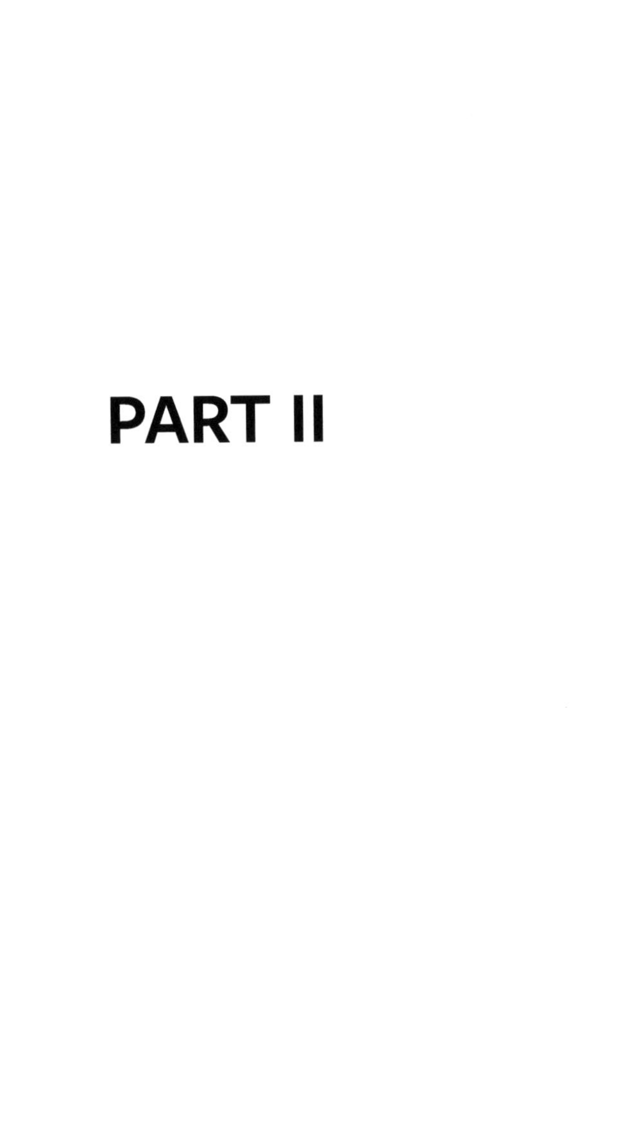

5
A PERIOD OF CHANGES

The beginning of the 1990s has been regarded as a period of profound crisis for France. The slowdown of economic growth, the worsening of the public deficit, and the dramatic rise in unemployment rates seemed to threaten the structural foundations of the French social model.[1] The early 1990s were also a difficult period for French Catholicism, which was weakened by a dramatic drop in vocation, a sharp decline in attendance at religious practices, and the increasing rejection by French citizens of the conservative positions on sexual morality sustained by the Church.[2] However, the most apparent features of this double crisis of the French welfare state and French Catholicism should not lead the observer to overlook the ongoing structural transformations that were happening in these domains. The second part of this book provides a critical perspective on these transformations.

The initial hypothesis of the second part of this book is the claim that the process of secularization has not implied the disappearance of Catholicism from the public sphere in secular France.[3] Catholics and Catholic-inspired organizations still play an important public role and sometimes exert a subtle influence on social policy decisions, even though the French do not crowd out churches every Sunday, disregard the teachings of Catholic hierarchies, and reinterpret Catholic principles in accordance with their own values. In this sense, following a suggestion proposed by Émile Poulat a long time ago, the

1 Rosanvallon, *La nouvelle question sociale*, 7-12; Smith, *France in Crisis*, 1-2.

2 Pelletier, *La crise catholique*, 7-8.

3 Ibid., 7.

second part of this book aims to understand the new 'place' of Catholicism in post-Christian France.[4] Before undertaking such an enterprise, however, we would like to provide several empirical findings that question the apparently irreversible demise of French Catholicism.

While this chapter presents several observations on the recent developments of French Catholicism, Chapters 6 and 7 discuss some transformations of the French social model by studying the influence of Catholicism on housing and family policies, two fields that have traditionally been crucial areas for the projection of Catholic values into the social domain.

The second part of this book is an integration of the first part. Whereas Chapters 2, 3, and 4 studied the mobilization of Catholicism in the political domain, which has been the main terrain through which Catholic norms were instilled in the social policy sphere, this second part of the book explores the mobilization of Catholicism in civil society, as that seems to have become a primary channel through which Catholic-inspired organizations and movements are defending their values in the social policy sphere.

This chapter is divided into two main parts. The first one provides several empirical findings on contemporary Catholicism in France, and the second part suggests some theoretical considerations based on the data presented in the previous sections.

Catholicism in Contemporary France: Some Observations

In the Medieval period, France was called *la fille aînée de l'Église* ('the eldest daughter of the Church'). This title was intended to emphasize the deep religiosity of the French population and the political bonds between the Carolingian kingdom and the Papacy. Social and political reality has dramatically changed since those times and nowadays France is generally considered a prototypical example of a secular country, to the extent that saying that Catholicism is increasingly irrelevant in France has become commonplace.[5] Does this mean, though, that Catholicism has lost all its influence in the public sphere?

Although the declining religiosity of French people is undeniable, several signs show the resilience, if not a strengthening, of religion in the public sphere.[6] With this purpose in mind, the following sections integrate data on individual religiosity with what Karel Dobbelaere defines as the meso- and macro-level of secularization: some evidence on the changing organizational characteristics of religious associations and their role in different social fields.[7]

4 Poulat, *L'ère postchrétienne*, 15.
5 Hervieu-Léger, *Catholicisme, la fin d'un monde*, 13-16.
6 Hervieu-Léger, 'Sécularisation', 1152-1153.
7 Dobbelaere, 'The Meaning and Scope of Secularization', 600-603.

Weakening Values?

Statistics on individual religiosity, notably Church attendance, are generally used to highlight the degree of secularization in a given country. Table 4 shows that affiliation to Catholicism in France has dramatically declined in the last three decades. From 1990 to 2018, the percentage of regularly practising Catholics dropped from 15 per cent to 7 per cent, irregularly practising Catholics from 14 per cent to 6 per cent and non-practising Catholics from 28 per cent to 19 per cent. In contrast, the share of those who belong to other religions increased from 4 per cent to 10 per cent, principally as a consequence of the growth of Muslim communities, and the share of those who consider themselves without religion registered a dramatic increase by changing from 29 per cent and 10 per cent in 1990 to 37 per cent and 21 per cent respectively in 2018.[8] These contrasting trends in religious belonging highlight the deepening of the process of secularization in contemporary France and its increasing religious pluralism.

However, the data reported in Table 4 should be critically evaluated. Attendance at Mass is not probably the most reliable indicator of religiosity as it describes a rather superficial attachment to religion that does not consider the multifaceted aspects of religious behaviour.[9] This indicator seems more

TABLE 4
RELIGIOUS BELONGING IN FRANCE FROM 1990 TO 2018 (% FIGURES)*

	1990	1999	2008	2018	Change from 1990 to 2018
Regularly Practising Catholics	15	10	9	7	-8
Irregularly Practising Catholics	14	12	10	6	-8
Non-practising Catholics	28	31	23	19	-9
Other Religion	4	5	8	10	+6
Without Religion	29	30	33	37	+8
Atheist	10	12	17	21	+11
Total	100	100	100	100	–

* Dargent, 'Recul du Catholicisme, croissance des non-affiliés et des minorités religieuses', 223.

8 Dargent, 'Recul du Catholicisme, croissance des non-affiliés et des minorités religieuses', 229.
9 Michelat, 'Ce que se dire Catholique veut dire', 132-135; Hervieu-Léger (in collaboration with Champion), *Vers un nouveau Christianisme?*, 24.

suited to describing the religiosity of traditional societies in which there is a strong social pressure to attend collective religious rituals. Nowadays, people consider themselves religious even if they do not participate in a weekly Mass and they increasingly tend to create their own individual religiosity made up of a sort of bricolage of values, prescriptions, and rituals.[10] The individualization of religious beliefs and the so-called retreat of faith in the personal sphere make it necessary to look for other evidence derived from quantitative and qualitative analysis to reach more fine-grained conclusions on the level of attachment to religion.

Some further insights into the religiosity of France can be derived from consideration of other macro-level indicators, such as the perception of the importance of God in life and attitudes on morality issues, notably those pertaining to intimacy that have long focused the magisterium of the Catholic Church.

Figure 4 shows the number of French adults that claim that God is somehow important (either 'very important' or 'important') rose from 33 per cent (9 per cent plus 24 per cent) in 1990 to 34 per cent (21 per cent plus 13 per cent) in 2018 whereas those that believe that God is somehow not important (either 'not important at all' or 'not important') decreased from 66 per cent (27 per cent plus 39 per cent) to 65 per cent (35 per cent plus 30 per cent) in the same period. In other words, we may see substantial stability between 1990 and 2018. However, if we give a closer look at the figures, there seems to be a pattern of dualization on the idea about the importance of God. Those who considered God 'important' in their lives declined from 24 per cent to 21 per cent while those who considered God 'very important' grew from 9 per cent to 13 per cent. Data show that the percentage of those who considered God 'not important' in their lives dropped from 39 per cent in 1990 to 30 per cent in 2018 whereas in the same period those who considered God 'not important at all' rose from 27 per cent to 35 per cent. In this sense, we can contend that a growing part of the population is becoming completely indifferent to religion, but, at the same time, a minority (roughly one tenth) is showing a stronger attachment to faith.[11] This latter minority can become the reservoir for those campaigns, initiatives, and mobilizations organized by Catholic traditionalist groups.

Close scrutiny of the impact of secularization also shows that belief in Catholic teaching, most notably on bioethical, gender, and sexuality-related issues is greatly affected by secularization. These questions have been the central concern of the Catholic Church as "for the past twenty years, bioethics and gender issues constitute the new front line for the mobilization of Catholic

10 Hervieu-Léger, 'Bricolage vaut-il dissémination?'.
11 Dargent, 'Et Dieu dans tout ça?', 244.

FIGURE 4
ANSWERS TO THE QUESTION OF THE IMPORTANCE OF GOD IN LIFE FROM 1990 TO 2018 IN FRANCE (% FIGURES)*

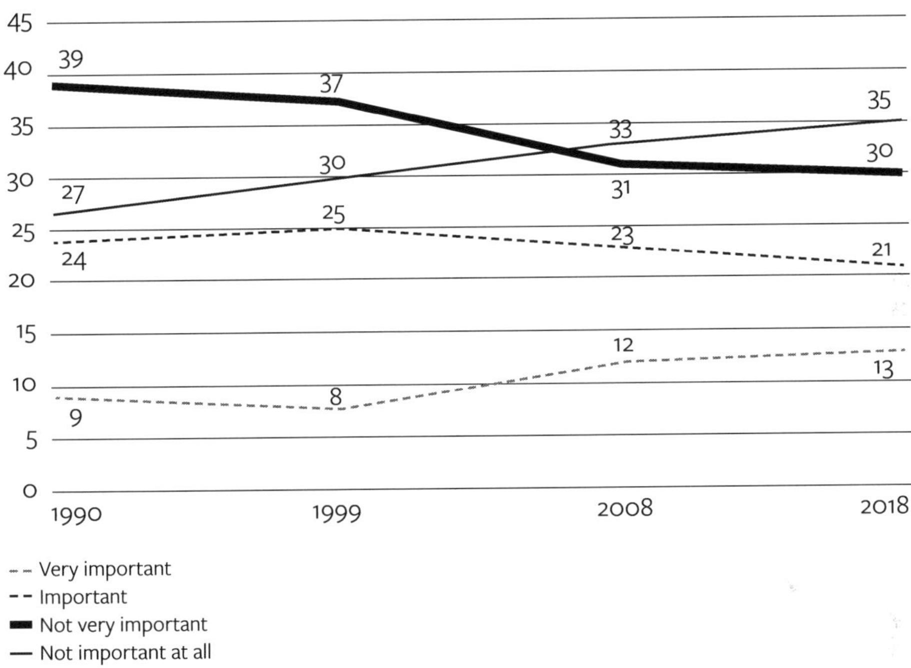

* Dargent, 'Et Dieu dans tout ça?', 245.

authorities".[12] However, the doctrinal closure of the Vatican on gender and sexually-related issues has further distanced Catholics from the doctrine of the Church on these matters.

The relationship between Catholicism and sexuality is the subject of a burgeoning body of scholarship.[13] One of the earliest works on the sexual morality of French Catholics was a book entitled *L'Amour, le sexe et les Catholiques* (Love, sex and Catholics) published in 1994 by Frédéric Mounier, head of the religion division of the Catholic newspaper *La Croix*. Using data from the surveys carried out by the INED, Mounier pointed out that not only did the largest majority of French people not follow the sexual norms prescribed by the Church, but neither did Catholic women, traditionally more attached to religious values. For instance, the data showed that in 1953, 53 per cent of Catholics thought that doctors should not offer advice on contraceptive methods,

12 Dobbelaere, Pérez-Agote and Béraud, 'Comparative Synthesis', 200.
13 Buisson-Fenet, *Un sexe problématique*; Bethmont and Gross, *Homosexualité et traditions monothéistes.*

but in 1966, 19 per cent of Catholics maintained the same opinion.[14] Although in 1988, 10 per cent of women considered religion very important in their lives, only 11 per cent of them employed natural contraceptive methods (particularly abstinence) and around 64 per cent used birth control pills.[15]

A more recent survey by the Institut Français d'Opinion Publique (IFOP), carried out in March 2013, confirms the widespread disregard by French people of Catholic sexual morality. The results of the survey, presented in Table 5, highlighted that the overwhelming majority of respondents believed that the Church should change its positions in relation to contraception (90 per cent), abortion (80 per cent), and homosexuality (65 per cent). In this sense, permissive values on gender, reproductive, and sexually-related matters are prevailing among French Catholics. Interestingly, the data indicated that the main division was between practising and non-practising Catholics. While the opinions of the latter are almost similar to those of all the French, the former have tended to assume more conservative positions.[16] In other words, nowadays, the main divide is not between Catholics and non-Catholics but between people with different levels of intensity of belief.[17]

Furthermore, the data presented in Table 5 also show that the attitudes of practising Catholics have become more conservative. Between March 2009 and March 2013 the percentage of practising Catholics who believed that the Church should revise its position on contraception declined from 75 per cent to 71 per cent, from 68 per cent to 45 per cent on abortion, and from 49 per cent to 44 per cent on homosexuality. In other words, an increasing number of practising Catholics believe that the Church should not abandon the traditionalist positions on sexuality that are grounded on the natural law tradition and which have been reaffirmed by the theology of Jean Paul II.

Drawing on the data briefly discussed in this section, two main observations can be made. First, French people show an increasing detachment from institutional participation in the Church and from the Church's sexual morality. Second, a minority of people are rediscovering a stronger sense of attachment to religious values and traditionalist ethical norms.[18] This paradoxical outcome seems to define the current situation of French Catholicism. Whether and to what extent these attitudes can influence political actors and the Catholic Church is a topic of ongoing debate.

14 Mounier, *L'amour, le sexe et les Catholiques*, 111-112.
15 Ibid., 122-125.
16 IFOP, *La position souhaitée de l'Église Catholique sur différents sujets*, 10.
17 Gauchet, *Le désenchantement du monde*, 5.
18 Raison du Cleuziou, *Une contre-révolution catholique*.

TABLE 5
'YES' ANSWER TO THE QUESTION "DO YOU BELIEVE THE CATHOLIC CHURCH SHOULD CHANGE ITS POSITIONS?" (% FIGURES)*

	All French	All Catholics		Practising Catholics		Non-Practising Catholics	
	2013	2009	2013	2009	2013	2009	2013
On Contraception	90	85	91	75	71	88	93
On Abortion	80	83	79	68	45	87	83
On Homosexuality	65	69	62	49	44	75	64

* IFOP, *La position souhaitée de l'Église Catholique sur différents sujets*, 10. <https://www.ifop.com/publication/la-position-souhaitee-de-leglise-catholique-sur-differents-sujets/>.

A Church in Decline?

To better understand the situation of contemporary Catholicism in France, it is important to have some idea of the changing organizational structure of the Church. One of the most pressing problems for the Catholic Church in France is the dramatic decline in membership. From 1990 to 2018 the numbers of seminarians dropped from 1,219 to 828, even though there was a steep increase between 2015 and 2018. The number of diocesan priests dramatically declined too, going from 25,203 in 1990 to 10,923 in 2018.[19] As a consequence of the lack of replacements, active priests have been forced to stay in service beyond the formal retirement age of seventy-five. The outcomes of this phenomenon are particularly evident in the countryside, a traditional stronghold of French Catholicism. In small villages, it is getting more common to find churches closed because no priest is living in the parsonage or because he has to divide his time between different places.[20] The decline in the numbers of nuns in the past decades is even sharper than that of priests. Whereas there were 62,208 nuns in France in 1990, by 2018 there were 22,128.[21] This drop in Church membership has led to the erosion of the parish culture, the capillary presence of members of the Church in various social realities.[22]

However, the figures shown in Table 6 should be interpreted within a broader framework to provide a more accurate picture of the Church membership. While the numbers of priests have declined in the post-war years,[23] those

19 Église Catholique en France, *Statistiques de l'Église Catholique en France*.
20 'La carte de France des prêtres', *La Croix*, 21 May 2010.
21 Église Catholique en France, *Statistiques de l'Église Catholique en France*.
22 Hervieu-Léger, *Catholicisme*, la fin d'un monde, 183.

TABLE 6
STATISTICS ON THE CATHOLIC CHURCH IN FRANCE FROM 1990 TO 2018*

	1990	1995	2000	2005	2010	2015	2018	Change from 1995 to 2018
Seminarians	1,219	1,155	976	784	732	653	828	-32,1%
Diocesan Priests	25,203	22,199	19,234	16,075	14,112	11,908	10,923	-56,7%
Nuns	62,208	52,420	49,871	44,340	33,340	24,971	22,128	-64,4%
Deacons	514	973	1,478	1,934	2,410	**2,656**	**2,833**	**+451,2%**

* Église Catholique en France, *Statistiques de l'Église Catholique en France*; Comité National Diaconat, *Statistiques sur la population des diacres permanents*; Conférence des Évêques de France, *Guide 2013 de l'Église Catholique en France.*

of deacons have steadily increased. From 1990 to 2018, the figures of deacons grew from 514 to 2,833.[24] In view of the fact that there is a certain level of substitution of roles between the different members of the Church,[25] deacons can be a great resource for a Church and their increase is a sign of its structural transformation.[26] The greater recognition of the role of lay people in the life of parishes is leading to a declericalization of the Church that may have some far-reaching consequences for this institution.[27]

The foundation of several charismatic religious communities and movements in France since the early 1970s is another telling social phenomenon that suggests the renovation of the Church in this country. Since the late 1990s these movements have become more institutionally organized and integrated into the Catholic Church of France. This argument deserves an exhaustive treatment that, unfortunately, cannot be undertaken here. However, some observations may suffice for the scope of this book.

One of the most successful new Catholic organizations in France is the Communauté de l'Emmanuel. Founded in Paris in 1972, and formally recognized by the Vatican in 1992, this organization has three main goals: adoration, compassion, and evangelization. Although this community has gener-

23 According to the Catholic hierarchy, a deacon is a layperson, whose tasks are mainly related to assisting priests in their administrative responsibilities. The duties of deacons were reformed by the Second Vatican Council as part of the *aggiornamento* of the Church to make them more involved in the life of their parishes.

24 Comité National Diaconat, *Statistiques sur la population des diacres permanents.*

25 Bourdieu and de Saint Martin, 'La sainte famille', 18.

26 Béraud, *Prêtres, diacres, laïcs.*

27 Pasture, 'Christianity in a detraditionalising world', 119.

ally been considered a charismatic movement, it would be reductive to just present it as a charismatic association because it draws its inspiration from the long-standing mystical tradition of French Catholicism and it is engaged in a large variety of social activities.[28] An intense communitarian life experience, based on sharing common moments, is offered to its members because, as pointed out by Laurent Landete, former President of the Communauté de l'Emmanuel, "the experience of God is made in contact with others".[29] In 2022, the Communauté de l'Emmanuel had 11,500 members and it was represented in sixty countries, where it was involved in a wide range of social initiatives (e.g. organization of study and missionary groups, provision of accommodation to students, charity activities and publishing religious books) that were completely funded by private donations and legacies.[30] This community was also composed 100 seminarians and 275 priests and 10 bishops came from its ranks.[31]

The Communauté Saint-Martin is another example of a new religious community active in France today. This community was founded by Abbé Jean-François Guérin, who intended to provide a stronger religious formation to seminarians and priests. Unable to find a diocese in France that would accept his community because it was considered too conservative, Abbé Guérin received the support of Cardinal Siri, Archbishop of Genova, and in 1976 he established a community in Voltri in Italy, with the name of Communauté Saint-Martin.[32] Since then, and after moving to France, the number of seminarians who have joined the community has steadily grown to the point that the Communauté Saint-Martin decided to reopen a huge formerly abandoned seminary. The influence of this community in the life of the Church has been increasingly recognized. An article published in September 2021 by *La Croix* entitled 'Communauté Saint-Martin, l'avenir de l'Église de France?' (Communauté Saint-Martin, the future of the Church of France?) pointed out that this community is one of the main 'providers' of the French clergy as its members accounted for roughly 40 per cent of the new ordinations of the Catholic Church of France.[33] This is quite a high number that is likely to give this community, as noted by *La Croix*, a remarkable influence on the Church.

The statistics and the observations presented in this section are aimed at providing some critical considerations of the Church of France and questioning the commonly held assumption about its irreversible decline. Though

28 Laurent Landete, former President Communauté de l'Emmanuel, 25 January 2015, personal interview.

29 Laurent Landete quoted in *La Croix*, 19 August 2007.

30 Laurent Landete, former President Communauté de l'Emmanuel, 25 January 2015, personal interview.

31 Communauté de l'Emmanuel, *Qui sommes nous?*.

32 Landron, À la droite du Christ, 147.

33 'Communauté Saint-Martin, l'avenir de l'Église de France?', *La Croix*, 20 September 2021.

the Church shows some signs of crisis, its situation also presents some elements that reveal a process of renovation. Some further considerations on the presence of religion in the political and civil society may deepen our understanding of the transformations that characterize contemporary French Catholicism.

Do Catholic Values Still Play a Role in French Politics?

Since the Liberation, the relationship between the Church and French political society has been characterized by a sort of double relaxation: the Church has generally restrained itself from intervening in political debates and Catholic-minded politicians have tended to pay limited attention to the positions of the Church.[34] The principle of *laïcité* was enshrined in the Constitution approved in 1946 and reaffirmed in the Constitution of 1958. With the constitutionalization of the *laïcité* the conflict between the 'two Frances' that had begun with the French Revolution was over.[35]

The idea of *laïcité* that post-war French politicians had in mind did not resemble any kind of militant anti-clericalism.[36] Political actors considered the *laïcité* as the independence of the state from all authorities that were not recognized by the whole population, to allow public institutions to be impartial [37] At the same time, the *laïcité* granted some autonomy to the Church from the interferences of secular authorities. In this sense, the French regime of *laïcité* granted a mutual separation between the political and the religious field.

Nowadays, the separation between the state and the Church is a paradigm of French politics to the point that France does not present a religious cleavage any more.[38] This result was also the outcome of the final disbanding of the MRP in 1967 and the absence of an electorally consistent Christian democratic party in France since the disappearance of the MRP. In contrast with other countries, notably Italy, the idea of the political union of Catho-

34 Rémond, *Le Catholicisme français et la société politique*. However, the Church has always pointed out the importance of political engagement. A document from the Commission Sociale de l'Épiscopat Français entitled *'Réhabiliter la politique' (Revitalize politics)* issued in 1999 affirmed that politics is a noble and difficult activity and those who are engaged in it need to be encouraged. See Commission Sociale de l'Épiscopat Français, *Réhabiliter la politique*.

35 Baubérot, 'La laïcité française et ses mutations', 182.

36 Baubérot, *Histoire de la laïcité en France*, 123.

37 Ibid., 101-102.

38 Jérôme Vignon, former President of the Semaines Sociales de France and President of the Observatoire National de la Pauvreté et de l'Exclusion Sociale, 8 January 2012, personal interview. A report presented in 1996 by the French Episcopal Conference entitled 'Proposer la foi dans la société actuelle' (Proposing the faith in current society) pointed out that the opposition between the counter-revolutionary and conservative Catholic tradition and a republican anticlerical tradition does not exist anymore. See Conférence Épiscopale Française, *Proposer la foi dans la société actuelle*, 10.

lics into a unique Christian democratic party has never had great appeal for French electors, and after the early 1950s, the Catholic electorate started to spread their preferences throughout the political spectrum. However, French Catholics have never been absent from political life[39] and since the mid 2000s, particularly following the election of Nicolas Sarkozy in May 2007, the French Right has proposed a revision of the conception of the *laïcité*.[40]

In his book-interview *La République, les religions, l'esperance* published in 2004, Sarkozy wrote that "the place of religion in France at the beginning of the third millennium is central".[41] The space that Sarkozy intended to accord to religion is not certainly a formal role in the political sphere, but rather that of being an enduring source of inspiration for political questions. In his speech at Lateran Palace on 20 December 2007, the newly elected president of the Republic emphasized the Christian roots of France, asked for their valorization, and remarked on the superiority of Christian morality over secular morality by saying that the primary school teacher could not replace the clergyman in the transmission of values.[42] Sarkozy also stressed the need for a transition from a negative to a positive kind of *laïcité*.

The resilient influence of Catholicism on the mainstream Right was confirmed by the victory of the Catholic and socially conservative François Fillon in the primary elections of Les Républicains (LR) in November 2016 and the election for the presidency of this party in December 2017 of the devout Catholic Laurent Wauquiez, who was one of the leading political figures in opposing the legalization of same-sex marriage in France.[43] Following a dramatic defeat at the 2018 European elections, at the beginning of June 2019 Wauquiez resigned from his position at the head of the LR and was replaced in October 2019 by Christian Jacob.[44] Although the new president of the LR intended to adopt a different political platform from that of his predecessor, he continued to support conservative positions on family and morality questions.[45] In a let-

39 They have continued to hold senior government positions, particularly in 'social ministries'. Just to mention some of them: Philippe Seguin, Minister of Social Affairs and Employment between 1986 and 1988; Philippe Douste-Blazy Minister of Health from 1993 to 1995 and Minister of Solidarity, Health, and Family from 2004 to 2005; Hervé Gaymard, Secretary of State for Health and Social Security from 1995 to 1998 and Minister of Economy, Finance and Industry from 2004 to 2005; and Christine Boutin, Minister of Housing from 2007 to 2009.

40 Baubérot, *Les sept laïcités françaises*, 110.

41 Sarkozy, *La République, les religions, l'espérance*, 15.

42 'Discours de Nicolas Sarkozy au Palais du Latran le 20 décembre 2007', *Le Monde*, 21 December 2007.

43 'Laurent Wauquiez gagne haut la main l'élection à la présidence des Républicains', *Le Figaro*, 10 December 2017.

44 'Laurent Wauquiez démissionne de la présidence du parti Les Républicains', *Le Monde*, 2 June 2019; 'La victoire sans triomphalisme de Christian Jacob à la tête de LR', *Libération*, 14 October 2019.

45 'Petit à petit, Les Républicains se déwauquiezisent', *L'Opinion*, 1 December 2019.

ter sent in 2017 to the AFC's Federation of Melun, before the upcoming political elections, Jacob wrote that he considered parents to be the first educators of their children, he wanted to allow artificial reproductive technologies only for heterosexual couples affected by infertility problems, and he opposed any proposal for medical research on human embryos.[46]

The impact of Catholicism on political leaders also found a formal channel of transmission in the Entente Parlamentaire pour la Famille,[47] an informal inter-parliamentary group established in 2006 that was composed of roughly 140 deputies after the 2017 legislative elections.[48] The Entente has generally tended to promote family laws that bear the imprint of conservative Catholic values. In consideration of the resilient influence of Catholicism on the French Right, we may claim, as Sarkozy did, that the place of religion "is not a place external to the Republic [...] it is a place in the Republic", which is sustained by the Catholic moralism that inspired a part of French political elites.[49]

The influence of religious values on political actors is also promoted by the fact that religion is one of the main criteria that influence voting behaviour.[50] In other words, the Catholic symbolic system has a strong explicative power over political attitudes and behaviours.[51] This conclusion is corroborated by the electoral choices for the first round of the presidential elections in 2017, as shown by Table 7.

According to a survey by IFOP, in 2017 Catholics tended to position themselves on the centrist (Emmanuel Maron) or right-wing side of the electoral spectrum (François Fillon, Nicolas Dupong-Aignan and Marine Le Pen). As shown in Table 7, the centrist candidate Emmanuel Macron collected 22 per cent of the Catholic votes, the three right-wing candidates (François Fillon, Nicolas Dupong-Aignan, Marine Le Pen) received 56 per cent of their votes (28 per cent plus 6 per cent plus 22 per cent), and the two left-wing candidates (Jean-Luc Mélenchon, Benoît Hamon) only 18 per cent (14 per cent plus 4 per cent) of their votes. The most telling result shown in the table is the vote of practising Catholics, which diverged from the overall vote of Catholics. Regularly practising Catholics gave stronger support to the moderate right-wing candidate (Fillon), who collected the majority of their votes (55 per cent), while far-right candidates (Nicolas Dupong-Aignan, Marine Le Pen) received 14 per cent (12 per cent plus 2 per cent) and the leftist candidates (Jean-Luc Mélenchon, Benoît Hamon) only 10 per cent (8 per cent plus 2 per cent).

46 AFC de Melun et sa Region, *Letter by Christian Jacob.*

47 Jean-Luc Roméro, PS politician and LGBT activist, 12 July 2013, personal interview.

48 'L'entente parlementaire pour la famille resserrée sur ses piliers', *La Vie*, 20 June 2017.

49 Sarkozy, *La République, les religions, l'espérance,* 15.

50 Le Bras and Todd, *Le mystère français*; Bréchon, 'La religion, le facteur le plus explicatif du vote!', *Le Figaro*, 7 May 2012.

51 Michelat and Dargent, 'Système symbolique catholique et comportements électoraux', 27.

TABLE 7
ELECTORAL PREFERENCES IN THE FIRST ROUND OF THE 2017 PRESIDENTIAL ELECTION (% FIGURES)*

	Jean-Luc Mélenchon	Benoît Hamon	Emmanuel Macron	François Fillon	Marine Le Pen	Other Candidates
Total Catholics	14	4	22	28	22	10
Regularly Practising	8	2	19	55	12	4
Occasionally Practising	17	2	18	37	18	8
Non Practising	14	5	23	25	23	14
Without Religion	28	8	24	9	23	8
Total French	20.1	6.3	23.3	20.1	21.6	8.6

* IFOP, *Le vote des électorats confessionnels au 1er Tour de l'élection présidentielle*, 6.

Although those Catholics who are more integrated into the symbolic system of Catholicism are still reluctant to vote for far-right candidates, Table 7 highlights that the Front National (FN), rebranded Rassemblement National (RN) in 2018, has made significant inroads among Catholic electors as Marine Le Pen was voted by 18 per cent of occasionally practising Catholics and 23 per cent of non-practising Catholics.

It may be argued that the Catholic vote could have only a marginal impact on the final outcome of elections, given that regularly practising Catholics are a small minority of the French electorate. However, this objection can be partly rejected for two reasons. First, the likelihood of regularly practising Catholics to vote is greater than that of other French voters.[52] Second, the impact of the vote of a minority of the electorate is increased by the majoritarian electoral system that tends to amplify the effects of the aforementioned factors.

Catholicism and Civil Society

Presenting a clear definition of civil society is challenging. This concept has multiple meanings and it is often presented with normative (positive) connotations. This is why the concept of civil society may conceal more aspects of the relationship between the public sphere and the state than elucidate them.[53] In order to avoid methodological shortcomings, this book adopts a broad definition of civil society and considers it an intermediate social field between state authorities and individuals, whose precise boundaries and interactions are subjected to historical changes and whose role is the establishment of a space

52 Bréchon, 'La religion, le facteur le plus explicatif du vote!', *Le Figaro*, 7 May 2012.
53 Therborn, 'Ambiguous Ideals and Problematic Outcomes', 142-143.

for discussion, collaboration, and mediation between individuals, intermediate groups, and public institutions.

Catholics have always created a dense network of civil society associations composed of charity organizations, workers' organizations, sports clubs, and so on. Sometimes these actors were ancillary organizations of the Church and supported the electoral campaigns of Christian democratic parties.[54] In contrast to other Western European countries, French civil society organizations have generally been weak and without much political influence.[55] On the other hand, the dramatic crisis of political parties and labour unions, the crisis of legitimacy of public authorities, the increasing public trust benefitting non-profit associations have strengthened the public role of civic society associations. An aspect that has been seldom studied by the scholarship is the fact that faith-based groups and Catholic-inspired organizations active in the provision of social services are becoming not only important institutional partners for public bureacracies, but also new tools for the promotion of anthropological and ethical values bearing the imprint of religious ideals in contemporary secular or post-secular societies. This subject is investigated in more detail in Chapter 6 with regard to housing policies. However, this section provides some observations on Catholic civil society organizations in France today.

The Catholic press has traditionally been an important channel for the diffusion of Catholic ideas.[56] Some Catholic and Catholic-inspired publications have always contributed to the dialogue between the Catholic and the socialist and communist subcultures (e.g. *Esprit* and *Témoignage Chrétien*) and right-wing and liberal circles (e.g. *Valeur Actuelles*). Still today, in France there is a vast array of Catholicism journals and Catholic cultural associations. Like the print media in most Western countries, Catholic journals are currently coping with a period of crisis. However, it seems that they are facing it relatively well. In 2018, *Esprit* registered a respectable monthly circulation of 10,000 copies, and that was almost the same as the well-known *Les Temps Moderns* founded by Jean-Paul Sartre. According to the Alliance pour les Chiffres de la Presse et des Médias (ACPM), between 2000 and 2018 the daily circulation of *Le Figaro* dropped by 13 per cent (from 369,547 to 321,157), that of *Le Monde* by 22 per cent (from 403,892 to 316,895), and that of *Libération* by 58 per cent (from 171,596 to 72,397). However, in the same period, the daily circulation of *La Croix* declined only by 7 per cent (from 105,216 to 97,512).[57]

Catholic education institutes are another channel that has traditionally been used by the Church to reproduce its social and cultural influence. The overall number of Catholic schools is quite relevant in France. In 2018-2019 there

54 Kalyvas, *The Rise of Christian Democracy in Europe*, 113.

55 Pasture, 'Syndicats et associations en France et en Europe, une interrogation sur les originalités françaises', 469.

56 Rémond, 'Un chapitre inachevé (1958-1990)', 402.

57 ACPM, *Classements de presse payante.*

were 7,364 institutes enrolling 2,099,476 students (around 20 per cent of the total student population).[58] Although Catholic primary and elementary schools registered a noticeable drop in students of 3 per cent between 1996 and 2002, and again by a similar percentage between 2008 and 2013, in the following four years they dramatically increased their student population and reached almost the same numbers that they had in 1998 (see Figure 5). As for Catholic secondary schools, after having lost roughly 3 per cent of students between 1995 and 2005, they have registered a steady increase since 2006. The upward trend of the student population enrolled in Catholic secondary schools became steeper after 2008, to the extent that in 2018 these schools had 5 per cent more students than they had in 1996. The data on Catholic secondary schools are more striking when they are compared with the figures for students in public secondary institutes, which dramatically dropped by 9 per cent until 2008. Even though since 2009 the number of students enrolled in public secondary schools has increased, the trend has been less dynamic in comparison with Catholic secondary schools.

During the Third Republic, schooling was the ground for intense struggles between Catholics and the political elites that intended to secularize France. However, following a process of internal secularization of Catholic schools, education has increasingly become an area of mutual recognition and collaboration between Catholicism and public authorities, to the extent that the cooperation between the minister of education and the Enseignement Catholique has become an established orientation of education policies in France. This cooperation is exemplified by the fact that in 2018 roughly 90 per cent of Catholic institutes were contracted-in schools.[59] This implies that they are part of the national education system, even though they continue to maintain some autonomy in defining their educational projects, the salary of the teachers in these schools is paid by the state, and national and local public authorities contribute to the operating costs of Catholic institutes.[60]

In spite of this recognition of Catholic institutes by public authorities, schooling still remains a sensitive topic that can easily reopen ideological conflicts. This happened in 1984 when François Mitterrand attempted to combine private institutes into a unique grand public service, but he had to retreat from his original proposal in the face of strong protests from the Catholic schools. A more recent example of resurgent conflicts is provided by the vehement accusations launched in November 2012 by left-wing political parties at the Secretary for Catholic Education, Érik de Labarre because he sent a letter to all headmistresses and headmasters of Catholic institutes asking them to open a debate on the law on same-sex marriage.[61]

58 Enseignement Catholique (issues from 2012-2018), *Les chiffres clés de l'enseignement catholique*.
59 Ibid.
60 Poucet, *L'enseignement privé en France*, 71-75.
61 'Enseignement catholique, les chefs d'établissement invités à ouvrir le débat sur le mariage homosexuel', *La Croix*, 28 December 2012.

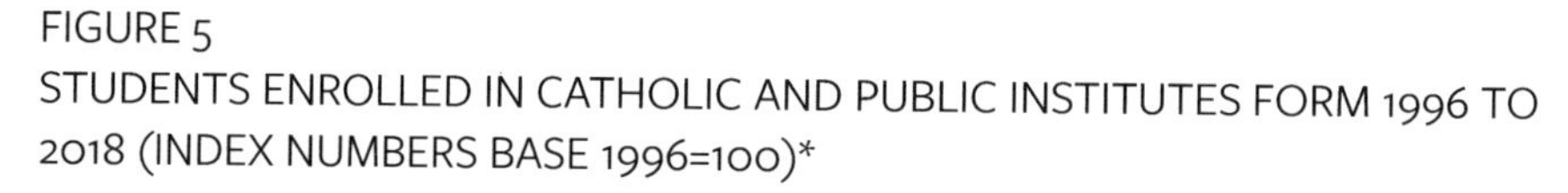

FIGURE 5
STUDENTS ENROLLED IN CATHOLIC AND PUBLIC INSTITUTES FORM 1996 TO 2018 (INDEX NUMBERS BASE 1996=100)*

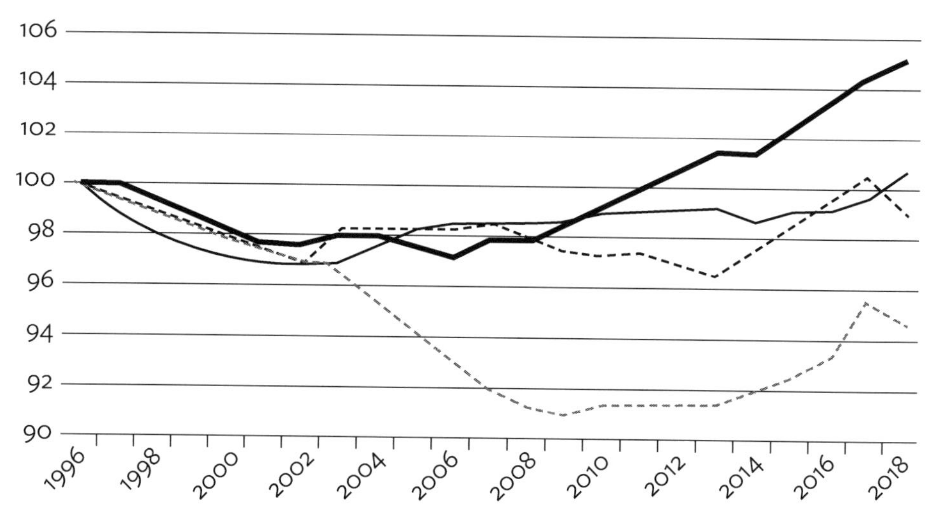

-- Catholic primary and elementary schools
▬ Catholic secondary schools
— Public primary and elementary schools
-- Public secondary schools
* Enseignement Catholique, *Les chiffres clés de l'enseignement catholique*. iv.

The non-profit sector has generally been another field characterized by a strong and capillary presence of Catholicism. Some of the major French non-profit organizations in France have a Catholic background.[62] Since the early 1990s, voluntary associations have gradually become stable partners of public authorities in the provision of social services in various areas, such as housing (Emmaüs France, FAP, Habitat et Humanisme), family services (AFC), social assistance (Secours Catholique), and so on.[63]

62 It is difficult to find reliable data on the social economy in France because the academic scholarship has traditionally paid limited attention to the topic, and the few reliable statistics on the topic do not classify associations according to their denomination. However, case studies, interviews, and expert opinions can supplement the lack of quantitative data.

63 Habitat et Humanisme was founded in 1985 by the then real estate agent Bernard Devert, who became a priest in 1987. The mission of the association is the provision of houses to economically deprived families. Since its foundation, more than 12,000 families have benefited from the support of the association and now Habitat et Humanisme is a medium-sized enterprise. In 2012, the Federation Habitat et Humanisme had an annual budget of 285.5 million euros, it managed 7,000 houses throughout France, and it had 2,300 volunteers and 200 employees. See, 'Bernard Devert, président d'Habitat et Humanisme', *Le Monde*, 23 September 2013. Given the chronic inefficiencies of French public job centres (pole d'emploi), the major voluntary groups are also promoting job insertion branches.

A telling example of a partnership between a Catholic-inspired association and public authorities is provided by the so-called Les Chantiers-éducation[64], managed by the AFC. The aim of Les Chantiers is the establishment of a network of families that discuss and attempt to find solutions to common problems related to the education of their children. The project had immediate success and the initiative was soon adopted all over France. In 2010, there were 630 Chantiers in 80 departments involving around 1,000 volunteers and 5,000 families. Given the good results of the initiative, in 2008 the ministry of national education signed an agreement with the AFC to further develop the project.[65] The case of Les Chantiers-éducation is particularly revealing because it is related to two policy areas, family and education, that in the past have triggered strong conflicts between the Church and the state as they were considered crucial policy fields, both for Catholic groups and state authorities, for projection of their influence into the social domain.

Since the mid 1990s, religious-inspired non-profit organizations have increasingly tended to be considered collaborators with rather than competitors of public institutions. This development was the outcome of complementary interests. While recognition by public authorities permits associations to receive public funding, the purpose of state authorities is to find reliable partners that may experiment with new policy programmes, provide the expertise that they sometimes lack, and manage social programmes in a more flexible and cheaper way than they do.

Civic associations may even become new instruments for the renovation of political participation, even though this has seldom been their stated purpose.[66] The capacity of voluntary groups to defend the interests of socially marginalized people not represented by political parties and their capacity to earn the trust of public opinion dissatisfied with traditional political actors is making them the reference point for new forms of political participation[67] and civic activism aimed at renewing social bonds and solidarity networks.[68]

The political role of civic associations is not new. At least since the early 1980s, for example with Solidarność in Poland, social scientists have pointed out the positive impact of civic activism in the political sphere. However, this argument should be critically considered. Not all kinds of engagement pro-

For example, Secours Catholique established a central office dealing with employment issues, whose activities were similar to those of a job placement centre.

64 It is difficult to translate this French expression. The English translation could be 'construction sites for an education project'.

65 Vincent Porteret, Delegate General of the Confédération Nationale des Associations Familiales Catholiques, 22 September 2013, personal interview.

66 Barthélémy, *Associations*.

67 Rosanvallon, *La contre-démocratie*.

68 Annie Orsoni, Head of the Secours Catholique-Caritas 11th arrondissement of Paris, 1 February 2014, personal interview.

moted by civil society associations have beneficial effects for democracy.[69] For instance, in 2012-2013 the social protests against same-sex marriage in France, led by civil society associations, opened highly divisive debates characterized by the emergence of strong ideological conflicts. The defence of normative principles inspired by traditional Catholic anthropological doctrines reopened social and political cleavages, originated forms of anti-systemic politics, and provoked episodic acts of violence in the attempt to impede the approval of a project of law proposed by a democratically elected Parliament.

Entering a Post-secular Era: Secularization, Civic Engagement, and New Social Mobilization

This chapter has presented some empirical findings on the presence of Catholicism in various social spheres in contemporary France. Given the breadth of the topic, our attention has necessarily focused on several key changes that have interested current Catholicism and on some important fields for the projection of Catholic influence in society. This chapter did not aim to reject the widespread thesis that France is an increasingly secular country, but rather to offer a nuanced outlook on the process of secularization in this country. Two opposite conclusions can be drawn from the consideration of the findings presented in the chapter. First, a large majority of French people are less involved in religious organizations than in the past and they tend to disregard Catholic principles on morality issues. These signs highlight the declining influence of Catholic values in contemporary France.[70] Second, a minority of French people show an enduring or even greater attachment to Catholic ideals, that religious principles still have a great influence on voting behaviour, and that Catholic-inspired organizations are still largely present in civil society. These facts demonstrate the enduring vitality of Catholicism in secular France. Although this may involve just a small minority of the French, the resilience of Catholicism should not be underestimated.

Though the French regime of *laïcité* has imposed a strict separation between the Church and the state, some recent developments may strenghten the influence of religions in the public sphere.

First, the disappearance of the religious cleavage has lessened the ideological constraints on the involvement of religious-inspired actors in the management of public services (e.g. social assistance, health care, and education). Second, religious actors may acquire greater influence in the public domain because of the crisis affecting its traditional opponents: public authorities,

69 Therborn, 'Ambiguous Ideals and Problematic Outcomes', 147.

70 To these cases, it is possible to add the disappearance of traditional Catholic associations such as the Jeunesse Ouvrière Chrétienne and the Jeunesse Agricole Catholique.

secular political elites, and their assertive, if not militant, secularism.[71] Third, the extension of political regulation to fields with high symbolic relevance (e.g. bioethics, gender questions, and reproductive technologies) can reactive forms of protests aimed to defend long-standing anthropological Catholic norms. In these cases, religion may provide the intellectual and symbolic resources for mobilizations in defence of moral and cultural values that are shared by a part of the population that is not affiliated to any Catholic organization, but is attached to Catholic traditional values.

The possible stronger role of religion in secular France had already been pointed out by René Rémond at the beginning of the 1990s. The French historian challenged the paradigm of secularization by arguing that since the 1960s the relationships between Catholicism and public powers have ameliorated.[72] More specifically, Rémond remarked an apparent paradox of French political life by claiming that when France was a profoundly Catholic country and the Catholic Church was powerful, the Church was marginalized in the public life. In contrast, when the Church became weaker, Catholicism received increasing institutional recognition and greater attention from the mass media.[73] This paradox has also characterized some central values of the Christian democratic tradition (e.g. subsidiarity, family values, and decentralization of the state) that have become increasingly widespread in France and in Europe since the disappearance or relative decline of some European Christian democratic parties.[74] The principal reason for the changing attitudes of public institutions depends on the fact that they do not perceive Catholicism as a contender for their authority, as they did in the past, and they can now better understand the contribution that Catholicism and Catholic-minded actors can provide to the collective life through public services and normative elements that sustain the foundation of public institutions.

Two main scenarios in relation to the changing role of Catholic groups in the public sphere can be envisaged. The first one is characterized by greater cooperation between Catholic-inspired actors and public authorities. The increasing social engagement of Catholic associations will open up new forms of collaboration between public authorities and religious-inspired groups. The new cooperation is based on reciprocal recognition for mutual autonomy. The state and religious-inspired actors acknowledge their dissimilar ethical backgrounds, but this does not prevent them from establishing various forms of cooperation in the interests of citizens, particularly the most socially vulnerable. Even though religious-inspired actors accept the rules prescribed by public powers, their stable partnerships with public authorities lead them to

71 Gauchet, 'Laicitá e ruolo pubblico delle religioni', 148.
72 Rémond, 'Un chapitre inachevé (1958-1990)', 395.
73 Ibid., 401.
74 Invernizzi Accetti, *What is Christian Democracy?;* Pouthier, 'Émergence et ambiguïtés de la culture politique démocrate-chrétienne', 305.

become part of the public institutional system and this may provide them with the opportunity to exercise a subtle influence on policy decisions.

The second scenario that was partly sketched out by Suzanne Berger is defined by the re-emergence of strong ideological conflicts between state authorities and religious-inspired actors.[75] In this case, Catholic-inspired social movements and public authorities do not recognize the full legitimacy of the other. Their contrasting views may provoke new divisions or the reactivation of the social cleavages that characterized French political history. Single-issue movements could thus become the agents of anti-system politics.

While an example of the collaboration between Catholic-inspired organizations and public authorities will be discussed in the next chapter, a case of ideological conflicts between public powers and newly mobilized religious-inspired actors will be investigated in Chapter 7.

75 Berger, 'Religious Transformations and the Future of Politics', 142.

6
SOCIAL CATHOLICISM IN AN AGE OF PERMANENT AUSTERITY

Since the mid 1990s there has been a proliferation of studies on the crisis of the Western welfare states.[1] The recognition of the need to reform contemporary systems of social protection and adapt them to budgetary constraints has become a largely accepted paradigm of the scholarship and the political debate.[2] Like most other mature welfare states, French social security has undergone some remarkable changes since the mid 1990s. To some extent, the reforms implemented since the mid 1990s have been paradigmatically different compared with those introduced in the early years after the Liberation. While in the second half of the 1940s Keynesian ideas contributed to expanding social expenditure, fifty years later the state attempted to cut back social expenditure. Though the neoliberal policies adopted by several governments have not significantly reduced overall welfare spending, they have led to the implementation of austerity measures that recalibrated the intervention of the state, introduced stricter budgetary criteria to evaluate social services, and reformed the governance of social programmes.[3]

A shift in the private/public mix in service provision has been one of the most remarkable institutional transformations of welfare states.[4] Since the 1990s, public authorities have made some efforts to call on the market and

1 Armingeon, Guthmann and Weisstanner, 'Choosing the path of austerity'; Castles, *The Future of the Welfare State*; Castel, *La montée des incertitudes*; Rosanvallon, *La nouvelle question sociale*; Taylor-Goody, *The Double Crisis of the Welfare State and What We Can Do About It*.

2 Levy, 'Vice into virtue?', 241.

3 OECD, *Social Expenditure*. See <https://doi.org/10.1787/data-00167-en>.

non-profit associations to assume increasing competences in delivering social services.[5] This chapter investigates some developments of French social security by discussing several changes to the housing legislation from the early 1990s to the mid 2010s and the influence of non-profit associations in shaping policy outcomes. In doing that, this chapter wishes to fill in a gap in the academic literature. Despite some notable noteworthy studies on the French third sector have deepened our understanding of it,[6] the policy influence of non-profit organizations is still an under-researched field.

The choice of studying housing policies was motivated by four principal reasons. First, housing has been a policy field characterized by dramatic changes in the last decades.[7] Second, one of the most salient developments has been the increasing participation and influence of voluntary groups at different policy levels.[8] Third, the major non-profit associations active in housing issues have a Catholic cultural background (FAP and Secours Catholique). Fourth, housing has generally been an important policy field for French Christian democracy and social Catholicism.[9] Therefore, the study of housing policies provides an intriguing perspective to understand the new institutional influence of Catholic-minded actors and their values and their values in shaping a field at the centre of policy innovation.

Three main ideas are presented in this chapter. First, the development of French housing legislation since the early 1990s has been characterized by the increasing participation of voluntary groups at different policy levels. Second, the greater involvement of non-profit organizations was not just motivated by the crisis in the welfare state, but mainly by the capacity of these organizations to offer valuable resources for elaborating public policies and presenting themselves as reliable interlocutors for public administrations. Third, the establishment of closer relationships with public authorities provided the values that inspired voluntary organizations to exercise a subtler, but nonetheless relevant, multi-level impact on social legislation.

Like the chapters in the first part of this book, this chapter aims to propose a critical reading of the role of religious values in social policy developments. However, two characteristics distinguish this chapter (and the following) from the previous ones. First, we propose a more thematic approach to the study of values in the social policy domain. Second, we focus our analysis

4 Alber, 'A framework for the comparative study of social services'; Beaumont and Dias, 'Faith-based organisations and urban social justice in the Netherlands'; Manuel and Glatzer, eds, *Faith-based Organizations and Social Welfare*; Ranci, Il volontariato; Williams, Cloke and Thomas, 'Co-constituting neoliberalism'.

5 Bäckström et al, eds, *Welfare and Religion in 21st Century Europe. Volume 1.*

6 Archambault, *The Nonprofit Sector in France*; Tchernonog et al, *Le paysage associatif français.*

7 Driant, *Les politiques du logement en France*, 152-160.

8 Fijalkow, 'Le tiers secteur associatif dans la régulation de l'habitat en France'.

9 Irving, *Christian Democracy in France*, 87-88.

on civil society organizations instead of political actors and parties to better explore the relocation of religious activism from the political sphere to civil society that has occurred in the last decades.[10]

This chapter devotes specific, but not exclusive, attention to the FAP. Although the FAP was founded by a religious man, the charismatic Abbé Pierre, it is a secular association whose public engagement nevertheless takes inspiration from Catholic social ideals.[11] Among the several voluntary associations active in housing policies, the FAP is one of the most well-known, influential, and organized, and its developments anticipated some of the main evolutions that are currently being experienced by French non-profit organizations.[12]

The chapter is divided into two parts. The first one is composed of three subsections that discuss the three main stages in the development of French housing legislation since the early 1990s. The concluding paragraph summarizes the arguments of the previous parts and it presents some theoretical observations on the new role of religious values in the social policy sphere from the early 1990s to the mid 2010s.

Housing Policies and Social Catholicism

Welfare state scholarship has extensively written on 'core' social policy areas (e.g. employment, health care, social assistance, and pensions), but it has paid less attention to housing policies. For a long time, this lack of interest from the academic community was often matched by the limited interventions of governments that devoted a small share of their social budgets to housing. In France, until the late 1980s, housing questions did not occupy a central place in the political debate, and in the rare cases when they did, they were generally subordinated to the need to promote macro-economic developments.[13] However, since the early 1990s, housing issues have attracted greater attention following a dramatic increase in housing prices, the intensification of the lobbying activity of voluntary organizations, and the recurrence of episodes of transgression of the law related to housing problems (e.g. squatting and urban riots in deprived metropolitan areas)[14]. These events gave stronger political relevance to housing and new policies began to be introduced. This

10 Casanova, *Public Religions in the Modern World.*

11 Yves Colin, Director of Communication of the FAP, 18 December 2013, personal interview.

12 Edith Archambault, Emeritus Professor at the Université Paris 1 Panthéon-Sorbonne and Deputy President of the Association pour le Developpement des Données sur l'Economie Sociale 26 January 2014, personal interview.

13 The 1981 Mitterrand presidential manifesto considered housing policies a branch of the macro-economic politics or a specific sphere of social intervention to alleviate the difficult social conditions of some categories of people, such as the elderly, disabled, and young couples. See Balchin and Rhoden, *Housing policy*, 17-85.

14 Bigot and Hoibian, *Les difficultés des français face au logement*, 9.

chapter individuates three main stages in the evolution of French housing legislation since the beginning of the 1990s:

- Early and contradictory developments (1990-1995);
- Increasing activism (1995-2010);
- Informal alliance between voluntary associations and public authorities (2010-2015).

These different stages are defined in accordance with two criteria: the attitudes of public authorities and the policy innovations that they implemented. It is thus possible to recognize a policy trajectory defined by the increasing activism of public powers and their greater openness toward the participation of voluntary organizations in the policy process.

Bruno Palier has claimed that social policy reforms introduced in France after the early 1990s have gradually changed the institutional settings of French social security. According to Palier, social policy innovations followed a trajectory thereby they were "at least partly, based on the consequences of the previous one. Each stage in the process opens up new reform opportunities, by changing the political context in which reforms take place."[15] Though Palier's description elucidates the long-term transformations of several policy fields, it overlooks the complexity of the various steps that compose a reform trajectory. His argument shows a typical weakness of several theories that focus on path dependency, which are sometimes affected by some degree of determinism. Excessive attention to self-reinforcing institutional mechanisms may lead to overlooking the agency of social and political actors. Governments can decide to follow a different policy trajectory from the one previously taken and policy changes can sometimes be characterized by ruptures motivated by new prevailing social values, electoral purposes, the capacity of new actors to mobilize social consensus, and so on. In our study of housing policies, we noticed that these causal factors were often at work.

Early and Contradictory Developments

As we noted in Chapters 3 and 4, French housing reforms achieved limited success. The developments in housing legislation until the late 1990s were often incoherent and lacked coordination with other social policy domains. Furthermore, the enactment of new laws was sometimes followed by the proposal of past policy solutions. Housing was a kind of garbage can policy field, a rather uncoordinated set of policies that were sometimes the by-product of interventions made in other socio-economic areas. The austerity measures introduced by Mitterrand after 1983 worsened the living conditions of the lower social

15 Palier, 'Ordering Change', 32.

strata and increased economic inequalities.[16] On 24 February 1984, Le Nouvel Observateur published a long article entitled 'La faim est entrée dans Paris' (Hunger has entered Paris). According to this magazine, people in lower social classes it was becoming harder and harder to obtain enough resources to buy food and find a place to sleep.[17]

In the 1980s the leading role in lobbying for the amelioration of housing conditions was taken up by some of the principal voluntary associations belonging to the Catholic subculture (e.g. Secours Catholique and Emmaüs France). The great majority of the activities of these groups consisted of charity initiatives or episodic events aimed at raising public awareness of the precarious housing conditions of a part of the French population. One the most well-known of these events was the operation Noël de la Charité, a distribution of free meals in the winter of 1984 organized by Banque Alimentaire, Emmaüs France, Secours Catholique, and l'Armée du Salut in collaboration with the newspaper *France Soir*.

Later on, the mobilization on housing questions was joined by other organizations, collectives, and groups that were driven by the leftist counterculture of the 1970s (e.g. Droit au Logement and Jeudi Noir) or by humanitarian values but without any distinct religious or political affiliation (e.g. Les Enfantes de Don Quixote). The links between older and newer associations have generally remained strong. A sort of collaborative attitude has always characterized the various voluntary groups involved in housing problems, regardless of the fact that these groups have different backgrounds.[18] What motivates the social engagement of activists the most is a concern for the increasing deterioration of social conditions rather than the religious belonging of the people in need, as remarked by Bruno Morel, Director General of Emmaüs France of Emmaüs Solidarité:

> although there are many religious references in our documents, we have never claimed to function as a Catholic association...above all what matters to us are the values of dignity, respect and hospitality. I am not going to welcome someone in a centre because he is Catholic, Jewish or Arab. I'm going to welcome him because he is on the street.[19]

This capacity to leave aside their religious beliefs and focus on the needs of people has allowed non-profit organizations to acquire the trust of religious and non-religious people alike. The gradual internal secularization of vol-

16 Le Puill and Le Puill, *La décennie des nouveaux pauvres*.
17 'La faim est entrée dans Paris', *Le Nouvel Observateur*, 24 February 1984.
18 Annie Orsoni, Head of the Secours Catholique-Caritas 11th arrondissement of Paris, 21 February 2014, personal interview.
19 Bruno Morel, Director General of Emmaüs Solidarité, 11 February 2014, personal interview.

untary associations in Western countries since the early 2000s[20] is not only a consequence of the increasing professionalization of their services, but it is also an indirect outcome of the willingness of the third sector to accept the challenges posed by multicultural societies. To better help people of different cultural and religious origins, volunteers leave aside their religious and ethical values and replace them with a kind of ecumenic approach that puts great emphasis on fraternity, solidarity, and attention to the psychological needs of human beings. This also permits philanthropic organizations to rebuild citizenship bonds and a sense of fraternity among people from different religious backgrounds.[21]

Social problems can sometimes instigate the elaboration of innovative solutions. The early 1990s were characterized by one of the most relevant developments of the associational movement: the foundation of the FAP. This new association was officially established in January 1992 and recognized as an organization of public interest by decree on 11 February 1992.[22] Apart from Abbé Pierre, the 'founding fathers' of the FAP were André Chaudiéres, Raymond Étienne, and Serge Colonni. The FAP originated from the different currents of the Emmaüs movement, an organization founded in 1949 that "has been firmly rooted in its ethos of putting solidarity into action, whilst challenging policy at the same time".[23] In other words, supporting people in need and pushing public authorities to intervene were the principal aims of the Emmaüs movement.[24]

The idea to establish a specialized voluntary organization exclusively dealing with housing problems had come from several people in the Emmaüs movement some years before, in light of the increasing complexity of housing problems. The first announcement of the plan to create the FAP was made in October 1987 during the first meeting of the Rencontres Humanitaires Internationales. This event, which was part of the initiatives of the World Year for Homeless People proclaimed by the United Nations, gathered together national politicians, local administrators, and a number of voluntary groups that were working on various aspects of housing issues. The establishment of the FAP also found an institutional sponsor in several MPs who took part in that meeting.

20 Archambault, 'Les institutions sans but lucratif hier et aujourd'hui', 9-11.

21 Annie Orsoni, Head of the Secours Catholique-Caritas 11th arrondissement of Paris, 21 February 2014, personal interview; Laurent Kapel, volunteer for Secours Catholique 18th arrondissement and responsible for the thérapie communautaire intégrative, 4 March 2015, personal interview.

22 Décret du 11 février 1992, *Journal Officiel de la République Française, Lois et Décrets*, 15 February 1992, 2417.

23 Emmaüs International, *The History of the Emmaüs Movement*.

24 Desmard, Étienne and Delahaye, *L'Abbé Pierre*, 91.

In contrast with many other voluntary groups, the FAP decided to hire specialized professional figures rather than just relying on activists. André Chaudiéres, for instance, was president of the company that manages social housing for Emmaüs France; Patrick Doutreligne, who has been the Managing Director of the FAP from 2013 to 2015, was the former Secretary General of the Haut Comité pour le Logement des Personnes Défavorisées, a government consultative body on the housing problems of disadvantaged people; and Yves Colin, the Director of Communication at the FAP, worked for several years in advertising companies before taking up this position.

Another aspect that differentiated the FAP from most other French non-profit organizations was its legal status. The large majority of voluntary groups in France are associations rather than foundations.[25] The founding members of the FAP decided to establish it as a foundation because this legal status allowed their organization to be more autonomous from public authorities than other associations working in the field.[26] In France, foundations could not receive public funding. Though this could be financially problematic, it meant they were not subject to the rules imposed by the public administrations that provide financial resources. In this sense, it was the aim of the FAP's founders that the greater autonomy of their organization would allow it to preserve its critical attitudes vis-à-vis national and local political authorities. As pointed out by Patrick Doutreligne,

> trying to bring association into the mould of service providers 'sponsored by public powers' led to a form of dependence, and therefore of weakening of associations vis-à-vis these political sponsors [...] local authorities will instil a look, a pressure, a control, much less neutral and objective under the precept that 'who pays is who decides' [...] The counter-associative power is weakened by gaining proximity to the elected.[27]

Maintaining some autonomy from public authorities can pay off.[28] Even after the death of the Abbé Pierre in 2007, the FAP continued to benefit from the great public trust that is demonstrated by the contributions it collects every year from thousands of private donors. For example, at the end of the 2018 fiscal year (closed on 30 September 2018), the funding collected by the FAP amount-

25 In 2012 in France there were roughly 1,300,000 associations, but only 1,988 foundations. See Tchernonog et al., *Le paysage associatif français*, 28, 224.

26 Yves Colin, Director of Communication of FAP, 18 December 2013, personal interview.

27 Doutreligne, 'Rôle de plaidoyer des fondations et capacité financière ou statutaire à alerter les pouvoirs et l'opinion publics', 2-3, author's translation.

28 The quest for autonomy is problematic not only for financial reasons, but also administratively, because several social initiatives in the housing sector, for example managing local sheltering centres, are often managed by associations in collaboration with national or local public administrations. The complexity of tasks and the unclear legal framework make it quite difficult to distinguish precisely the roles and competences of voluntary groups from those of public powers.

ed to more than 47.5 million euros, the overwhelming majority (95 per cent) of which came principally from small private donations and legacies.[29] These are quite respectable figures in view of the fact that in 2011 only 2 per cent of French non-profit associations had financial resources above half a million of euros.[30]

In spite of the activism of voluntary associations, at the beginning of the 1990s political awareness of the housing problems was still limited. A policy reform that, at least in part, changed the attitude of public authorities was the Besson Bill, which was the first law to introduce innovative instruments and new institutional settings to address housing issues.[31] Besides permitting non-profit organizations to collaborate with public bureaucracies on housing-related problems, the new law impressed a dramatic change to the legal paradigm adopted by public powers when considering housing problems. This can be seen by reading the first article of the Besson Bill, which states that "guaranteeing the right to housing constitutes a duty of solidarity for the whole nation".[32]

The right to housing is not mentioned in the French Constitution of the Fifth Republic and it is only vaguely indicated in the laws enacted before the 1990s. By emphasizing, for the first time, a specific right to housing for everyone and considering it a duty of national solidarity, the legislator intended to establish a clear symbolic distance from past policies. There were three main reasons for this. First, housing problems were considered causes of social distress, and not just an economic problem, as had been affirmed in the previous policies. In this sense, the Besson Bill adopted the typical approach of voluntary organizations that have regarded them as the outcome of multiple causes of social exclusion affecting human beings whose needs had to be placed at the centre of the policy intervention.[33] For example, a slogan of the 'Mobilisation Générale pour le Logement' (General Mobilization for Housing), a broad campaign organized by the FAP in 2011-2012, was the idea that the housing problems were not just a problems of housing.[34] In other words, housing is not just a material problem but is first and foremost a social question affecting the well-being of citizens. Second, the law seemed to assimilate the right to housing into the category of other social rights that define social citizenship. Third, the novel normative approach to housing problems was accompanied by the affirmation of a voluntaristic attitude, as the Besson Bill stated that the right to housing had to be guaranteed. However, the policy solutions envisaged by the law were undermined by the limited public funding invested by public administrations.

29 FAP, *Rapport du Commissaire aux comptes sur les comptes annuels*.

30 Tchernonog et al., *Le paysage associatif français*, 148.

31 Loi n° 90-449 du 31 mai 1990, *Journal Officiel de la République Française, Lois et Décrets*, 2 June 1990, 6551-6554.

32 Ibid., author's translation.

33 Christophe Robert, Delegate General of the FAP, 18 December 2013, personal interview.

34 Fondation Abbé Pierre (2013), *L'état du mal logement en France*.

The innovations introduced by the Besson Bill were not just limited to acceptance of the intellectual framework adopted by voluntary groups. They were also extended to the establishment of new institutional settings for dealing with housing affairs. To reach its goals, the new law required a department plan that mapped out local conditions of social precariousness. State authorities, local administrations, voluntary organizations, family associations, and other social partners (e.g. water and energy supply agencies) were asked to participate in the drafting of department plans. The bill thus introduced the first organic participation of associations in the policy making process.[35] In this sense, it created a quasi-corporatist institutional setting, which has an approach traditionally sponsored by social Catholicism.

The new openness of public authorities was the outcome of four strictly interrelated developments: the inability of public powers to overcome the increasingly negative impact of housing problems, the professional reliability of associations, the strong public trust that benefited non-profit organizations, and the possibility for public authorities to save money by using the services of non-profit organizations. In the early 1990s, the French welfare state showed several signs of inadequacy in dealing with social risks that were not directly related to the employment questions of the so-called labour market 'insiders' (i.e. workers employed in public administration or big companies and hired with open-ended contracts). French social security, like other continental welfare regimes, was aimed at preserving the income of 'insiders' instead of dealing with long-term unemployment, precarious employment, and the structural causes of social exclusion, which are at the root of housing problems. The inability of the then existing policies to cope with housing questions was worsened by the cognitive weakness of public bureaucracies that did not know much about housing. The habit of recruiting senior civil servants from the ranks of the elitist *grandes écoles* further increased the distance between decision makers and social problems. An example of this cognitive weakness in understanding housing questions is provided by the poor reliability of the early statistics on housing produced by INSEE.[36] In spite of the Jacobin spirit that has generally led public bureaucracies to distrust non-state actors, public administrations gradually accepted the contribution of voluntary groups.[37] In addition, during periods of budgetary constraint the cheap services provided by philan-

35 Driant, *Les politiques du logement en France*, 156.

36 INSEE, *Les conditions de logement en 2006*.

37 The greater openness of public authorities depended on the reliability of the major voluntary associations, whose capacities were sometimes acknowledged by public authorities in administrative reports. For example, in speaking of the FAP the Cour des Comptes observed that "The Fondation Abbé Pierre, in relation to the French associative fabric, has developed true expertise and know-how that allows it to act in partnership or through agreement with a large number of local associations". See, Cour des Comptes, *Fondation Abbé Pierre pour le logement des défavorisés*, 7.

thropic organizations were highly valued by state authorities that could not take the risk of investing funds in new policies whose social return was difficult to forecast. By delegating the study and the implementation of new measures to voluntary groups, public administration could thus avoid this risk.

The provision of expertise is quite an effective lobbying strategy because knowledge is never neutral.[38] Experts may help frame the ways in which a problem is understood, emphasize some aspects of a question to the detriment of others, convince decision makers of the importance of taking some initiatives, and so on. Civil society actors have exercised a crucial contribution to policy developments by providing their expertise to public authorities that need it. A distinction elaborated by Christian Lequesne and Philippe Rivaud can be useful to understand the advisory role and political influence of the expertise of voluntary groups.[39] Lequesne and Rivaud distinguish three typologies of expert: the expert who is a specialist in an area or a question, the expert who is a mediator, and the expert who gives some meaning to the policy process. While the third typology of expert in Lequesne and Rivaud's classification seems a little bit too vague to be used to study a policy process, the first two could be employed to figure out the lobbying activities of voluntary organizations. The illustration of the activities of the FAP may exemplify those kinds of expertise.

The expert-specialist can offer technical information deriving from some direct experience. Since its foundation, the FAP has developed this expertise. Its annual report, entitled 'L'état du mal logement' (The state of poor housing), "can be considered an institutional publication in the sector of housing policies" in France.[40] Furthermore, the FAP has established a specialized research branch that collaborates with public administrations or external research institutes, such as the Fondation pour la Recherche Sociale. This research activity of the FAP has greatly benefited from the capillary presence of the Fondation throughout the country in managing sheltering centres, and initiatives in support of homeless people. Having demonstrated great flexibility in interlinking technical knowledge and daily experience, the research activity of the FAP has received considerable scientific recognition, as pointed out in a report by the Cour des Comptes.[41]

The second type of expertise provided by the FAP is its ability as a mediator. The concept of mediator has a variety of meanings. Here, we use it in a broad sense by referring to the capacity of a social actor to reduce the distance and to create some dialogue between two parts. In this case, the expert does not use its technical knowledge, but its reputation. The role of an expert as a

38 Grossman and Saurugger, *Les groupes d'intérêt*, 17.

39 Lequesne and Rivaud, 'Les comités d'experts indépendants', 874.

40 Cécile Duflot, Minister of Territorial Equality and Housing, 1 February 2013, at the conference for the presentation of the report 'L'état du mal logement', personal recording.

41 Cour des Comptes, *Fondation Abbé Pierre pour le logement des défavorisés*, 7.

mediator is important in situations that involve questions of public order. In relation to housing issues, this was particularly relevant when squatting in vacant buildings was a modality of action employed by several collectives that organized people affected by precarious housing conditions. On several occasions, Abbé Pierre became an expert–mediator who was called on by public authorities to convince squatters to leave peacefully some of the buildings that they occupied.

Public trust can be a crucial factor in influencing policy developments and it may also lead to institutional developments. An example is provided by the constitution of the Haut Comité Comité pour le Logement des Personnes Défavorisées.[42] The establishment of this administrative body dealing with the housing problems of deprived people was a long-standing demand of voluntary groups that was eventually accepted at the end of 1992. To cope with the social consequences of the economic crisis that hit France at the beginning of that decade, the government of the time had to demonstrate to public opinion its willingness to do something about social precariousness. Accepting the requests of voluntary organizations working on housing problems seemed a good way to show the activism of public authorities. At the inaugural session of the Haut Comité the national press was invited. In front of a crowd of journalists, Abbé Pierre was sitting next to the President of the Republic and the Prime Minister. Though the creation of this administrative body was an opportunity for political forces to exploit the popularity of the Abbé, it was also an important victory for the associational movement. The law only attributed a consultative role to the Haut Comité and the power to suggest new laws on its own initiative or after a request of the government. However, the regular hearings, consultations, and meetings organized by the new institution put the delegates of voluntary organizations, who were members of the new consultative body, in direct contact with the high ranks of the public administration. It should not come as a surprise that the idea of introducing an enforceable right to housing, enacted by a law in March 2007, came from the Haut Comité, as its formal and informal meetings offered to voluntary organizations the opportunity to advance their ideas and convince decision makers of the validity of their proposals.

Though the economic crisis that affected France in the first half of the 1990s gave great resonance to housing problems and the related question of urban segregation, the awareness of the seriousness of these issues was shared more by intellectual and administrative elites than by political leaders. At a conference organized in October 1990 by the Délégation Interministérielle à la Ville, the Institut Français d'Architecture, and *Esprit*, the sociologist Alain Touraine remarked on the strict links between social exclusion and spatial segregation.

42 Décret n° 92-1339 du 22 décembre 1992, *Journal Officiel de la République Française, Lois et Décrets*, 22 December 1992, 17561.

According to Touraine, the main problem facing contemporary societies is not exploitation, as it had been in the past, but exclusion. Touraine believed that we are in a phase of transition from a vertical society, distinct in social classes, to a horizontal society, where people staying at the centre tend to be separated from those living at the periphery.[43] The contemporary form of class struggle is not between people belonging to upper and lower classes, but between people spatially separated. Urban segregation is the new social question.[44]

The debate for the presidential election in 1995 revolved around social cohesion.[45] This indirectly made housing a topic discussed by the candidates. However, the political proposals of the major parties did not show the foresight of the Besson Bill and the insight of Touraine's ideas. In this regard, the election of 1995 was a deviation from the policy trajectory that was initiated by the Besson Bill. The influence of neoliberal ideas on the French Right and part of the Left, the inadequate understanding of left-wing parties of the changing characteristics of social problems, and the absence of organized political constituencies in support of the reform of housing legislation were some of the main causes that prevented mainstream parties to pay adequate attention to housing problems and advance innovative policy solutions. Reading the presidential programmes of Jacques Chirac and Lionel Jospin is quite telling. Both Chirac and Jospin claimed that the construction of social housing and the promotion of private ownership were the two main strategies to cope with housing problems. For instance, in his presidential manifesto, Chirac declared his commitment to "urgently create logements d'insertion[46] [...] create a new homeownership loan [...] grant tax incentives",[47] while Jospin suggested "a relaunch of social housing [...] an incentive for homeownership".[48]

In a period of economic crisis characterized by widening economic inequality, the promotion of private ownership would advantage only the most affluent social classes.[49] Eventually, the policy proposals of Chirac and Jospin created the basis for a greater dualization of housing legislation, consisting of the provision of social housing for the poor and public funding for the most-well off.

43 Touraine, 'Face à l'exclusion', 8-9.

44 Ibid., 12.

45 In a public speech on 17 February 1995, Chirac spoke of the social fracture that characterized France. The future President of the Republic denounced that the French machine was not working for all French and a social fracture was widening. See Chirac, 'Le marie de Paris présente son project presidentiel, «La France pour tous». Jacques Chirac: «Il est temps de renoncer au renouncement», *Le Figaro*, 18-19 February 1995.

46 This is housing rented at low rates to specific categories of people facing particularly difficult social situations in order to favour their social reintegration.

47 Chirac presidential manifesto, Archives Électorals du Cevipof, Fonds Election Présidentielle des 23 Avril et 7 Mai 1995, Archives Électorals EL 209, author's translation.

48 Jospin presidential manifesto, Archives Électorals du Cevipof, Fonds Election Présidentielle des 23 Avril et 7 Mai 1995, Archives Électorals, EL 209, author's translation.

49 Bigot and Hoibian, *Les difficultés des français face au logement*, 81.

Increasing Activism

The second period in the development of French housing legislation individuated in this chapter runs approximately from the second half of the 1990s to the end of the 2000s. The distinct characteristics of the reforms introduced in these years were the increasing activism of public authorities that implemented a vast array of policy solutions that addressed the social causes of housing problems and the establishment of closer forms of cooperation between public administrations and voluntary groups. Despite the poor understanding of housing problems shown by Jospin and Chirac in 1995, the legislation introduced since the mid 1990s returned to the policy trajectory indicated by the Besson Bill, characterized by a stronger voluntaristic approach in addressing housing questions by public powers.

The current scholarship has widely accepted Bruno Palier's thesis that the welfare reforms enacted since the mid 1990s were defined by the strengthening of the role of the state, which was mainly motivated by the inadequacy of social partners in managing the increasingly complex French system of social security.[50] Though our research on housing policies corroborates this conclusion, it also identifies that the new prerogatives assumed by state authorities were often accompanied by the introduction of new flexible ways of governing social security programmes. In the housing sector, for example, public authorities not only strengthened their role, but they also increasingly opened up the policy process to the participation of non-state actors at various policy levels.

The previous section of this chapter pointed out that non-profit associations exercised a perceivable impact on the cognitive approach adopted by public authorities. This influence has strengthened since the mid 1990s when it was possible to see a steady change to the conception of housing problems so that they were not treated in isolation from other social questions or as mere economic issues, but they were considered the outcome of a process of social exclusion. This cognitive approach characterized the Solidarity and Urban Renovation Bill (Loi relatif à la Solidarité et au Renouvellement Urbains, SRU) elaborated by the Jospin government and enacted on 13 December 2000.[51] This law aimed at reinforcing the coherence of urban and territorial policies as it considered urban renovation, social solidarity, and political citizenship as strictly interrelated questions that could not be treated separately because the "deepening of social inequalities within spatial segregation could lead to undermining the social bond and the basis of the republican contract and the functioning of democracy."[52]

50 Palier, *Gouverner la sécurité sociale*, 387-388.

51 Loi n° 2000-1208 du 13 décembre 2000, *Journal Officiel de la République Française, Lois et Décrets*, 14 December 2000, 19777-19829.

52 Ibid., author's translation.

The importance of the SRU Bill was not just related to the intellectual approach that put at its centre social solidarity and political citizenship, but also to the fact that it introduced some remarkable reforms to the then existing legislation. They included Article 55, which established that 20 per cent of new residential constructions in all municipalities with more than 3,500 inhabitants or 1,500, if they were situated in the Île de France, had to be social housing. A set of administrative sanctions was introduced against those municipalities that did not respect the quota of 20 per cent. Finally the law imposed the social destination of a consistent part of private property, which has been a traditional goal of social Catholicism.

After the return to power of the Right in 2002, the SRU Bill came under discussion. Like most of other Western neoliberal political coalitions, the French centre-right parties demonstrated greater preference for policies aimed at supporting access to private ownership rather than inverning on the causes of poor housing conditions. For example, a report by the Direction des Études de l`UMP, issued in 2006, was entitled 'Contre la précarité, permettre à chacun d'être propriétaire' (Against precariousness, enable everyone to become a homeowner). The two main proposals in this study included the selling off of some of the social housing belonging to public administrations and the introduction of new fiscal incentives for access to private ownership, mostly through tax breaks.[53] Behind these policy solutions there was not only the intention to fulfil people's legitimate aspiration of becoming owners, but also a neoliberal ideological approach. As noted by Christophe Robert, Deputy Managing Director of the FAP,

> promoting access to private property is a privatization of the housing problem. If you are an owner, you do not benefit from some credit for social housing, social benefits, and so on. When people buy a house that is too expensive and they do not have the financial capacity to pay for it, the problem is theirs. It is clear. In this way you privatize the housing problem. It is a very ideological approach. It is also ideological in another sense. Once you are an owner, you are in an individualized relation with society. In social housing, there are associations that gather people and social movements. Instead, owners are all by themselves and interested only in their questions.[54]

The new ministers in power after Chirac's re-election in 2002 also showed stronger sensitivity to the protests of several local administrations that, since

53 Direction des Études de l'UMP, *Contre la précarité, permettre à chacun d'être propriétaire*, 39-44. The proposal by the UMP reminds one of the flagship policies of the first government of Margaret Thatcher, who with the Housing Act of 3 October 1980 authorized the sale of council houses to their tenants at discounted rates. A similar policy was considered by David Cameron in 2013.

54 Christophe Robert, Delegate General of the FAP, 18 December 2013, personal interview.

the introduction of the SRU Bill, had been lobbying for a flexible interpretation of the quota of 20 per cent of social housing or were even asking for a reduction in this threshold. In consideration of that, the right-wing government presented a proposal for a law that wanted to consider the quota of 20 per cent at the intermunicipal rather than at municipal level.[55] In this sense, the law did not formally reduce the quota of 20 per cent, but it relieved some local administrations of the need to build social housing. Voluntary associations and left-wing parties immediately opposed that proposal for a law. The FAP, through the charismatic figure of its founder, assumed a leading role in voicing the discontent to the proposal. During the weeks that presented a proposal for a law that the parliamentary discussion of the law, the old abbot made a public appeal to the President of the Republic, Jacques Chirac, asking him to put some pressure on the deputies to impede any reform of the SRU Bill. On 24 January 2006, the Abbé Pierre attended the parliamentary debate on the reform of the law. In front of the numerous journalists and MPs who flocked to meet him at the National Assembly, he declared that he was there because the honour of France was in question and then he added that not respecting the SRU Bill was shameful.[56] At the end of the morning, the proposal of the right-wing deputies to change the way of calculating the quota of 20 per cent of social housing was withdrawn.[57]

The example of the debate on the SRU Bill is quite telling, not only because it shows the closeness between the non-profit actors and left-wing parties at that time, but also because it reveals the capacity of voluntary groups to become public actors involved in the political debate. Martine Barthélémy has noted this new 'political role' of voluntary organizations and she contended that civic associations may change the forms of political participation in contemporary societies.[58] We believe that Barthélémy's observations were probably too prudent, in view of the most recent evolutions of political activism. Our study of the mobilization of voluntary organizations on housing policies and the activism of civil society groups during the anti-gay marriage campaign shows that associations are not only primary actors engaged in political debates, but they can also substitute traditional social and political actors (e.g. political parties and labour unions). This new public role of voluntary groups is sometimes acknowledged by the senior members of civil society associations themselves. In an interview in *Le Monde*, Christophe Robert underlines the importance of the FAP's activism by saying that "only public questioning

55 'Quand les élus UMP cherchent à démolir la loi SRU', *Libération*, 19 November 2006.
56 L'abbé Pierre sonne les cloches des députés', *Libération*, 25 January 2006.
57 'La majorité renonce à alléger la loi sur le logement social', *La Tribune*, 25 January 2006.
58 Barthélémy, *Associations*.

could force politicians to position themselves for a real change of direction, even if it is not necessarily our responsibility to take on this role."[59]

The new public role of voluntary organizations has been indirectly favoured by several long-term political developments. The declining popularity of political parties, labour unions, and public bureaucracies is becoming a crisis of legitimacy of these institutional actors. The decreasing relevance of political cleavages has promoted the influence of social actors whose identity is not primarily defined by political ideologies, as is the case for several civil society associations. Finally, the skilful capacity of several voluntary organizations to use the mass media has greatly promoted their public image and their presence in the public sphere. Communication has acquired a crucial importance for philanthropic associations and it has been arguably been one of the main drivers of their popularity and of gaining the attention of public authorities on social problems. This point was clearly explained in a reply to a question that we asked to Yves Colin during our interview. Colin's response is worth reporting extensively. The Director of Communication of FAP claims that

> there are two main reasons why communication actually matters. First of all, because it is our identity, it is what the Abbé Pierre mastered best. He has always done things to help the most deprived people, but he was first of all an extraordinary lobbyist and a man of communication. He had the ability to make society understand the problems of suffering people and he had the ability to question the public authorities, to put them in front of their responsibilities. We are in the path of the Abbé Pierre, we are his legitimate heirs. However, the use of communication is not related to a question of memory, but it is a method that we use because it works and we have every reason to continue working in this way. The second big reason is that the problems related to the housing sector are hidden. And we, therefore, need to show this problem so that it is understood, because we know well that the public authorities only regulate those problems that are known. [60]

The skilful use of communication techniques and the trust of public opinion contributed to the successful mobilization that led to the introduction of the Enforceable Right to Housing Bill (Loi au Droit au Logement Opposable, DALO) on 5 March 2007, one of the most relevant developments of French housing policy in the 2000s.[61]

This major reform established that some categories of socially vulnerable people, as defined by the law, have a right, upon the approval of their demand by a special commission, to ask for the intervention of judicial authorities to

59 Robert quoted in 'La crise du logement s'impose dans la campagne', *Le Monde*, 1 February 2012, author's translation.

60 Yves Colin, Director of Communication of FAP, 18 December 2013, personal interview.

61 Loi n° 2007-290 du 5 mars 2007, *Journal Officiel de la République Française, Lois et Décrets*, 6 March 2007, 4190-4206.

offer them a decent house. The novelty of the DALO Bill resided in the fact that it introduced an obligation of result enforceable by public authorities. This law fully assimilated the right to decent housing conditions into the category of social rights. Once again, the French legislator adopted the cognitive approach of voluntary organizations because the DALO Bill had a 'personalistic' approach because it considered a decent house as a kind of human right that public power had to provide.

The bill was the final outcome of long-term lobbying by voluntary organizations. The idea of an enforceable right to housing was an original demand by Abbé Pierre that was re-elaborated by the Haut Comité pour Logement de les Personnes Défavorisées. The 8th Report of the Haut Comité issued in 2002 stated that it was necessary to be "moving from an obligation of means to an obligation of result. This will require a law clearly establishing the content of the right and the remedies available to citizens".[62]

In spite of this formal acknowledgement of the need for a more assertive intervention against poor housing conditions, the legislator postponed the introduction of an enforceable right to housing. Right-wing governments were not keen on supporting the demands of voluntary associations. However, the lobbying by the third sector continued through the institutional channels provided by the meetings of the Haut Comité. In this sense, voluntary associations adopted the typical attitude of pressure groups, aimed at establishing closer formal and informal links with administrative elites in order to convince them of the validity of their proposals. The Haut Comité thus became not only a new type of quasi-corporatist body, but also an institutional venue for the exercise of the increasingly professional lobbying of non-profit associations. The outcome of the institutional pressure of voluntary organizations is shown by the strong tone of the text of the 12th Report of the Haut Comité that affirmed that "the enforceability of the right to housing, recognized as a legitimate principle, is increasingly regarded as necessary."[63]

The introduction of far-reaching reforms in settled institutional areas is challenging. The DALO Bill was met with great expectations, but it immediately became evident that the capacity of public administrations to apply an enforceable right to housing was limited, given the chronic shortage of social housing and the lack of public funding to build new houses.[64] Furthermore, the DALO Bill required the setting up of an administrative procedure that public bureaucracies were unable to manage without long delays. The new law

62 Haut Comité pour le Logement des Personnes Défavorisées, *8e Rapport*, 30, author's translation.

63 Haut Comité pour le Logement des Personnes Défavorisées, *12e Rapport*, 10, author's translation.

64 Statistics confirmed these criticisms. Between 2008 and 2011, only 37,686 people out of 96,189 favourable decisions were located in social housing in accordance with the DALO Bill. See FAP (2013), *L'état du mal logement en France*, 172.

did not significantly alleviate the poor housing conditions of a large part of the lower classes and did not prevent the evictions of those persons who did not meet the requirements prescribed by the bill, most notably in Paris, where there was an increase in evictions.[65] In this sense, the DALO Bill seems to be an example of agenda marketing rather than an effective policy change, that is, a policy measure that a government introduces to show to the public its engagement rather than implementing an effective reform.

It is difficult to provide a comprehensive evaluation of the housing legislation introduced between the mid 1990s and the late 2000s. However, the increasing tendency to put people at the centre of policy interventions, the promotion of quasi-corporatist arrangements, and the greater influence of civil society actors show a typical Catholic social imprint similar to that advocated by social encyclicals, even though neither public authorities nor voluntary associations explicitly claimed their intention to promote social Catholic values. In this sense, it is probably possible to conclude that an implicit social Catholicism inspired the housing legislation in the period considered here.

Toward a New Alliance?

The third period in the development of housing policies individuated by this chapter started approximately at the beginning of the 2010s. While the policy reforms introduced in the previous two periods contributed to a gradual change in the attitudes, strategies, and instruments adopted by public administrations, the more recent reforms have been characterized by the establishment of closer forms of collaboration between public authorities and non-profit organizations, to the extent that a sort of informal alliance between public administrations and associations can be noted. Furthermore, we think that the housing legislation in the first half of the 2010s represents an evolution of the previous two, as it developed along a policy trajectory characterized by greater acceptance of the demands of voluntary associations and their further integration into the policy process.

There have been several signs that show the closer cooperation between public actors and voluntary groups. In 2012, the FAP lauched the 'Mobilisation Générale pour le Logement'. This campaign aimed to push every candidate running for the presidential elections scheduled in May to take a clear position and make a formal commitment to address housing problems. Like most other public events organized by the FAP, the campaign was carefully managed to have a strong media impact. The advertising agency BDDP & Fils, one of the major advertising agencies in France, coordinated the various media events with the collaboration of the well-known photographer Olivier Roller, who had become famous for his artistic portraits of ministers, senior financial

65 'Hausse des expulsions de locataires DALO', *Le Figaro*, 8 June 2017.

managers, and public figures.[66] The mobilization had ample resonance and an immediate echo on the Left to the point that it became a topic of debate during the primary elections for the position of first secretary of the PS. Martine Aubry, one of the main contenders in those elections, affirmed her personal commitment to presenting some laws that would address housing problems. A similar statement came from François Hollande, the other main candidate in the primary elections.[67]

Housing questions occupied a prominent space in the political debate for the presidential campaign in 2012.[68] It was probably the first time that this policy issue had had such widespread coverage in the mass media. For example, housing was one of the main arguments in the speech given by François Hollande at Bourget on 22 January 2012, when the socialist leader sketched out the principal proposals of his presidential manifesto.[69] The centrality of housing questions in the electoral debate encouraged the FAP to exploit the momentum. It thus decided to invite all the candidates running in the presidential election, apart from Marine Le Pen, to the presentation of the annual report on 'L'état du mal logement' on 1 February 2012.[70] In front of the audience, all the invited politicians agreed to sign Le Contrat Social de la Fondation.[71] This document contained the major propositions suggested by the FAP: an increase in the construction of social housing, stricter application of the SRU Bill, the introduction of a more comprehensive urban policy, more severe controls on the increase of rents, and so on. On that day, in re-affirming his commitment to change precarious housing conditions, Hollande publicly declared: "I commit myself in front of the Fondation Abbé Pierre and above all in front of the French."[72]

The Hollande presidential manifesto confirmed the proximity between the PS and the positions of the FAP that largely summarized those of other voluntary associations working on housing policies. For example, proposition n° 21 of the Hollande manifesto stated that the PS candidate intended to in-

66 'La Fondation Abbé Pierre confie sa communication à BDDP & Fils', *La Correspondance de la Publicité*, 21 June 2013.

67 'Les prétendants à la présidentielle courtisent le monde HLM à Bordeaux', *Le Monde*, 30 September 2011.

68 'Le logement est devenu un thème majeur de la campagne présidentielle', *Le Point*, 23 January 2012; 'Le mal logement : enjeu majeur de la campagne présidentielle', *La Vie*, 23 February 2012.

69 'Je suis venu vous parler de la France, et donc de la République…', *Libération*, 22 January 2012.

70 François Hollande, Nicolas Sarkozy, François Bayrou, Jean-Luc Mélenchon, and Eva Joly were invited. Nicolas Sarkozy could not take part, but he sent his personal advisor Henri Guaino.

71 'M. François Hollande précise devant la Fondation Abbé Pierre ses propositions en matière de logement', *La Correspondance Économique*, 2 February 2012.

72 Parti Socialiste, *'Logement: «Je m'engage devant la Fondation Abbé Pierre et surtout devant les Français»*, author's translation.

crease the construction of new houses, particularly social housing, and proposition n°22 affirmed the need for the introduction of stricter controls in respect of the SRU Bill. Though, in principle, Sarkozy agreed to the propositions of the FAP, the main French right-wing parties that sustained Sarkozy's candidacy were not particularly concerned about the social problems related to housing issues.[73] As in the presidential campaign in 2007, the UMP did not pay much attention to social policies, housing policies included, and it continued to believe that access to private ownership was the best solution to the housing questions. For instance, one of the main proposals made in 2012 by Sarkozy in relation to housing was the announcement of a plan for reducing the cost of houses through the introduction of new tax breaks, to help the middle classes to access ownership.[74] The Sarkozy presidency supported this idea, which has not contributed much to solving the social problems related to the increasing costs of housing and urban segregation.[75]

The government of the socialist Prime Minister Jean-Marc Ayrault, in power after the victory of Hollande at the presidential elections held in 2012, confirmed the positions taken by the President of the Republic during the electoral campaign. The informal alliance between public authorities and voluntary associations was demonstrated not only by the acceptance of the proposals of the latter, but also by the closer institutional collaboration between associations and government authorities in drafting new housing policies. A crucial initiative for the elaboration of new policy proposals was the Conférence Nationale contre la Pauvreté et pour l'Inclusion Sociale held in December 2012, which put at its centre housing problems. On that occasion, several working commissions were set up whose tasks were the elaboration of new policy projects. These commissions were composed of senior bureaucrats, academics, politicians, and delegates of voluntary organizations (e.g. ATD Quart Monde, Croix-Rouge, Emmaüs Solidarité, and FAP), and one of them was headed by Christophe Robert. The membership of the various commissions showed the intention of the government to address housing problems within a broader framework, as had always been advocated by the third sector. Furthermore, the conference demonstrated at the symbolic and policy levels the willingness of the public administrations to elaborate policy solutions through a quasi-corporatist strategy that would consider the large variety of approaches and interests at stake. In other words, the Conférence Nationale was an example of that organic cooperation between civil society and political powers that social Catholics have always envisaged.

73 Neuilly-sur-Seine, one of the richest towns in France and a traditional stronghold of the Right, has one of the lowest rates of social houses in the country. In 2009, this town that was administered by Nicolas Sarkozy between 1983 and 2002 had just 3.6 per cent of social housing. See FAP, *Loi SRU pour le logement social*, 5.

74 'Hollande-Sarkozy: deux discours sur le logement', *Le Monde*, 27 April 2012.

75 Bigot and Hoibian, *Les difficultés des Français face au logement.*

Several proposals of the Conférence Nationale were included in the reform bill titled Accès au Logement et un Urbanisme Rénové, also known as the Duflot Bill.[76] This law, which was one the major policy reforms introduced by Hollande during the first two years of his mandate, took up many of the demands of voluntary associations: the establishment of a maximum level for rents, increase in social housing to be built by municipalities.[77]

Evaluating Values in Action

This chapter has discussed some developments in French housing policies from the early 1990s to the mid 2010s, when this policy area started to undergo several notable transformations. The research carried out for this chapter provided the opportunity to study a major field of the welfare state that has not received the attention it deserves by the academic literature and to explore the changing institutional influence of voluntary associations. Their increasing involvement at different levels of the policy process was one the crucial features of the policy trajectory followed by the development of the housing legislation described in the chapter. Studying the changing impact of non-profit organizations has offered a privileged point of view for understanding the current influence of Catholic social ideals.

This chapter has mixed together two analytical perspectives: a study of the principal reforms of the housing legislation and an investigation into the role of voluntary organizations in shaping policy developments. While the former was focused on presenting the main legislative innovations, the latter studied housing policy from a sociological angle and was interested in figuring out the policy impact of non-profit organizations. The combination of these two approaches was necessary to elucidate the intricate and multifaceted transformations of housing policies. The originality of the research presented in the chapter consisted of three main aspects. First, it illustrated the trajectory of housing policies by showing not only their macro-level changes, but also the most relevant contradictory developments that characterized their evolution. Second, it discussed the multi-level and changing institutional impact of voluntary associations across time. Third, it explored the influence of the values of voluntary groups on housing legislation.

This study corroborated the conclusions that values shape public policies by moulding the intellectual paradigm of decision makers and by provid-

76 The law took its name from the then Minister of Territorial Equality and Housing, Cécile Duflot.

77 Loi n° 2014-366 du 24 mars 2014, *Journal Officiel de la République Française, Lois et Décrets*, 26 March 2014, 5809-5925.

ing the skills and style of action that they may adopt.[78] Thus, the influence of ideas is subtle because the social actors that intend to promote them do not suggest specific values, but rather tool kits that bear the imprint of values. For instance, none of the Catholic and Catholic-inspired associations active in housing questions affirm their intention to promote Catholic social values, and some of them, like the FAP, even explicitly acknowledge their secular character. However, their cognitive framework and the policy instruments that they support are consistent with the ideals of social Catholicism. In this sense, they have tended to place concern for the personal well-being of people at the centre of their mobilizations, they remarked the importance of the principle of subsidiarity by claiming the importance of the involvement of civic associations in the policy process, they promoted quasi-corporatist policy arrangements, and they rejected the idea of addressing housing problems from an economic perspective to favour a more 'personalistic' approach that place at the centre of the policy intervention human beings. Through their institutional cooperation with public authorities, we think that voluntary associations have been able to instil some of their inspiring values into the housing legislation of secular France.

A final observation can be added here. Cultural elements may fall short of influencing policy decisions if the actors that bring them do not provide the resources that could contribute to solving social problems. For example, the study of the development of housing policies shows that the ideals of voluntary groups achieved some impact on the policy process because non-profit organizations provided valuable resources for public administrations in dealing with housing problems. The expertise, public trust, and professional capacities of associations were highly valued resources for public administrations that were coping with a lack of knowledge of housing affairs, a crisis of legitimacy, and limited resources to invest in social programmes.

78 Swidler, 'Culture in action', 282.

7
NEW IDEOLOGICAL CONFLICTS?

On 30 March 2018, *The Financial Times* published an article entitled 'The Return to Religion'. According to this British newspaper, "among atheists as well as believers, strident secularism is giving way to a renewed sense of faith's hold".[1] The increasing recognition of the resilience of religion has encouraged a paradigm shift in social sciences. Since the late 1990s, a growing number of scholars have turned their backs on the previously dominant paradigm of secularization to suggest a revision, if not a rejection, of it.[2] However, it is important to acknowledge that the process of secularization in Western societies can have paradoxical outcomes. Although secularization has weakened the authority of institutional churches[3] and has led to declining participation in religious practices,[4] it has also been accompanied by the diffusion of new religious movements[5] and their greater political assertiveness[6]: a phenomenon that can be defined as the return to religion. In this sense, secularization and the return to religion are not mutually exclusive phenomena, but they can be interrelated events.[7]

This chapter wishes to contribute to the ongoing debate on the renewed public role of religion. This will be done by studying the anti-gay marriage

1 'The return of religion', *Financial Times*, 30 March 2018.
2 Fox, *An Introduction to Religion and Politics*, Chapter 2.
3 Chaves, 'Secularization as declining religious authority', 750.
4 Dargent, 'Assistance aux offices et prière', 229.
5 Stark, 'Europe's receptivity to new religious movements: Round two', 390.
6 Toft, Philpott and Shah, *God's Century*, 74-79.
7 Reisebrodt, 'Religion in the modern world', 3.

campaign in France in 2012-2013 and the debate on the introduction of a bill that criminalized the online obstruction of abortion adopted by the National Assembly in 2017. The proposal for a law to legalize full marriage and adoption rights for same-sex couples (the so-called Taubira Bill)[8] was the origin of one of the broadest and most intense protests, principally coordinated by an umbrella organization called the Manif pour tous (The demo for everyone), about a societal question in the recent history of France.[9] The opposition of a large part of French society was unexpected. The introduction of same-sex marriage did not provoke any discontent in Sweden and Portugal, only limited protests in the UK, and in apparently Catholic Ireland a broad social movement mobilized in support of same-sex marriage.[10] Why did the opposition to same-sex marriage lead to the outbreak of a strong wave of social protests in France, one of the most secular countries in secular Western Europe? This chapter addresses this question. However, our analysis is not mainly aimed at understanding why mass protests broke out in France, but at why and how Catholic values and Catholic-inspired actors played a prominent role in them. For a long time social movement scholars have been mostly interested in the reasons for social protests, but they have neglected the more theoretically relevant question of what kind of social movement has been mobilized.[11]

The mobilization against same-sex marriage was not the only phenomenon that has shown the new kinds of public engagement of Catholicism in the public sphere. Catholic and Catholic-inspired actors have demonstrated a great ability to use new channels of communication to sustain their values. This has been highlighted by the proliferation of several websites managed by pro-life Catholic organizations that spread misleading information about abortion to deter young women from seeking an abortion. The study of the political debate on the bill that outlawed the online obstruction of abortion will allow us to understand the new strategies being adopted by traditionalist Catholic organizations against women's reproductive rights, which are

8 The name of the law derives from that of the then Minister of Justice Christiane Taubira.

9 Brustier, *Le mai 68 conservateur.* The campaign against same-sex marriage was characterized by the use of a large repertoire of contentious actions, including signing petitions, occupying premises, having sit-ins, disturbing public events, organizing protest marches, and so on. Two of the major collective actions that attracted the attention of the national and international mass media were the march on 13 January 2013, which assembled in Paris roughly 670,000 people, and the rally on 24 March 2013, when around 850,000 people protested against the Taubira Bill (the figures reported are the average between the data claimed by the police and those of the organizers of the demonstrations). These marches were the two biggest demonstrations on a societal question in the history of the Fifth Republic. See 'Manif pour Tous: combien de participants?', *Le Monde*, 6 October 2014.

10 'Sweden Church allows gay weddings', BBC, 22 October 2009; 'Le Portugal autorise le mariage homosexuel', *L'Express*, 8 January 2010; 'Gay marriage bill expected to complete passage through House of Commons', *The Guardian*, 16 July 2013; 'Irish's marriage equality moment', *The New York Times*, 18 May 2015.

11 Walder, 'Political sociology and social movements', 406.

increasingly threatened by conservative and populist governments in Europe and in the United States.[12]

The current scholarship has provided contrasting interpretations of the influence of religion on gender and sexuality-related matters. Some social scientists have argued that contemporary Western societies are becoming increasingly permissive. Although the outcomes of this wave of permissiveness vary between countries, in Western societies religion is a brake rather than a barrier to the liberalization of social legislation.[13] In contrast, other scholars have claimed that since the 1970s there has been *réenchantment du droit*. Public authorities have increasingly associated religious communities to the elaboration of policy solutions on value-laden issues with the result that the new policies that have been introduced bear the imprint of religious doctrines. This structural development in political life is a phenomenon of our post-secular era, in which public authorities, affected by a crisis of legitimacy, rely on the normative and symbolic resources provided by religious actors.[14]

Similarly to other sections of this book, this chapter avoids entering discussions about higher or lower levels of religiosity to devote greater attention to the new patterns of mobilization of Catholic authorities and Catholic-inspired actors. In doing so, we seek to understand the new forms of public engagement of Catholicism in France. This chapter sustains the idea that the sense of symbolic insecurity perceived by religious people when important references in their lives are put under discussion because of the secularization of social legislation can lead them to take action in defence of Catholic anthropological principles. In this sense, as observed a long time ago by Dietrich Bonhoeffer and Paul Tillich, secularization is not only a threat, but it can also become an opportunity for a renewed role for religion and it can lead to a stronger engagement by religious minorities in the public sphere.[15]

This chapter is an integration of the second part of this book that aims to understand the relocation of the mobilization of Catholicism from the political domain to civil society. While Chapter 6 studied the collaborative relationships between Catholic-inspired groups and public authorities, this chapter investigates the emergence of new ideological conflicts between religious-minded actors and political powers.

The chapter is divided into three main parts. The first one will study the mobilization against same-sex marriage. The second will consider the debate on the introduction of the crime of online obstruction of abortion. Finally, the third part summarizes the main conclusions of this chapter.

12 Council of Europe, *Women's Sexual and Reproductive Health and Rights in Europe*, 5.
13 Engeli, Green-Pedersen and Thorup Larsen, eds, *Morality Politics in Western Europe*; Knill, Adam and Hurka, eds, *On the Road to Permissiveness?*; Knill, Preidel and Nebel, 'Brake rather than barrier';
14 Feuillet-Liger and Portier, 'Religion et bio-droit en France', 345-346.
15 Bonhoeffer, *Widerstand und ergebung*; Tillich, *The Courage to Be*.

Against Same-sex Marriage

The anti-gay marriage campaign was not the first mobilization in which Catholic and Catholic-inspired groups took part in France. On several other occasions, French Catholics had taken to the streets to defend their values and interests. Catholics were the backbone of the Mouvement de l'École Libre in 1984, in 1998-1999 Catholic-inspired actors organized the protests against the introduction of civil partnerships (Pacte Civil de Solidarité, PaCS), and the *marches pour la vie* against abortion have become almost regular annual events since 2005.[16] In this sense, the anti-gay marriage campaign in 2012-2013 was just one the latest mobilizations organized by Catholic actors. If we adopt a long-term historical perspective, this campaign share two relevant characteristics with past protests on morality issues that had occurred in France. First, it was supported by the same coalition of actors that opposed other proposals of law that liberalize social legislation. Like past mobilizations against divorce, abortion, and civil partnerships, the anti-gay marriage campaign was sustained by Catholic hierarchies and right-wing politicians, it was organized by Catholic-inspired associations, and it saw the participation of integralist Catholic movements. Second, the arguments used by the opponents of same-sex marriage resembled those employed in the aforementioned protests: the disruption of family life, the negative impact of the new laws on children, and the subversion of supposedly universal anthropological principles of our civilization. What has changed in comparison with the previous protests is the structure of political opportunities that provoked the outbreak of social protests and the strategic interaction between the various actors engaged in contentious actions. These factors are discussed in the following sections of this chapter.

Troubles in the Church

In France, like in other European countries such as Ireland, Italy, and Spain, the Catholic Church was one of the staunchest opponents of the extension of LGBT rights, and its arguments, based on the natural law tradition, inspired the anti-gay marriage campaign. For this reason, it is appropriate to start our analysis by considering the role played by the Church in that campaign.

Since the Liberation, French bishops have generally avoided any direct intervention in national political life, except in extraordinary situations, such as when they repeatedly issued public statements against the Front National (FN) of Jean-Marie Le Pen. The *laïcité* of the state, the process of deconfessionalization of Catholic associations, and the increasing secularization of French society weakened the authority of the Church. In other words, the

16 Tartakowsky, *Les droites et la rue*, 176.

Catholic Church generally avoided initiating direct confrontations because it was almost sure to lose. However, this general rule was partly left aside when crucial interests and values for the Church were at stake (e.g. divorce, abortion, and education). On the other hand, in these situations, French bishops generally tried to conceal their involvement to prevent the resurgence of anti-clerical attitudes and the reopening of the religious conflicts that characterized the political history of France between the late nineteenth and early twentieth centuries. For example, in 1984 French bishops supported the Mouvement de l'École Libre, but the leadership of the social protests was taken up by the parents of the students of private schools, not by the Church.[17]

The legislative reforms dealing with family- and sexuality-related issues are grounds for confrontation between the Catholic Church and those political authorities that have attempted to democratize the sphere of intimacy. The growing intervention of public powers in this domain, a phenomenon that Denis Pelletier has defined as an anthropological transformation of politics, has put under discussion the magisterium of a Catholic Church that has made the defence of the natural law tradition a cornerstone of its authority.[18] The introduction of same-sex marriage posed a severe challenge for the Catholic Church for four principal reasons. First, same-sex marriage conflicts with a central tenet of the Catholic doctrine that states that a marriage is a sacrament celebrated between a man and a woman. Second, given the close linkage between civil and religious marriage in France, the legalization of the latter undermined the symbolic value of the former. Third, the question of same-sex marriage reactivated some internal tensions in French Catholicism. The radicalization, since the early 1980s, of several Catholic movements that presented themselves as the better defenders of Catholicism, could have further undermined the authority of the Church among the most devout Catholics.[19] Four, the legalization of same-sex marriage in France would have had a remarkable impact on other countries, where proposals for the extension of LGBT rights were under discussion. Although the national level is still the most signifi-

17 'Le succès de la manifestation en faveur de l'école privée', *Le Monde*, 26 June 1984. Following the success of the demonstration in Paris, Mitterrand's educational reform was withdrawn. In this case, the Catholic Church showed how it could be a veto player despite the *laïcité* of the French Republic.

18 Hervieu-Léger, *Catholicisme, la fin d'un monde*; Kuhar and Paternotte, eds, *Anti-Gender Campaigns in Europe*; Paternotte, van der Dussen and Piette, eds, *Habemus gender!*; Pelletier, 'Les évêques de France et la République de l'intime -1968-2005', 180.

19 Tartakowsky, *Les droites et la rue*, 158. In 2011 substantial media coverage was given to the mobilization of Civitas and the Society of Saint Pius X (founded by the schismatic Archbishop Marcel Lefebvre). On that occasion, these two Catholic traditionalist organizations were protesting against the play *Golgota Picnic*, which described some episodes in the life of Jesus. Civitas and the Society of Saint Pius X accused the play of being a manifestation of Christianophobia and they tried to disrupt its performances in Toulouse and Paris. See '250 catholiques manifestent en silence contre "Golgota Picnic"', *La Croix*, 8 December 2011.

cant political context for understanding social mobilizations, the increasingly closer transnational communications, interactions, and networks between countries have made easier the spillover of effects of a policy reform from one country into other countries.

In the summer of 2012, it became evident that François Hollande was committed to introducing same-sex marriage, as he had promised during the presidential electoral campaign. Given the aforementioned challenges posed by the question, French bishops decided to take a clear position against the Taubira Bill. The Church could not afford the high moral and political costs of inaction. Bishops abandoned their careful attitudes and expressed their discontent against the legalization of same-sex marriage and adoptions.

The first prominent voice of French Episcopacy to declare its opposition to the Taubira Bill was that of the Cardinal of Lyon, Mgr Philippe Barbarin, a notoriously conservative figure of the French Church. In an interview published in *Le Progrès*, this senior prelate asked public authorities not to intervene in a domain that, according to him, was beyond their competence. For Mgr Barbarin, the Parliament could legislate on security, health care, and peace related questions for example, but not on marriage because "the Parliament is not God the Father".[20] Two aspects of the declaration by the Cardinal of Lyon deserve particular attention: its self-contradictory character and its rejection of the principle of the *laïcité* of the state. Mgr Barbarin's affirmation asked the Parliament to avoid intervening in order to preserve the legislation, bearing the imprint of Catholic values, which had been introduced by previous Parliaments. Furthermore, he asked a democratically elected Parliament to restrict its power in a policy area that the principle of *laïcité* ascribes to the remits of public authorities. In this sense, the Cardinal of Lyon was asking for a radical change in French politics.

The declarations of Mgr Barbarin were followed by more moderate statements from Cardinal André Vingt-Trois, President of the Conférence des Évêques de France. For Assumption Day (15 August), Mgr Vingt-Trois sent a letter to all parishes in France to remind them to pray for the defence of the family and the protection of children.[21] Though Mgr Vingt-Trois did not make any reference to the proposal for a law on same-sex marriage, it was clear that his message intended to raise the awareness of Catholics on that question. In doing so, France's top Catholic bishop mixed up a political controversy with a liturgical calendar, a tradition that the Church of France had abandoned since the Second World War.[22] While Mgr Barbarin disputed the political sovereignty of the state on ethical matters, Mgr Vingt-Trois used a liturgical event to

20 'Mgr Barbarin contre le mariage gay: «Le Parlement n'est pas Dieu le Père»', *Le Progrès*, 14 August 2012.
21 'Contre le mariage gay, l'Église fait appel à Marie', *Libération*, 13 August 2012.
22 Béraud and Portier, *Métamorphoses catholiques*, 69.

intervene in a political debate. In both these circumstances, the *laïcité* of the French Republic seemed to be questioned.

Despite the declarations of Mgr Barbarin and the positions taken by Mgr Vingt-Trois, the Church maintained a prudent attitude on the debate on same-sex marriage until the end of September. In the early autumn of 2012, it still intended to avoid open confrontation with public authorities. For example, a document from the Council of the Family and Society of the Bishops' Conference of France of 28 September 2012 entitled 'Elargir le mariage aux personnes de même sexe? Ouvrons le débat!' (Extending marriage to homosexuals? Opening up the debate) affirmed the need for the introduction of a new legal framework for the recognition of stable relationships between same-sex partners.[23]

The heated political debate on the Taubira Bill and the increasing activism of Catholic traditionalist groups radicalized the positions of the Church. In the opening speech at the French Bishops' Plenary Assembly on 3 November 2012, Mgr Vingt-Trois defined gay marriage as "a vision of the human being without acknowledging the sexual difference [...] a deception that would shake one of the foundations of our society and would establish discrimination between children."[24] By further explaining what would become the official position of the French bishops on the Taubira Bill, Mgr Vingt-Trois also affirmed that the Church was not primarily interested in defending the sacrament of marriage, but "the social function of marriage that does not depend on any religion [...] [and is] the fruit of the cumulated wisdom of our civilization."[25]

The arguments supported by Mgr Vingt-Trois were consistent with a traditionalist interpretation of the natural law tradition. Even though this body of thought has been increasingly criticized for confusing cultural prejudices on gender issues with religious principles, it still represents the primary intellectual reference through which conservative Catholicism understands gender and morality questions.[26] Marriage should be thus reserved for heterosexual couples because it is finalized to the biological reproduction that represents the alliance between God and men. In this sense, for the Church, the materialistic reality of sexual complementarity has a spiritual meaning that has to be preserved by civil laws.[27] This combination of gender prejudices, theological arguments, and political claims that inspired the positions of French bishops closely resembled the conservative moralism of the Vichy regime that defended a traditionalist conception of the family and rejected the evolution of social values.

23 Conseil Famille et Société, *Élargir le mariage aux personnes de même sexe?*
24 Vingt-Trois, *Discours d'ouverture de l'Assemblée Plénière de novembre 2012*, author's translation.
25 Ibid.
26 Lustig, 'Beginning of Life', 547.
27 Hervieu-Léger, *Catholicisme, la fin d'un monde*, 229-265.

Two further elements of Mgr Vingt-Trois' declarations should also be drawn out because they inspired the anti-gay marriage campaign: the effort to avoid any explicit reference to formal Catholic doctrines and the recourse to a secular vocabulary. French bishops made a great effort to present their engagement not as a mobilization in support of Catholic values, but rather as a defence of supposedly universal anthropological principles that were the basis of French civilization. The aim of this effort at concealing the Catholic ideals behind the mobilization against same-sex marriage was the attempt to broaden the resonance of the message of the Church beyond traditional Catholic groups so that it could reach wider social constituencies that were not closely attached to the moral doctrine of the Church, but that still considered themselves culturally Catholic.

To strengthen the impact of their message, French bishops also remarked how their engagement was motivated by their willingness to oppose inequality, which is a cornerstone of French political culture, and that it was not directed against homosexual people. These two aspects constituted crucial elements of the several declarations released by the bishops during the debate on the Taubira Bill. By recalling the principle of equality, the bishops claimed that the introduction of same-sex marriage and adoption would create discrimination between children. To avoid any possible suffering to them, bishops argued, it was appropriate to avoid the introduction of the Taubira Bill. Despite this staunch opposition to the extension of LGBT rights, the Church intended to show a tolerant attitude toward homosexual people. This position was consistent with established doctrinal principles. Since the publication of the declaration *Persona Humana* in 1975, the Vatican had made a clear distinction between homosexual acts and homosexual persons: while homosexual acts were unequivocally rejected, homosexual persons were considered deserving of compassionate understanding.[28] In other words, homosexuals could be accepted within the community of believers upon abstaining from the exercise of their sexuality.

The declarations of the Assembly of Lourdes of November 2012 stopped the internal debate within the Church. It was paradoxical that the bishops closed down the discussions within their own ranks at the moment they were asking the government to open a broad public debate on same-sex marriage.[29] However, the unanimous position of the Church was apparent and it was stronger at the highest ranks than at its grassroots level. Several members of

28 Congregation for the Doctrine of the Faith, *Persona Humana*, § 8.

29 Monique Baujard, former Director of the Service National Famille et Société of the Conférence des Évêques de France, 23 July 2014, personal interview.

the clergy, Catholic associations, and a large part of the Catholic public opinion did not share the position of their bishops.[30]

The distance between the Church and French Catholics was shown in an opinion poll carried out by IFOP for the Catholic magazine *Le Pèlerin* in January 2013, when the wave of contentious actions against the Taubira Bill reached its peak. According to the results of this survey (see Table 8), the majority of Catholics (54 per cent) were in favour of same-sex marriage and their approval rate was just six points lower than that of the average French population (60 per cent). The preferences of Catholics tended to diverge in accordance with the frequency of their religious practice. Whereas practising Catholics were the least in favour of same-sex marriage (41 per cent), non-practising Catholics had very similar preferences (56 per cent) to those of the average French population (60 per cent). The frequency of religious practice was also positively correlated to the intensity of opposition to same-sex marriage, even though this effect was not particularly strong. One-third of practising Catholics (29 per cent) was absolutely against same-sex marriage while the corresponding figures for all French were just a few points below (23 per cent).

TABLE 8
ANSWERS TO THE QUESTION "WOULD YOU GIVE THE RIGHT TO MARRY TO HOMOSEXUAL COUPLES?" (% FIGURES)*

	Total "Yes"	Absolutely "Yes"	Rather "Yes"	Total "No"	Absolutely "No"	Rather "No"
Total Catholics	54	26	28	46	19	27
Practising Catholics	41	19	22	59	30	29
Non-Practising Catholics	56	27	29	44	17	27
Other Religions	47	25	22	53	18	35
Without Religion	76	46	30	24	12	12
Total French	60	32	28	40	17	23

* IFOP, *Les Français et le mariage homosexuel*, 19.

30 The internet was the principal channel for the diffusion of dissenting opinions. In several blogs, members of the clergy and Catholic associations criticized the closure of the Church and they manifested their acceptance of the law on gay marriage. For example, Lionel Laot, priest of Quimper, wrote an open letter in which he criticized the Catholic Church for the absence of any internal debate on the question of gay marriage. See 'Le curé de Quimper pour le mariage homosexuel', *l'Humanité*, 29 December 2012. The Dominican Lionel Gentric, a students' tutor at the convent of Saint-Thomas-d'Aquin in Lille, posted on the website of the Province of France of the Dominican Order a long article in which he denounced the fake unanimity of the Church and he explained the reasons why the Church should approve gay marriage. A few days after its publication, Gentric's text was removed from the website. See 'L'article du dominicain a été retiré', *Riposte Catholique*, 1 January 2013.

Several reasons can be advanced to explain the approval of same-sex marriage by the majority of French Catholics. First, non-practising Catholics were less informed about the consequences of the introduction of same-sex marriage. Their weak integration in the Catholic community prevented them from acquiring a critical opinion on the impact of the Taubira Bill.[31] Second, French Catholics, particularly those without strong beliefs, were influenced by the mass media that were sympathetic toward same-sex marriage.[32] Third, as noted by Monique Baujard, former Director of the Service National Famille et Société of the Conférence des Évêques de France,

> non-practising Catholics are very close to all people and they do not see why the Church is against gay marriage. They just do not make the point. Instead, practising Catholics, some of them, I think, understand better because they are more involved, but they show to some extent that they do not agree with what the Church said.

In the end, according to Baujard, most Catholics are probably against same-sex marriage, but they still agree that it should be legalized.[33]

The beginning of the parliamentary debate on the Taubira Bill in the autumn of 2012 was accompanied by the outbreak of a wave of protest actions against this law that lasted until the middle of 2013. The social mobilization against the bill created a division not only in French society, but also within the Catholic milieu.

While several bishops took part in demonstrations and some priests urged churchgoers to attend them, other senior prelates were against the Taubira Bill, but uneasy about taking to the streets.[34] Though many Catholics participated in the social mobilization, some Catholics were shocked by the

31 Philippe Ariño, writer and spokesperson for the Manif pour Tous, 25 January 2014, personal interview.

32 This idea was shared by several bishops. On 30 October 2012, by making an indirect reference to the debate on the Taubira Bill, Cardinal André Vingt-Trois spoke of the need to defend the freedom of consciousness against the lobbies that saturated the space of communication. See Vingt-Trois, *Homélie du Cardinal André Vingt-Trois lors de la messe pour les responsables politiques et les parlamentaires.*

33 Monique Baujard, former Director of the Service National Famille et Société of the Conférence des Évêques de France, 23 July 2014, personal interview.

34 Several appeals to participate in the first national march against the Taubira Bill on 13 January 2013 in Paris were launched by the Bishops of Lyon, Dijon, Avignon, Beauvais, Blois, Créteil, and so on. The Archbishop of Chambéry, Mgr Philippe Ballot, suggested to his colleagues that they should play a more proactive role in supporting this protest march. An enquiry by the magazine *Le Canard Enchaîné* reported that some parishes in the suburbs of Paris (e.g. Saint-Cloud, Guyancourt, Malakoff, Châtillon, and Orsay) accommodated the people who took part in the Parisian march in the premises of those parishes. See 'Mobilisation générale dans les couvents, les paroisses, les évêchés l'église sort le grand jeu pour faire capoter la diabolique loi sur la mariage gay', *Le Canard Enchaîné*, 18 January 2013.

warnings of their priests and left their parishes.[35] Some Catholic associations (e.g. David & Jonathan, Femmes et Hommes, Égalité, Droits et Libertés dans les Églises et la Société, FHEDLES) were even in favour of the introduction of same-sex marriage. This internal division in the broad Catholic community was a big problem for the Church and was a cause of great concern to bishops.[36]

The radicalization of the Manif pour Tous that was increasingly managed by Catholic traditionalists,[37] politicization of the protests and the final approval of the law on same-sex marriage changed the structure of the political opportunities that had led the Church to assume 'militant' positions against the Taubira Bill. The wish to avoid being involved in a permanent struggle against the political authorities and the attempt to restore the unity of French Catholicism encouraged bishops to set aside the confrontational attitudes they had adopted until early 2013. The importance of an open dialogue with public authorities was a key aspect of Mgr Vingt-Trois' message at the bishops' conference in April 2013. In addressing the high prelates of France, Mgr Vingt-Trois admitted that the Church should not expect civil laws to defend Catholic values. The real struggle, Mgr Vingt-Trois believed, did not consist of an ideological or political battle, but was in the effort of finding in ourselves the profound motivations of the faith.[38] Another example of the more conciliatory attitudes adopted by the Church after mid 2013 is offered by the confirmation of Mgr Jean-Luc Brunin as President of the Conseil Famille et Société of the Conférence des Évêques de France. In contrast with the more conservative bishops, Mgr Brunin maintained a moderate position during the debate on the Taubira Bill. In presenting his candidacy, he stated that he intended to promote a dialogue between the Church and society in line with the ideas of Vatican II, by going beyond the contrapositions that characterized the debate on the Taubira Bill.

The Political Support for the Anti-gay Marriage Campaign

The French campaign against same-sex marriage was supported by some major political groups who became important allies of the social protesters. This outcome surprised many observers. As pointed out, among others, by the socialist politician and LGBT activist Jean-Luc Roméro the promotion of LGBT rights has become an electioneering subject in France. According to Roméro, the support for these rights does not undermine the popularity of their pro-

35 Monique Baujard, former Director of the Service National Famille et Société of the Conférence des Évêques de France, 23 July 2014, personal interview.
36 Monique Baujard, former Director of the Service National Famille et Société of the Conférence des Évêques de France, 23 July 2014, personal interview.
37 Béraud and Portier, '"Marriage pour tous"', 74.
38 Vingt-Trois, *Discours d'ouverture de l'Assemblée Plénière d'avril 2013*.

moters, as in the past, but it brings consensus.[39] Likewise, for Éric Fassin, in Western countries, there has been a reversal of the homosexual question as political actors do not look for the vote of homophobic people, as happened before, but they search for the support of homosexual groups. In other words, the previous political homophobia has been replaced by a kind of political homophilia.[40]

Though Roméro and Fassin have identified an important change in the political attitudes in several Western democracies where the support for same-sex marriage became mainstream, their conclusions in relation to France were probably affected by some excessive optimism. This was shown by the mass demonstrations against same-sex marriage in 2012-2013 and the fact that the opposition to LGBT rights engaged senior right-wing politicians.

Before considering the role of the French Right in the mobilization against the Taubira Bill, it seems appropriate to note that the legalization of same-sex marriage provoked some discontent also in the ranks of the Left. For a long time, left-wing parties have been reluctant to extend LGBT rights. Until the late 1980s, in the UK the Labour party did not give much support to the demands of LGBT organizations, and in Italy the introduction of civil partnerships were promoted by some left-wing parties only after the early 2000s.[41] Likewise, several groups of the French Left have always been deeply sceptical of extending LGBT rights as heterosexual couples. The late introduction of same-sex marriage in France in comparison with other European countries have depended not only on the opposition of Catholic-minded groups and right-wing parties, but also on the morally conservative attitudes of several leftist politicians. For example, when the PS won the political elections in 1997, the law on civil partnerships was not among Lionel Jospin's priorities. Eventually, the PaCS became one of the flagship policies of his government, but that was not the original intention of the socialist leader. The introduction of the PaCS was mostly the result of the popularity of the law among the French electorate and the successful lobbying by several PS subgroups and LGBT organizations. Furthermore, the law on civil partnerships did not give to the couples that signed a PaCS the same rights as married couples, because they could not adopt a child nor were they entitled to any pension benefit in the case of the death of the partner. In that sense, the PaCS was a half step toward equality or, to look at it another way, an example of half inequality.

For the 2012 presidential election, the socialist candidate François Hollande made a formal commitment to introduce full marriage and adoption

39 Roméro, *Homopoliticus*, 3.

40 Fassin, *L'inversion de la question homosexuelle*, 235.

41 Brooke, *Sexual Politics*, 253; Ozzano and Giorgi, *European Culture Wars and the Italian Case*.

rights for same-sex couples.[42] This decision was the outcome of a long evolution of the programmatic platform of the PS that, since the mid 2000s, had put increasing emphasis on societal reforms and equality of rights for same-sex people. While the PS macro-economic policies tended to become increasingly similar to those of moderate right-wing parties, on societal questions the PS intended to mark its difference from the Right.[43] As a result, the moral liberalization of family laws has become a distinguishing characteristic of the political platform of French socialists.

However, there was a generation gap in opinions on societal questions within the PS. Some socialist leaders of the 'old generation' were very critical of the Taubira Bill. In an interview for the TV programme Grand Journal in November 2012, the former socialist Prime Minister Lionel Jospin said that he was against same-sex marriage. In his view, humanity is divided between men and women and not in relation to sexual preferences.[44] In an interview in February 2013 in the conservative Catholic magazine Valeurs Actuelles, Michel Rocard, a senior historical figure of the PS, expressed his disapproval of the proposal that same-sex couples could adopt children. For Rocard, a law on this matter was dangerous and not desirable.[45] Georgina Dufoix, the socialist Secretary of State for Family Affairs in the first Rocard government, gave her public endorsement of the protests against same-sex marriage and took part in the national march against the Taubira Bill on 13 January 2013.[46]

Though it is always difficult to understand the original intentions of political actors, we may assume that Hollande probably underestimated the possibility that the legalization of same-sex marriage could meet strong opposition.[47] The high approval rates for this issue shown in the opinion polls and the limited protests in other Western countries that introduced same-sex marriage probably suggested to him that the approval of the Taubira Bill would not encounter any major difficulties.[48] As on many other occasions during his presidency, Hollande made a big mistake in his judgement of the attitudes of French people. The principal error was related to the fact that French citizens had mixed opinions on the possibility granted by the Taubira Bill to provide full adoption rights to same-sex couples, and adoption was a highly sensi-

42 The 31st engagement of Hollande's presidential manifesto stated the intention of the socialist leader to give "the right of marriage and adoption to homosexual couples". See Hollande, *Le changement c'est maintenant*, 22.

43 Bergounioux, *Les socialistes*, 122-123.

44 Dusseaulx 'Les réserves de Jospin sur le mariage pour tous', *Le Journal du Dimanche*, 10 November 2012.

45 'Michel Rocard: ses confidences à "Valeurs actuelles"', *Valeurs Actuelles*, 7 February 2013.

46 Elkaim 'Georgina Dufoix, contre le mariage pour tous', *La Vie*, 4 January 2013.

47 Gamson and Meyer, 'Framing Political Opportunity', 285.

48 From June 1996 to February 2013 the approval rate for homosexual marriage rose from 48 per cent to 66 per cent. See IFOP, *Les Français et les droits des couples homosexuels*, 6.

tive topic in French public opinion.[49] In this sense, the extension of full adoption rights to same-sex couples made French citizens more critical toward the Taubira Bill, even though the great majority of them were in favour of same-sex marriage.

The acceptance of same-sex marriage and adoption varied in accordance with political preferences, as shown in Table 9. Even though the great majority, 84 per cent, of the left-wing electorate in January 2013 was in favour of same-sex marriage, 33 per cent of leftist electors were against the idea of giving adoption rights to same-sex couples. These figures remained substantial stable between August 2012 and January 2013. The opposition of the left-wing electorate to same-sex adoption was confirmed by many of the people that we interviewed at the national march in support of the Taubira Bill on 17 December 2012. Although they decided to take to the streets to defend this law, many of them told us that they were strongly opposed to the idea of opening up adoption to same-sex couples and they tended to justify their opinion with similar arguments to those used by the opponents of the Taubira Bill: the possible negative impact on the well-being of children, the need to open up a broad public debate on the question before extending adoption rights, and the concern about the subversion of the long-standing anthropological norms of French society.[50]

In January 2013, the electors of the UMP and the FN were the least in favour of same-sex marriage. However, the most hostile were the voters of the UMP, whose approval rate went down from 46 per cent in 2012 to 38 per cent in 2013 for same-sex marriage and from 38 per cent to 25 per cent for adoptions.

Interestingly, the electors of the FN were quite divided on same-sex marriage and adoptions. In relation to the first question, in August 2012, 49 per cent of them were in favour of same-sex marriage and this percentage increased to reach 52 per cent in January 2013. As for adoption, only 38 per cent of the electors of the FN were in favour of same-sex adoption in August 2012, but this figure decline to 34 per cent in January 2013. Although since the early 2010s, the FN has made significant inroads among French Catholics, this party

49 Jérôme Brunet, spokesperson for the Manif pour Tous and President of the association Appel des Professionnels de l'Enfance, 4 July 2014, personal interview, 4 July 2014, personal interview.

50 For example, we interviewed Mr Jean Toniolo, who has been a member of the PS for a long time. He is deputy mayor of Homécourt, a small village situated in the department of Meurthe-et-Moselle, and an activist for LGTB rights. Mr Toniolo participated in the march in support of the Taubira Bill because he believed that the new law enhanced equality of rights, he was a member of the PS, and he was homosexual. However, when we asked him his opinions on homosexual adoptions, he replied that he preferred that the government did not legislate on this issue because it was such a sensitive topic, given that it could have a negative impact on the life of children. Therefore, it would have been better had the government opened up a broad public debate on the topic. Jean Toniolo, deputy mayor of Homécourt, LGBT activist, 17 December 2012, personal interview.

has attracted a minority of Catholic electors and mostly non-practising Catholics.[51] In view of the mixed opinions of her voters, it is understandable why the FN President, Marine Le Pen, had ambivalent positions on LGBT rights, though several FN leaders, like the Marion Maréchal Le Pen, Jean-Marie Le Pen's niece, endorsed the positions of the Manif pour Tous and took part in the protest marches against the Taubira Bill.

Another relevant aspect shown in Table 9 is the partial hiatus between the official positions of the main political parties and the opinions of their electors. This was not only the case in relation to leftist electors on adoption rights, as we have previously pointed out, but also on same-sex marriage and adoption among rightist voters. Although the UMP strongly rejected the Taubira Bill and the FN was critical of it, in January 2013 a total of 41 per cent of the voters of the UMP and 52 per cent of those of the FN approved the idea of giving marriage rights to same-sex couples. These discrepancies between ethical beliefs and political identifications show the limited ability of political parties to establish a strong identification with their electors, whose individualism on morality issues may lead them to assume ethical choices that diverge from those upheld by the parties that they vote for.

We should not be surprised that the majority of the UMP's electors rejected same-sex marriage and adoption. Catholicism was a crucial factor for understanding the sociology of the UMP[52] In contrast to some other European right-wing parties, and with the partial exclusion of the period of the second half of the 1970s, since the early 1980s, the French mainstream Right has strengthened its moral conservatism. For instance, in 1982 the overwhelming majority of right-wing political elites voted against the decriminalization of homosexuality, in 1999 against civil partnerships, and in 2013 against same-sex marriage.

The transformations underwent by the French mainstream Right in the early 2000s have not much changed its ethical background. As pointed out by René Rémond, the identity of the UMP was constituted by the implicit reference to the Christian democratic legacy that enabled the aggregation of the RPR and the UDF into the UMP in 2002.[53] The cultural background of most right-wing French leaders has been profoundly influenced by Catholic family traditions or by their socialization in Catholic organizations. The Sarkozy

51 Dargent, 'Les catholiques français et le Front national', 27.
52 Haegel, *Les droites en fusion*, 233.
53 Rémond, *Les droites aujourd'hui*, 237.

TABLE 9
APPROVAL RATE FOR SAME-SEX MARRIAGE AND ADOPTION ACCORDING TO POLITICAL PREFERENCES (% FIGURES)*

Political Party	Marriage		Adoptions	
	Aug 2012	Jan 2013	Aug 2012	Jan 2013
Left	81	84	68	67
UMP	46	41	38	25
FN	49	52	38	34
Total French	65	63	53	49

* IFOP, *Les Français et les droits des couples homosexuels*, 7-8.

presidency reinforced the influence of Catholic values on French politics[54] and the UMP, whose *Charte des valeurs* (a mission statement), approved at the National Congress in 2012, explicitly affirmed the inspiration for the party of the Christian democratic tradition and its commitment to defend traditional family values.

The debate on same-sex marriage contributed to reactivating the deeply rooted Catholic background that permeated the political identity of the UMP and it stimulated a defensive reaction in support of Catholic anthropological values that a large number of the militants and electors of this party considered a component of their identities. In relation to that, it is possible to understand the radicalization of the ideological positions of the UMP during the political debate on the Taubira Bill.

In January 2013, the President of the UMP, Jean-François Copé, argued that the socialist government should not legislate on marriage, an institution, Copé pointed out, which is based on the complementary union between a man and a woman. He then launched the idea of a petition for a referendum on same-sex marriage.[55] In spite of the strong presence of Catholic values in its cultural background and the radicalization of the party positions on same-sex marriage, the UMP largely remained external to the anti-gay marriage cam-

54 Haegel, *Les droites en fusion*, 231. The UMP's *Charte des valeurs* also noted that the family was the primary place of solidarity, parents should be supported in their educative mission, and the promotion of demographic dynamism was a primary purpose of the party See UMP, *La Charte des valeurs*, 3. The returning importance of Christian values has not been a phenomenon only related to the idiosyncrasy of Nicolas Sarkozy and the UPM. For example, David Cameron declared that his project of the Big Society was not invented by him but by God, and then he added: "I'm just continuing God's work". See Cameron quoted in *The Independent*, 10 April 2014.

55 'Mariage gay: l'UMP lance une pétition pour un référendum', *Le Point*, 31 January 2013.

paign.[56] The party became a crucial institutional ally of the Manif pour Tous, it was engaged into a parliamentary struggle to oppose the approval of the Taubira Bill and several of its leaders took part in the protest marches against this law. Some activists of the Manif pour Tous also established a new political movement, called Sens Commun, aimed at shaping the agenda of the mainstream Right, that was integrated in the UMP.[57] However, a sort of mutual distrust divided the UMP and the Manif pour Tous, which was accompanied by the exchange of harsh declarations by Copé and the President of the Manif pour Tous, Ludovine de la Rochère.[58] While large sectors of the UMP did not want to be identified with a social protest that was acquiring radical conservative attitudes, the Manif pour Tous, like all new social movements, gave great importance to its autonomy, particularly from political parties. The effort by the Manif pour Tous to avoid any formal political affiliation was also motivated by the attempt of its leaders to provide wider resonance to its message beyond the conservative and rightist constituencies.

Although the Manif pour Tous did not have any formal political linkages, it entered the field of electoral politics. For example, on 19 November 2013, coinciding with the opening day of the Congress of the mayors of France, the Manif pour Tous launched a *Charte* for the candidates in the municipal elections to be held on 23 and 30 March 2014. This document was essentially a concise collection of the main demands from the anti-gay marriage campaign: the commitment to abrogate the Taubira Bill, oppose the extension of assisted reproductive technologies to lesbian couples, support local family policies, and the rejection of the teaching of the so-called gender theory in schools.[59] According to the leaders of the Manif pour Tous, the *Charte* was not a step toward the politicization of their movement, but rather just a reminder of the universal principles that should engage all politicians concerned with the common good.[60] In other words, the commitment of the Manif could be considered political if by politics we mean a high and noble activity interested in

56 Some senior female leaders of the UMP such as Nadine Morano and Roselyne Bachelot held more conciliatory positions on the Taubira Bill than the rest of their party. However, their opinions were soon marginalized. As long as the debate on same-sex marriage continued, the radicalization of the positions of the UMP caused the dissociation from the party of the association GayLib, on 11 January 2013. This association, which had been part of the UMP since the foundation of the party, announced the rupture of its links with the UMP because the progressive, liberal, and humanist stances represented by GayLib were not taken into consideration within the UMP any more.

57 Bolzonar, 'Conservative Catholicism versus social Catholicism?'.

58 She became the president of the Manif pour Tous at the beginning of May 2013.

59 'Charte d'assaut pour la Manif pour tous', *Liberation*, 26 February 2014.

60 Ludovine de la Rochère, President of the *Manif pour Tous*, 24 March 2014, personal interview.

ameliorating the life of citizens. However, it was not a partisan engagement because it did not take the side of any political party.[61]

The political collocation of the candidates that signed the *Charte* provided some further insights into the political profile of the mobilization against same-sex marriage. The question was the object of an inquiry by the newspaper *Libération* at the end of February 2014. By taking into consideration the then still provisional electoral lists for the forthcoming local elections in a few of the major cities of France, the left-leaning journal noticed the overrepresentation of candidates from the FN.[62] We replicated the analysis by *Libération*, but we refined it by considering the definitive electoral lists and by extending the cases taken into account to the twenty-five largest French cities.[63] In the twenty-five most populous cities in France, seventy-seven heads of the electoral lists for the 2014 municipal elections had signed the *Charte* of the Manif pour Tous.[64] The largest number of the signatories, forty-nine out of seventy-seven, were at the head of the FN's list, fifteen belonged to various groups of the Right, twelve to the UMP, and one to another far-right right party (see Figure 6).

This overrepresentation of the FN highlighted the ambivalence of this party to the mobilization against same-sex marriage. Although Marine Le Pen declared she would abrogate this law in the event of her victory at the next presidential election, she has always refused to openly support the Manif pour Tous[65] Restrained by an electorate that showed mixed opinions on LGBT rights and animated by the intention to pursue the *dédiabolisation* (de-demonization) of the FN, namely giving a more modern and less radical image to her party, the President of the FN preferred to avoid establishing any close relationships with the associations that organized the protests against the Taubira Bill. On the other hand, several local candidates of the FN endorsed the positions of the anti-gay marriage campaign. The closeness of the FN to the Manif pour Tous is even more evident when some local cases are considered. For example, in Lyon, all the heads of the nine lists of the FN signed the *Charte*. Marie-Christine Arnautu, Deputy President of the FN in charge of the elaboration of the social policy platform of the party, signed the *Charte* and she was elected to the city council of Nice. The head of the list of the FN in the

61 Jean-Pier Delaume-Myard, writer and spokesperson for the Manif pour Tous, 24 March 2014, personal interview.

62 'Le FN à Fond sur la Charte de la Manif pour Tous', *Libération*, 27 February 2014.

63 The cities included in our inquiry were: Paris, Marseille, Lyon, Toulouse, Nice, Nantes, Strasbourg, Montpellier, Bordeaux, Lille, Rennes, Reims, Le Havre, Saint-Étienne, Toulon, Grenoble, Dijon, Angers, Saint-Denis, Villeurbane, Nîmes, Le Mans, Clermont-Ferrand, Aix-en Provence, and Brest.

64 This large number of heads of lists is partly due to the fact that Paris, Marseilles, and Lyon are divided into several electoral districts and the major political parties generally presented a list in each of them.

65 'Mariage gay: Marine Le Pen a annoncé qu'elle abolirait le mariage pour tous si elle arrivait au pouvoir', *Huffington Post*, 19 May 2013.

FIGURE 6
HEADS OF THE LISTS WHO SIGNED THE CHARTE OF THE MANIF POUR TOUS IN THE TWENTY-FIVE LARGEST CITIES IN FRANCE, BY POLITICAL PARTY*

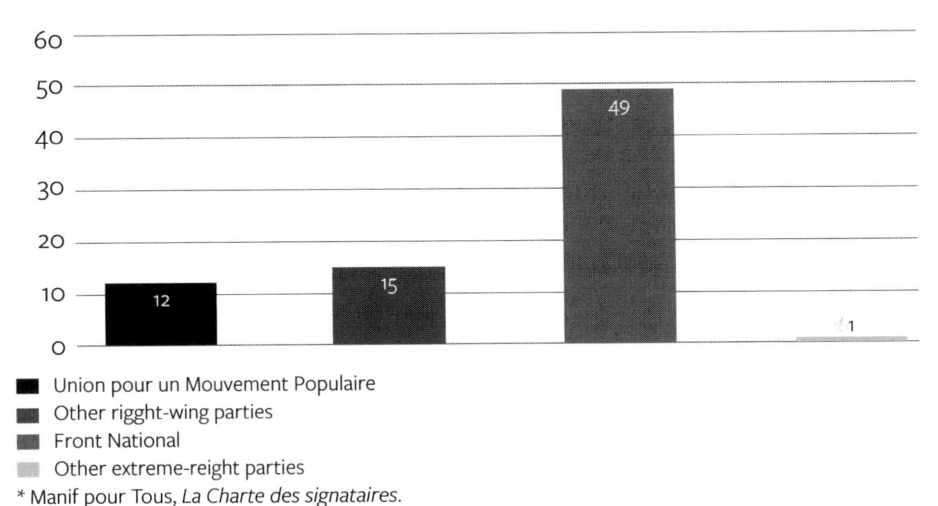

* Manif pour Tous, *La Charte des signataires.*

10th arrondissement of Paris was a former militant of the Manif pour Tous who was responsible for security at the demonstrations.

In a press communication on 31 March 2014 the Manif pour Tous triumphantly announced the election of 85 per cent of the 672 heads on the electoral lists that signed the *Charte*.[66] The largest majority of the new administrators came from small rural villages. This result indirectly confirms the enduring entrenchment of Catholic anthropological values in the countryside, a traditional fief of French Catholicism. However, among the newly elected there were also politicians and mayors of large or medium-sized cities situated in areas with strong left-wing traditions, such as the mayor of Limoges (a city administrated by the Left since 1921) or Nîmes.

The observations presented here are intended to illustrate the complexity and ambiguities that characterized the role of the main political actors during the debate on the law on same-sex marriage. In order to get a more comprehensive understanding of the anti-gay marriage campaign, it is important to pay closer attention to the mobilization of civil society associations.

The Opposition of Civil Society

Catholics have never been absent from French political life. Their engagement has been directed not only toward conventional forms of political participa-

66 'Charte LMPT: parmi les 672 têtes de liste signataires, 85% ont été élus', *Le Salon Beige*, 31 March 2014.

tion (e.g. voting, belonging to political parties, and serving in public offices), but also toward unconventional modes (e.g. demonstrating, boycotting, and occupying public spaces). Albeit social scientists have paid greater attention to the involvement of leftist activists in social movements, conservative, right-wing, and Catholic actors have always participated in social movements.[67] The protests against same-sex marriage in 2012-2013 were an example of that.

The wave of contentious actions against the Taubira Bill began in October 2012 and acquired greater coordination with the foundation of the Manif pour Tous on 17 November 2012. The name Manif pour Tous was chosen to emphatically mark its contrast to the Taubira Bill, which was commonly defined as *mariage pour tous* (marriage for everyone). The selection of a name for a protest movement is often motivated not only by the need to attract mass media attention, but also by the effort to provide a symbolic identity to it. Social mobilizations are generally engaged in the production of symbols by evoking emotions, using rhetorical arguments, or drawing on collective memories. These symbols contribute to the definition of a collective identity, building solidarity and encouraging participation in protest actions.[68] In this sense, the decision to name Manif pour Tous the anti-gay marriage campaign revealed the intention to emphasize the universal salience of heterosexual marriage and the contraposition to the Taubira Bill that, according to its opponents, would have undermined the anthropological foundations of marriage that they considered a pillar of French civilization.

From the start the Manif pour Tous assumed a modular organizational structure. It became an umbrella association that coordinated the actions of its various associations, collectives, and small groups at the local and national levels. At the beginning of 2013, at the peak of the social protests, the Manif pour Tous was composed of thirty-seven different associations and it had several branches or delegates in every department of metropolitan France, as well as representatives in several other European countries that were mostly drawn from local French communities. Even though the various associations and collectives had great autonomy from each other, their weak links were counterbalanced by the fact that most activists belonged to the same informal social networks, notably the same religious associations, local communities, and voluntary groups.[69] Informal networks and cross-membership have always helped to strengthen the cohesion of a social movement and to encouraging participation. This was also the case for the Manif pour Tous.

Three people assumed the leadership of this umbrella association: Frigide Barjot, who was the main spokeswoman, Laurence Tcheng, spokes-

67 Tartakowsky, *Les droites et la rue*, 7-10.

68 Della Porta and Diani, *Social Movements*, 100-110; Tarrow, *Power in Movement*, 156.

69 We acquired this information by interviewing more than 40 people who participated at the national protest marches of the Manif pour Tous on 13 January 2013 and 23 March 2013.

woman of the group La Gauche pour le Mariage Républicain, and Xavier Bongibault, a member of the association Plus Gay sans Mariage.

The media exposure of the leaders of social movements means that the image of a movement tends to be aligned with its leaders, who become public figures and represent the values of a mobilization. This observation is particularly valid for those new movements whose social basis and ideology still need to be consolidated. Therefore, the personal biographies of leaders acquire an important role in building up the reputation of a social mobilization, in attracting new members, and finding allies. The composition of the leadership of the Manif pour Tous was a strategic choice aimed at creating a public image of a mobilization inspired by the values of tolerance, pluralism, and open-mindedness. This is how we may interpret the decision to place at the head of the Manif pour Tous the charismatic figure of a singer/humorist who used to play in the nightclubs of Paris (Frigide Barjot), a supposedly leftist Catholic teacher (Laurence Tcheng), and a young homosexual student (Xavier Bongibault). In this sense, the organizers of the social protests against same-sex marriage wished to challenge the stereotypical portrayal of the campaigns against LGBT rights as gatherings of homophobic, bigoted, and reactionary religious people.

The image of tolerance that the Manif pour Tous gave of itself was also conveyed by its Charte, which affirmed that "La Manif Pour Tous is a profoundly pacific movement which is non-partisan and non-denominational. It determinedly opposes the 'marriage for all' law and homophobia."[70]

Ludovine de la Rochère, who became its president following the resignation of Frigide Barjot from her role at the beginning of May 2013, gave us a less formal definition of the Manif pour Tous than that provided by its official statement. According to her, "The Manif pour Tous is a civic movement, a citizen movement, a disinterested, spontaneous, popular movement, truly a movement of simple citizens very determined to defend the common good".

In other words, according to its president, the Manif pour Tous was a movement that does not include celebrities and renowned politicians, but only common people concerned about the threat to widespread social values.[71] This portrait of the Manif pour Tous by its leaders contrasts with that of its antagonists: the LGBT community and those cultural and social elites that supported LGBT rights. According to Jean-Pier Delaume-Myard, another spokesperson for the Manif pour Tous, "in France [the LGBT community] is an ultra-minority community, but they have financial structures, people who help them in the media, on the television, in the newspapers, etc. Therefore, they are ultra-minorities, but ultra-powerful."[72] Although devoid of an explicit

70 Manif pour Tous, *Our Ethics*.

71 Ludovine de la Rochère, President of the Manif pour Tous, 24 March 2014, personal interview.

72 Jean-Pier Delaume-Myard, spokesperson for the Manif pour Tous, 24 March 2014, personal interview.

political imprint, these descriptions of the Manif pour Tous show two prototypical features that define the populist radical right: the contrast between the 'pure' people and the 'corrupted' elites and the 'pure' people's effort to defend the general will that is ignored by the elites.[73]

To the pacific, non-partisan and non-denominational features should also be added heterogeneity. Among the thirty-seven associations that composed the Manif pour Tous, there were religious organizations, profession-based groups, family associations, organizations of adopted children, a feminist group, a collective of mayors, and two LGBT organizations. The emphasis of social movements on their heterogeneous character is generally a powerful rhetorical argument because it permits their spokespersons to present their protests as the symptom of widespread popular discontent.

The apparently popular, anti-elitist, and heterogeneous character of the campaign against gay marriage is put under discussion when the biographies of its leaders are considered.[74] For example, Frigide Barjot was born into a rich Catholic family from Lyon. Her father was a personal friend of the former President of the FN, Jean-Marie Le Pen, and Le Pen was a guest at her marriage, which was celebrated by the Pétainist Abbé de Nantes, the founder of the integrist Catholic group Contre-Réforme Catholique. During her studies at Science Po in Paris, Madame Barjot became a supporter of the RPR, and in particular of Jacques Chirac, and later of the rightist Gaullist Charles Pasqua. After graduating, she started work in the advertising company that managed the electoral campaigns of the Gaullist party. For several years, Barjot was a singer/humourist in two groups, Jalons and Dead Pompidou, and they performed at protest actions organized by right-wing or far-right organizations. In 2006, Madame Barjot converted to Catholicism. In her book entitled *Confessions d'une Catho Branchée* (Confessions of a trendy Catholic), which tells of her spiritual itinerary and how she rediscovered the faith, she defined herself as a press secretary of Jesus and explained how she intended to give public relevance to the ethical principles of traditional Catholicism that, according to her, are fully compatible with the values of the secular French Republic.[75] With these aims in mind, in 2009 she organized the campaign 'Touchez pas à Mon Pape' (Don't Touch My Pope) that aimed to encourage Catholics to defend Benedict XVI, who was being criticized for his conciliatory positions toward the negationist Mgr Richard Williamson.[76]

Like Frigide Barjot, Laurence Tcheng also came from an economically privileged background and graduated from the elitist Science Po in Paris. Before becoming a teacher, she worked in an advertising company and then as

73 Mudde and Rovira Kaltwasser, 'Populism'.
74 'Les surprenants opposants au mariage gay', *Le Figaro*, 21 September 2012.
75 Barjot, *Confessions d'une catho branchée*.
76 '1er «Benoîthon» sur le parvis de Notre-Dame de Paris – Frigide Barjot : «Cette défiance vis-à-vis de Benoît XVI m'est insupportable»', *Famille Chrétienne*, 17 April 2009.

a senior manager at McDonald's. Although she frequently repeated her political preference for the PS, she has never been member of this party and she has always rejected the propositions of François Hollande on the extension of LGBT rights.[77] Madame Tcheng's supposedly leftist movement, La Gauche pour le Mariage Républicain, is an unknown organization that was created on 13 November 2012, just four days before the first local demonstration by the Manif pour Tous.

When we broaden our analysis from the leaders of the Manif pour Tous to the groups that composed it, we have a further confirmation of its entrenchment in the French traditionalist Catholic cultural milieu. This conclusion was originally advanced in an inquiry by *Le Monde*, which was published on 21 April 2013 under the provocative title 'Derrière la grande illusion de la Manif pour Tous' (Behind the great illusion of the Manif pour Tous).[78] The great illusion *Le Monde* was speaking about was the apparent, but largely misleading, representation of the anti-gay marriage campaign as a non-confessional and non-partisan mobilization. The research carried out for this chapter replicated the inquiry of the French newspaper, but it corrected some empirical inaccuracies and oversimplification in the classification of the organizations of the Manif pour Tous. Our analysis thus refined the inquiry made by *Le Monde* by paying attention to the stated principles of every association as they were presented in their official publications and it considered the initiatives organized by them. To collect further information, in some cases we interviewed the senior members and some activists of the groups that composed the Manif pour Tous in order to acquire a fine-grained understanding of their cultural and ideological positions.[79] After this empirical research, it was decided to classify the associations of the Manif pour Tous into six distinct categories in accordance with the leading principles that inspired their actions. These categories were: Catholic associations, associations with Catholic leadership, other religious associations, conservative associations, 'empty shells', and a residual category named other associations. The distinctions that are proposed here are not clear-cut classifications, however. For example, several religious associations tend to assume conservative positions on family issues. On the other hand, their prevailing mission and activities suggest that they should be considered religious associations rather than conservative. Figure 7 shows the results of our inquiry.

77 'Anti-mariage gay: qui est la caution «de gauche» de Frigide Barjot?', *Le Nouvel Observateur*, 9 January 2013.

78 'Derrière la grande illusion de la "Manif pour Tous"', *Le Monde*, 21 March 2013.

79 We could not record most of the interviews with grassroots activists of these associations because they firmly refused that our conversation would be recorded because they were concerned that any recording could eventually be used by the government against them or their families.

The relative majority, eleven out thirty-seven, of the associations that composed the Manif pour Tous in 2013 were Catholic-inspired associations. By this, we mean those associations whose state principles bear the imprint of Catholic values, but they do not have any formal affiliation with the Church. In this sense, they can be considered culturally Catholic because their background is shaped by Catholic values, even though they are not formal Catholic associations. The group of eleven Catholic-inspired associations we identified is composed of a large variety of organizations. Some of them prefer to reject any denominational affiliation (e.g. Familles de France) or they frame their inspiring principles in vague solidaristic and humanitarian terms (e.g. Alliance Vita, Collectif pour l'Humanité Durable). For example, Alliance Vita was one of the leading associations of the Manif pour Tous. Founded in 1993 by the then leader of the Christian democratic party, Christine Boutin, Alliance Vita had campaigned against abortion, the PaCS, same-sex marriage, and the liberalization of bioethical laws. However, the engagement of the association was not motivated by the defence of formal Catholic doctrines, but by the belief in protecting human dignity or struggling against the causes that could lead to human suffering. In accordance with that belief, Alliance Vita has never promoted pastoral activities, but it has devoted its efforts to providing social services to people and families facing hardship situations related to health problems. Only two associations of the Manif pour Tous openly acknowledged their Catholic inspirations and their intention to defend Catholic moral doctrines: AFC and Dialogue and Humanisme. The AFC is one of the oldest family associations in France. In 2013 it counted around 30,000 families as members and it is often involved in elaborating or consulting on family-related laws.[80] Dialogue and Humanisme is an association created in 1999 that organizes meetings and conferences to discuss and promote the social doctrine of the Church, especially among those who are engaged in professional fields and in the voluntary sector.

The second largest group in our classification include ten associations that we called, following *Le Monde*, 'empty shells', namely formal structures that have never organized any events in the course of their existence (e.g. Homovox.com, David et Eugenia, and Juristes pour l'Enfance) or their activism was mainly limited to their affiliation to the Manif pour Tous (e.g. Médecins et Pédiatres pour l'Enfance, La Gauche pour le Mariage Républicain, and Plus Gay sans Mariage). Most of these groups had been established some months before the outbreak of the protest against the Taubira Bill. The lack of information about these new organizations led us to suppose that they were just fake groups that were created to support the idea that the Manif pour Tous was a heterogeneous movement composed of a large variety of different civil society associations. The third largest category in our classification is made up of six conservative orga-

80 Vincent Porteret, Delegate General of the Confédération Nationale des Associations Familiales Catholiques, 22 September 2013, personal interview.

nizations. It included those associations whose rejection of same-sex marriage was based on a broad conservative political ideology. For example, in this category we placed the Collectif des Maires pour l'Enfance that represented around 20,000 mayors of France, mostly from the UMP and from small villages, and the Fédération Nationale de la Médaille de la Famille Française, an old family association that was inspired familism and nationalism. In the Manif pour Tous four non-Catholic associations were also involved: the Comité Protestant Evangélique pour la Dignité Humaine, Fédération Nationale des Associations Familiales Protestantes, the Muslim association Fils de France, and Les Musulmans pour l'Enfance. This common front of religious organizations against same-sex marriage emphasized conservative ethical principles on family-related issues rather than religious values.[81] In this sense, they defended a sort of culturalized kind of religious beliefs rather than formal religious norms.

An argument that was largely prevalent in left-wing public opinion was the idea that the Manif pour Tous was deeply influenced by religious charismatic associations. Among others, this thesis was advanced by *Le Monde*.[82] To demonstrate the role of charismatic communities behind the Manif pour Tous, *Le Monde* just pointed out that several leading members of the Manif pour Tous worked, were affiliated to, or had close relationships with the Communauté de l'Emmanuel, one of the largest Catholic communities in France. For example, Jean-Baptiste Maillard, who managed the communication activities of the Communauté de l'Emmanuel, was one of the co-founders of the collective Homovox and helped to organize the national protest marches for the Manif pour Tous. However, his engagement in the social protests against the Taubira Bill was at the personal level and not in the name of Communauté de l'Emmanuel. Although many members of this community were firmly against same-sex marriage and they organized some internal debates to discuss this question, the Communauté de l'Emmanuel had never encouraged its members to protest against the Taubira Bill and it did not take part in the public debate on this law.[83] The reasons for this positioning are rather simple. The community intended to avoid the possibility that the outbreak of a conflict with public institutions could reopen old political cleavages that might have undermined its social activities.[84]

The engagement of the Catholic camp in the protests against the Taubira Bill became more apparent when considering the role of several civil society organizations that indirectly supported the social protests, although they were not part of the Manif pour Tous. In this sense, the public debate on the reform of family law activated established Catholic organizations that had generally refrained from taking sides in political questions.

81 Béraud, 'Un front commun des religions contre le mariage pour tous?', 339.
82 Laurent 'Derrière la grande illusion de la "Manif pour Tous"', *Le Monde*, 21 March 2013.
83 Laurent Landete, former President Communauté de l'Emmanuel, 25 January 2015, personal interview.
84 Ibid.

FIGURE 7
CLASSIFICATION OF THE ORGANIZING ASSOCIATIONS OF THE MANIF POUR TOUS, BY TYPE*

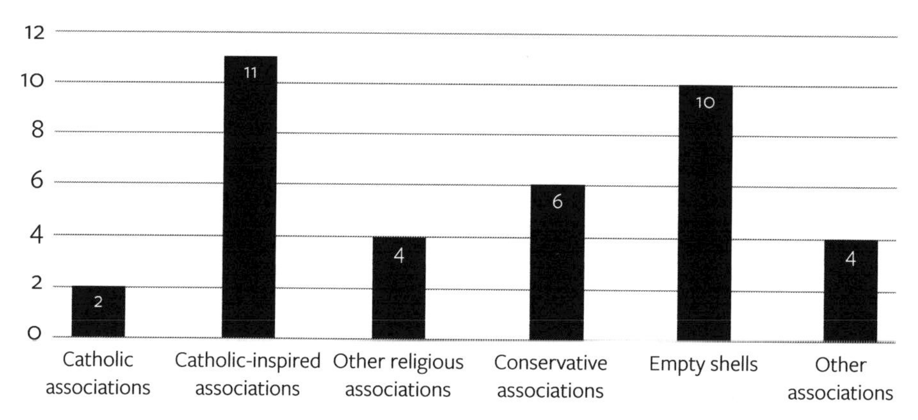

* 'Derrière la grande illusion de la "Manif pour Tous"', *Le Monde*, 21 March 2013.

For example, the theme of the 2012 annual national meeting of the Semaines Sociales de France was changing gender relationships in contemporary societies. The question of same-sex marriage was addressed by several interventions during the three days of this big convention of French social Catholics. In his closing speech, the President of the Semaines Sociales de France, Jérôme Vignon, remarked on the opposition of the majority of the members of his association to same-sex marriage.[85] In 2012, Vignon, who was also Président de l'Observatoire National de la Pauvreté et de l'Exclusion Sociale, gave his public endorsement to the Manif pour Tous and participated in several debates organized all over France by the Manif pour Tous, to explain the reasons for his opposition to the Taubira Bill.

Another prominent Catholic organization, the CFTC, was quite sympathetic to the protests against the Taubira Bill, even though the questions opened some internal divisions in the main French Catholic union. For example, Joseph Thouvenel, Deputy President of the CFTC, made fervent speeches against the family reforms implemented by the socialist government during the public meetings organized by the Manif pour Tous. However, on 7 January 2013 the Syndicat National de l'Enseignement Chrétien (SNEC), the most influential branch of the CFTC, released an official statement in which it said that "For SNEC-CFTC, the question of marriage for all pertains to the private sphere [...] the SNEC-CFTC is a professional trade union and not a political party."[86]

85 Vignon, *Conclusions de la session 2012 des Semaines sociales de France*, 2.
86 'Mariage pour tous: le Snec-CFTC réagit', *Ouest France*, 11 January 2013, author's translation.

The concise analysis of the profiles of the leaders of the Manif pour Tous and the organizations that supported it offers an understanding of how the supposedly heterogeneous movement that opposed same-sex marriage included a large variety of Catholic or Catholic-inspired. Two common aspects characterize their identity: their attachment to a conservative understanding of the family and their autonomy from Catholic authorities.[87] The organizations of the Manif pour Tous defended conservative anthropological principles that bore the imprint of the natural law tradition rather than Catholic doctrines. Furthermore, they did not have any formal affiliation with the Catholic Church. By adapting a well-known formula employed by the British sociologist Grace Davie,[88] we may conclude that the social activism of civil society groups against same-sex marriage was an example of believing without belonging, the collective action of actors that were defending their cultural and sociological Catholicism without being formally affiliated to Catholic authorities.

The outbreak of social mobilizations of civil society groups in 2012-2013 was made possible not only because Catholic-inspired actors have always been widespread in the social sphere, but also because civic associations felt a strong ethical drive to intervene in the defence of diffused conservative values on family and gender issues.[89] In this sense, civic associations were exercising a vicarious role on behalf of a large part of a society whose demands, they believed, were poorly represented. This could happen because two additional factors were at work. First, in the French political context the Church has no formal authority and its public engagement may encounter a strong reaction from anti-clerical cultural and political elites. Second, in late 2012 and early 2013, the UMP, which generally defended conservative values on family matters, was extremely weak because of the double electoral defeat in 2012, the divisive internal struggle for the presidency, and several financial scandals. Within this general context, the Manif pour Tous partly filled a social and political void in the representation of those French Catholics who were still attached to conservative Catholic cultural values, but were not represented by any mainstream political party at a time when a fundamental principle of their Catholic cultural identity (heterosexual marriage) was under discussion. By doing that, the Manif pour Tous did not act very differently from many other past social movements that tended to consider their protests as an alternative form of political participation on behalf of inadequately represented social constituencies.

87 Jérome Brunet, spokesperson for the Manif pour Tous and President of the association Appel des Professionnels de l'Enfance, 4 July 2014, personal interview.

88 Davie, *Religion in Britain since 1945*.

89 Ludovine de la Rochère, President of the Manif pour Tous, 24 March 2014, personal interview.

Influence on Policy Outcomes

The policy impact of the anti-gay marriage campaign poses a puzzle. When social protests were intense, the anti-marriage camp faced a clear defeat; yet when the intensity of contentious actions waned, the opponents to the extension of LGBT rights achieved several successes. This apparent puzzle demands careful consideration. Social movement generally have far-reaching goals. Determining their success or failure should led us to take into account not only the stated goals, but also their other purposes. In other words, if the anti-gay marriage campaign affected the liberalization of the family legislation planned by the government, then it should not necessarily be considered a failure, even though the protest actions could not prevent the legalization of same-sex marriage.

On 23 April 2013 the French National Assembly adopted the Taubira Bill, with 331 votes against 225.[90] The introduction of same-sex marriage and adoption was an evident defeat for the social movement opposing the extension of LGBT rights. However, the most important target of the social protests against the Taubira Bill was not same-sex marriage, but the right of same-sex couples to adopt children and the possible further liberalization of family legislation following the introduction of same-sex marriage.[91]

During his electoral campaign in spring 2012, François Hollande did not just propose the introduction of full marriage and adoption rights for same-sex couples as stated in the 31st engagement of his presidential manifesto. He also intended to implement a comprehensive reform of family legislation that would have strengthened the rights of civil partners, reinforced the parental authority of non-biological parents, and introduce assisted reproductive technologies for lesbian couples. Support for reproductive technologies was reaffirmed a few weeks before the first round of the presidential election by Najat Vallaud-Belkacem, who was at the time the spokesperson for Hollande's campaign. On 31 March 2012, at the Meeting pour l'Égalité, Vallaud-Belkacem stated that Hollande was committed to introducing a broad reform of the family code by spring 2013 and added that the project of law was already on the table.[92] On the highly contentious issue of surrogacy, in 2011, during the debate for the primary election of the PS, Manuel Valls, who was appointed Minister of the Interior after the election of Hollande, and in 2013 Prime Minister, even proclaimed his personal support for surrogacy, which he defined an unavoidable evolution.[93]

90 'Le "mariage pour tous" définitivement adopté à l'Assemblée', *Le Monde*, 23 April 2013.
91 Jérôme Brunet, spokesperson for the Manif pour Tous and President of the association Appel des Professionnels de l'Enfance, 4 July 2014, personal interview.
92 Yaggvideo, 'Najat Vallaud-Belkacem (PS)/Meeting LGBT pour l'Egalité'.
93 'Gestation pour autrui: le spectaculaire retournement de Manuel Valls', *Le Monde*, 3 October 2014.

The policy proposals of the government dramatically changed after the approval of the Taubira Bill. Among several others, four examples show the evolution of government action on family questions. First, on 3 February 2014, the day after a demonstration by the Manif pour Tous in Paris that gathered roughly 100,000 people, the government withdrew the new proposal for a law on family matters and announced that such legislation would not be presented in 2014.[94] Commenting on the news, the socialist senator and rapporteur of the law on same-sex marriage Jean-Pierre Michel declared, "It is a victory for the reaction [...] If the government is scared of a few tens of thousands of protesters who roam the streets, it does not have to govern."[95]

Second, on 28 April 2014, the Minister of the Family, Children, and Women's Rights, Laurence Rossignol, met the leader of the Manif pour Tous and announced that the government would not table any proposal for a law on reproductive technologies.[96] Third, in mid May 2014 several socialist and green deputies presented a new proposal for a law on family issues. However, the new text did not address some highly controversial issues, including the extension of adoption rights and assisted reproductive technologies. To delay the debate on the law, the UMP, and particularly its deputies affiliated with the Entente Parlementaire pour la Famille, presented more than 700 amendments. Faced with the obstructionism of the Right, the government eventually decided to withdraw the proposal for a law under discussion.[97] Fourth, at the beginning of October 2014, two days before another protest march organized by the Manif pour Tous against assisted reproductive technologies for lesbian couples and surrogacy, Valls had his first interview with the Catholic newspaper *La Croix*, in which he said, "Surrogacy is and will be banned in France. This is the very firm choice of the President of the Republic and his government."[98]

Echoing the words of the Manif pour Tous, the prime minister added, "I believe that in these times of crisis of identity, the family is a point of reference, a pole of stability. It evolved, certainly, and it is our role to accompany it."[99]

What provoked the dramatic turn in the political action of the French government? Valls probably provided the clearest explanation of that. During a meeting with the press in early October 2014, the prime minister declared that the public debate on family issues had the merit of allowing a change in positions.[100] According to Valls

94 'La Manif pour tous se réjouit d'une «première grande victoire»', *Le Figaro*, 3 February 2014, author's translation.
95 Jean-Pierre Michel quoted in *Le Point*, 4 February 2014.
96 'Les anti-mariage pour tous se réconcilient avec le gouvernement', *L'Express*, 28 April 2014.
97 'L'UMP parvient à faire reporter l'adoption de la loi famille', *Le Point*, 22 May 2014.
98 Manuel Valls quoted in 'Manuel Valls : «La France entend promouvoir une initiative internationale sur la GPA», *La Croix*, 2 October 2014, author's translation.
99 Ibid.
100 'GPA: Valls assume avoir "changé d'avis"', *Les Échos*, 3 October 2014.

> Our society is fractured enough and each of us seeks appeasement [...] Probably we underestimated [...] the fact that in a period of economic crisis, confidence crisis, identity crisis, these debates [about same-sex marriage, reproductive technologies, and surrogacy] could rise political currents, especially from the extreme right, that sought to reconstitute themselves on the backs of those - many - who had sincere convictions.[101]

In other words, the government changed its political agenda concerning family issues because the intense social mobilizations against same-sex marriage opened a highly divisive public debate and the Hollande presidency did not want to see the strengthening of radical right parties, whose political platforms embraced the claims of conservative social constituencies that supported the protest against the Taubira Bill. To sum up, we can conclude that the anti-gay marriage campaign failed to prevent the legalization of same-sex marriage and adoption but it was successful to prevent, at least in part, the liberalization of the family legislation planned by Hollande.

Abortion: A Still Open Question

In Chapter 4 we pointed out that the revision of the family code in 1965, the introduction of birth control pills in 1969, the legalization of abortion in 1975, and the decriminalization of homosexuality in 1982 formed a wave of liberalization of French social legislation that weakened the long-lasting imprint of Catholicism on family legislation.[102] Some of these reforms were quite popular and the support for them increased over time. This has been notably the case for abortion, as shown in Table 10.

In September 1974 a total of 48 per cent of French people were in favour of authorizing abortion when a woman demanded it because she believed that having a child could affect her material and moral conditions, but in February 2014 this figure rose to 75 per cent. In the same period, the percentage of those who agreed to permit abortion only in limited and specific cases declined from 25 per cent to 19 per cent, and those who were in favour of authorizing abortion only when the woman's life was in danger dropped from 24 per cent to 6 per cent. These data highlight the increasing permissiveness of French society on abortion.

Religion, particularly the frequency of religious practice, continues to be the most influential factor in influencing social attitudes toward abortion, as those who practise less are more likely to sustain permissive positions on abortion. However, this correlation between religious practice and permissiveness

101 Manuel Valls quoted in *La Croix*, 2 October 2014, author's translation.
102 Feuillet-Liger and Portier, 'Religion et bio-droit en France', 334.

TABLE 10
ANSWERS TO THE QUESTION "AMONG THESE DIFFERENT SITUATIONS, WHICH ONE SEEMS TO YOU BEST SUITED TO OUR TIME?" A COMPARISON BETWEEN THE ANSWERS GIVEN IN 1974 AND IN 2014 (% FIGURES)*

	September 1974	February 2014
Authorizing the termination of pregnancy by a doctor when the woman asks for it because she believes that her material or moral conditions of existence do not allow for her to have a child	48	75
Authorizing the termination of pregnancy in certain limited and specific cases	25	19
Authorizing the termination of pregnancy only when the woman's life is in danger	24	6
No answer	3	-
Total	100	100

* IFOP, 'Les Français et l'interruption volontaire de grossesse', 8.

should not lead us to conclude that all Catholics hold restrictive positions on abortion. As shown by Table 11, some 75 per cent of non-practising Catholics are in favour of authorizing abortion when a woman demands it because she believes that having a child will affect her material and moral conditions, but only 22 per cent agree to authorize abortion in limited and specific cases, and 3 per cent when the woman's life is in danger. The preferences of non-practising Catholics are similar to those of the overall French population. Once again, here we have a confirmation that non-practising Catholics seem to be fully integrated into the normative system of French society. Interestingly, the majority of practising Catholics, 53 per cent, also hold permissive attitudes toward the authorization of abortion, despite the Church continuously reaffirming its condemnation of this practice that Catholic moral theology considers to be against the Fifth Commandment that prohibits murder.[103]

Even though these data show the inroads of liberal individualistic values into French Catholicism, they should not be overstated. As pointed out by Monique Baujard,

> most Catholics are not in favour of abortion. Instead, they are in favour of legislation that makes it possible when there is a situation of distress,

103 Cunningham, *An Introduction to Catholicism*, 236.

> which is not exactly the same thing. You can be against it [abortion], you can think it is not a good idea, but you prefer that it is still possible. I think that for abortion it is very clear. This is one of the things that bishops do not always understand very well.[104]

However, can the widespread permissive attitudes toward abortion lead us to assume, as noted by Simone Veil in an interview with *Le Monde* on 17 January 1995, the twentieth anniversary of the bill that carries her name, that abortion is no longer a political issue in France today?[105] The answer to this question is probably negative. Even though in France, like in other Western European countries, the campaigns by anti-abortion activists and anti-gender movements have not succeeded in restricting women's reproductive rights,

TABLE 11
ANSWERS TO THE QUESTION "AMONG THESE DIFFERENT SITUATIONS, WHICH ONE SEEMS TO YOU BEST SUITED TO OUR TIME?", BY RELIGION PRACTICE (% FIGURES)*

	All French	Practising Catholics	Non-Practising Catholics	Without Religion
Authorizing the termination of pregnancy by a doctor when the woman asks for it because she believes that her material or moral conditions of existence do not allow for her to have a child	75	53	75	85
Authorizing the termination of pregnancy in certain limited and specific cases	19	34	22	11
Authorizing the termination of pregnancy only when the woman's life is in danger	6	13	3	4
Total	100	100	100	100

* IFOP, *Les Français et l'interruption volontaire de grossesse*, 9.

104 Monique Baujard, former Director of the Service National Famille et Société of the Conférence des Évêques de France, 23 July 2014, personal interview.

105 'L'avortement ne représente plus aujourd›hui en France un enjeu politique', *Le Monde*, 17 January 1995.

much still needs to be done to provide safe and adequate access to abortion services.[106]

This is why French governments implemented several policies to further extend access to abortion. The legislator became increasingly aware that the legalization of abortion did not mean that all women had effective freedom of choice as social, medical, and economic constraints can significantly restrict access to abortion services and drugs, particularly for younger women. A law promulgated in December 2000 established that drugs for urgent contraception could be bought without a medical prescription and delivered for free to underage girls.[107] A bill enacted in 2001 extended the period during which abortion could be practised from ten to twelve weeks, removed compulsory consultation for adult women, and allowed underage girls to access abortion without parental approval.[108] A decree introduced in 2004 allowed the provision of drugs to induce abortion in outpatient medicine.[109]

Despite the broad reform of the family legislation of the Hollande presidency was affected by the anti-gay marriage mobilization, the socialist president was able to strengthen the permissiveness of abortion laws. For example, the 2013 Social Security Bill introduced full reimbursement for abortion expenses.[110] Following a recommendation made by the Haut Conseil à l'Égalité entre les Femmes et les Hommes, on 4 August 2014 the Parliament suppressed the condition of distress that previously was a necessary requirement for access to abortion.[111] This reform was highly symbolic. The recourse to abortion ceased to be a decision that women had to justify on the basis of their precarious health, economic, and social conditions to the medical personnel who evaluated the admissibility of their demands. On 26 November 2014, the National Assembly approved another highly symbolic document in which it

> reaffirms the importance of the fundamental right to voluntary termination of pregnancy for all women, in France, in Europe and in the world; [...] recalls that the universal right of women to freely control their own bodies is an essential condition for building real equality between women and men and a society of progress.[112]

106 Outshoorn, 'The Stability of Compromise', 145; Haut Conseil à l'Égalité entre les Femmes et les Hommes, *Rapport relatif à l'accès à l'IVG. Volet 1.*
107 Loi n° 2000-1209 du 13 décembre 2000, *Journal Officiel de la République Française, Lois et Décrets*, 14 December 2000, 19830.
108 Loi n° 2001-588 du 4 juillet 2001, *Journal Officiel de la République Française, Lois et Décrets*, 7 July 2001, 10824-10826.
109 Décret n° 2004-636 du 1er juillet 2004, *Journal Officiel de la République Française, Lois et Décrets*, 2 July 2004, 12061.
110 Loi n° 2012-1404 du 17 décembre 2012, *Journal Officiel de la République Française, Lois et Décrets*, 18 December 2012, 19821-19874.
111 Loi n° 2014-873 du 4 août 2014, *Journal Officiel de la République Française, Lois et Décrets*, 5 August 2014, 12949.
112 Texte adopté n° 2014-433 du 26 novembre 2014, author's translation.

Finally, the law for the modernization of the health care system approved on 26 January 2016 suppressed the requirement for a minimum reflection period of a week before women could access abortion services and it also allowed midwives to carry out abortions.[113]

The permissiveness of the Hollande presidency was not shared by all mainstream French parties. The internal debate in Les Républicains (LR), the major French right-wing party, showed that abortion was still a controversial political issue for the French Right. This became evident during the debate in the LR's primary elections for the presidency of this party held in late 2016. On 22 November 2016 Alain Juppé harshly criticized François Fillon, his competitor for the LR's presidency, for being ambiguous about abortion. In his book manifesto, entitled *Faire* (Doing), Fillon had written that he considered abortion a fundamental right, but during a meeting with his supporters in June 2016 he admitted that he had been wrong to write that and he added that his Christian faith led him to oppose abortion.[114] In his long political career, Fillon had generally taken conservative positions on abortion. In 1982 he voted against the reimbursement of abortion expenses by social security, in 1993 he was against the introduction of the crime of obstructing abortion, and in 2001 he opposed the prolongation of the gestational period during which abortion could be practised. Conservative political ideas on family and societal questions allowed Fillon to gain the support of the Catholic electorate during the LR's primary elections and the endorsement of the association Sens Commun.[115] Juppé, who intended to represent more liberal positions on societal questions than Fillon, was probably overstating the ambiguity of his adversary's position. However, the fact that abortion opened a debate in the LR showed the moral conservatism of some senior figures of the LR and the ambivalence of this party on women's reproductive rights.

The most controversial reform of abortion policies enacted by the Hollande presidency was the introduction of the crime of online obstruction of abortion. A bill that criminalized the obstruction of abortion introduced in 1993 established that whoever impeded or attempted to impede abortion or access to those clinics that practised abortion could be punished with a period of detention of up to two years and a fine of 30,000 French francs.[116] Thi law aimed to stop the growing number of commando actions against clinics and hospitals that pro-life groups, following the example of cognate associations in the Unit-

113 Loi n° 2016-41 du 26 janvier 2016, *Journal Officiel de la République Française, Lois et Décrets*, 27 January 2016.

114 Fillon, *Faire*, 169; 'Qu'a vraiment dit François Fillon sur l'avortement?', *Le Figaro*, 22 November 2016.

115 IFOP, *Le vote des sympathisants de droite catholiques à la primaire de la droite et du centre*, 6, 8.

116 Loi n° 93-121 du 27 janvier 1993, *Journal Officiel de la République Française, Lois et Décrets*, 30 January 1993, 1576-1588.

ed States, had been carrying out in France since the late 1980s. More recently, the strategies of pro-life groups have changed. Instead of organizing commando actions, they started to spread fake news on abortion on the internet, which is the principal source of information for women and young people.[117]

Until September 2013, French public administrations did not have any official website to provide information on abortion. Several pro-life groups and conservative Catholic associations took advantage of this lack of initiative by public powers to set up several websites that provided unreliable information on abortion questions. The scope of these websites, which generally did not declare that they were managed by pro-life organizations and traditionalist Catholic activists, was to exert subtle psychological pressure on women who were considering terminating their pregnancies. The formal layout, the provision of apparently neutral medical information, and a free phone number that often claimed to be the number of a national listening centre gave to many anti-abortion websites the appearance of official institutional websites. However, those who answered the phone calls were pro-life activists who emphasized the negative consequences of abortion or gave intentionally misleading information. Skilful use of internet indexation mechanisms enabled these anti-abortion websites to appear at the top of the pages shown by the most popular search engines so that the reader further had the impression that they were official institutional sites.

One of the oldest and most popular was ivg.net. This site was opened in 2008 by René Sentis, an entrepreneur in the IT sector who published some books on the Christian meaning of love and who claimed to be an expert in the Billings ovulation method, a natural contraceptive technique promoted by the Catholic Church, which is based on the individuation of fertility periods and abstinence.[118] Two other popular sites were écoute-ivg.org and sosbebe.org. Both of them were managed by Alliance Vita.[119] A special mention should also go to afterbaiz.com. In contrast to the aforementioned sites, afterbaiz.com was characterized by a colourful layout, the use of several videos, and an easy-going written style that closely resembles teenagers' websites. Afterbaiz.com was created by Émile Duport, an activist of the anti-gay marriage campaign who was in charge of communication for the Manif pour Tous, besides being

117 Haut Conseil à l'Égalité entre les Femmes et les Hommes, *Rapport relatif à l'accès à l'IVG. Volet 2*, 31.

118 'Ivg.net, le site très orienté d'un couple de militants catholiques', *Le Monde*, 7 December 2016.

119 Ibid.

the spokesperson for Les Survivants,[120] a pro-life association founded in 1998 to raise public awareness on the consequences of abortion.[121]

The debate on the proposal for a law for the crime of online obstruction of abortion was characterized by the contraposition along the right-left political cleavage. While the socialist government and various leftist parties considered the proposed bill to be a measure to defend women's reproductive rights, the right-wing parties rejected what they considered to be a threat to freedom. This latter argument was also sustained by the Catholic Church, which aligned itself with the positions of the Right.[122]

However, two important differences distinguished the debate on the law for the crime of online obstruction of abortion from the debate on the Taubira Bill. First, the mainstream Right was not as strongly mobilized against the new bill as it was against same-sex marriage. This was remarked on by the LR's deputy Hervé Mariton and the Christian democratic deputy Jean-Frédéric Poisson, who regretted the lack of ideological awareness of the Right.[123] The LR did not want to engage with a topic that could open an internal division between its morally conservative wing and its socially progressive side, as shown by the contrasts between Juppé and Fillon. Second, even though several pro-life associations opposed the new law, their social discontent did not provoke the outbreak of a wave of social protests. The Manif pour Tous was almost absent from the public debate. Even though several Catholic groups and the Catholic Church were firmly against the new bill, the great popularity of abortion among French people and the lack of initiatives by pro-life organizations impeded the mobilization of broad social constituencies against it.

The weak parliamentary opposition and the limited mobilization of Catholic associations led the Church to take an assertive position against the proposed law for the crime of online obstruction of abortion. On 22 November 2016, Mgr Georges Pontier, President of the Conférence des Évêques de France, wrote an open letter to Hollande in which he expressed his concern about the new law on abortion. Mgr Pontier supported his claims with two arguments. First, he argued that this new law did not mention the existential distress that abortion could provoke. Second, he pointed out that it

> puts into question the foundations of our freedoms and especially the freedom of expression [...] limitation all the more serious as it touches issues

120 The name of this association is inspired by the high number of abortions practised every year in France, which, according to organizers of this association, is roughly 200,000.

121 'Ils aiment les Pokémon mais pas l'IVG: qui sont les «Survivants»?', *Le Nouvel Observateur*, 22 August 2016.

122 'Internet et anti-IVG, un débat entravé', *Libération*, 1 December 2016.

123 'À l'Assemblée, une centaine d'amendements contre le délit d'entrave à l'IVG', *Le Figaro*, 29 November 2016.

> related to freedom of conscience. To me, this seems to be a very serious attack on the principles of democracy.[124]

Interestingly, Mgr Pontier justified his position by avoiding any mention of religious doctrines and by using secular arguments that appealed to the long-standing principles of French republican life, notably the freedom of expression, the freedom of conscience, and the defence of democracy. In this way, Mgr Pontier's letter showed how religious authorities not only use neutral and generally accessible language to 'translate' religious doctrines to enter the agendas of parliaments, courts and administrative bodies, as Jürgen Habermas claims, but they also tend to rely on secular principles.[125] However, the Catholic Church was quite isolated in its struggle against the new bill and Mgr Pontier's appeal did not have any influence on the political debate. The bill introducing the crime of online obstruction of abortion was eventually approved by the National Assembly on 16 February 2017 and validated by the Constitutional Council on 16 March 2017.[126]

New Ideological Conflicts?

This chapter has discussed the role of Catholic and Catholic-inspired actors in defending Catholic anthropological values in the social protest against same-sex marriage in 2012-2013 and the opposition to a new law on abortion. Three conclusions can be derived from the research presented in the previous sections. First, the effort of secularizing family legislation reactivated the latent social cleavage, provoked the outbreak of strong protest actions, and it prepared the ground for new intransigent kinds of political militancy. Second, traditionalist Catholic and Catholic-inspired organizations showed not only a great capacity to mobilize people, but also to defend Catholic anthropological values that were poorly supported by conservative political actors. Three, Catholicism, most notably integralist Catholic organizations, had a great ability to innovate their strategies. The leaders and the activists of the Manif pour Tous demonstrated impressive communication skills and the ability to use them to organize collective actions, broaden their message and obtain public visibility. Likewise, the pro-life organizations showed how the internet and the manipulation of information provided by online platforms can become a tool to further their ideals and reach their goals. In this sense, we can extend

124 Pontier, *Délit d'entrave numérique à l'IVG*, author's translation.

125 Habermas, '"THE POLITICAL". The Rational Meaning of a Questionable Inheritance of Political Theology', 25.

126 Loi n° 2017-347 du 20 mars 2017, *Journal Officiel de la République Française, Lois et Décrets*, 21 March 2017.

to France what Ilvo Diamanti and Luigi Ceccarini noted about Italian Catholicism.[127] In France too, Catholicism is a minority, but it is still an influential minority in the public sphere that can defend Catholic anthropologicalvalues through the mobilization of the public opinion and the promotion of new forms of social engagement in the secular French society.

127 Diamanti and Ceccarini, 'Catholics and politics after the Christian democrats', 48.

8
A CONTRIBUTION TO A THEORY ON THE MOBILIZATION OF CATHOLICISM IN SECULAR SOCIETIES

The influence of religious values on the development of welfare states has been increasingly acknowledged since the early 1990s. The number of publications on the topic has grown. The explanations have become more sophisticated. The empirical evidence is more reliable. The current scholarship, notably the works of Gøsta Esping-Andersen and Kees Van Kersbergen, has led to identifying a conservative or Christian democratic welfare regime, a distinct kind of welfare state bearing the imprint of Catholicism.[1] However, most of the academic literature that studied conservative or Christian democratic welfare states has been focused on the period of expansion of the systems of social protection during the 'Glorious Thirty', it has mainly considered the role played by Christian democratic parties and Catholic labour unions, and it has paid little attention to the identity, discourses and new strategies of action used by civil society actors to shape social policy in contemporary secular or post-secular societies. The point of departure of this book was the attempt to overcome these weaknesses in the current welfare state scholarship and to contribute to a theory of the long-term institutional influence of Catholicism in shaping social policies in Western Europe.

1 Bäckström et al, *Welfare and Religion in 21st Century Europe. Volume 1*; Castles, 'On religion and public policy'; Flora and Heidenheimer, 'Introduction'; Huber, Ragin and Stephens, 'Social democracy, Christian democracy, constitutional structure, and the welfare state'; Manow, 'The "good, the bad and the ugly"'; Manow and Van Kersbergen, 'Religion and the Western Welfare State'; Morgan, *Working Mothers and the Welfare State*; Opielka 'Christian Foundations of the Welfare State', 102-103; Therborn, 'Another way of taking religion seriously'; Van Kersbergen, *Social capitalism*; Wilensky, 'Leftism, Catholicism and Democratic Comporatism'.

Although the research carried out for this book was influenced by the cultural turn that has interested social sciences since the late 1990s, it was focused on policy developments rather than on cultural analyses. The developments of social security offer an intriguing perspective from which to unfold the changing impact of values on politics because welfare states are not just technocratic mechanisms: they are first and foremost powerful political institutions that shape the lives of people and societies.[2] As a consequence, welfare states are embedded in a normative dimension and social policies are a terrain for the struggle between competing values.

The closer attention to the influence of Catholic social values on several crucial policy debates, processes, and outcomes has resulted in a critical outlook on the role of Catholicism during the historical development of French social security that has highlighted the ambiguous relationships between policy decisions and Catholicism, the difficult interpenetration of Catholic norms into the French system of social protection, and the recent resurgent relevance of Catholic ideals in policy debates. Furthermore, the long-term historical perspective allowed recognition of the influence of a large variety of Catholic-inspired actors, the existence of multiple forms of mobilizations in defence of Catholic values, and several institutional arrangements promoted by Catholic-inspired groups.

This concluding chapter intends to draw together the main findings of this book to provide the reader with a comprehensive picture of the research. In addition, this chapter draws attention to some theoretical and empirical contributions from this book that may open new avenues in research areas that deserve further investigation.

Continuities and Changes in a Long Story

This book divided its investigation of the historical role of Catholicism in the social policy domain into two parts. Whereas the first part explored the years of expansion of social protection since the outbreak of the Second World War, the second part studied the period of welfare retrenchment that started in the early 1990s, although several signs of welfare cutbacks can already be individuated before this period. This way of presenting the argument may give the impression of some kind of artificiality because historical epochs are seldom defined by clear-cut boundaries. In consideration of that, in the following pages we would like to present the long-term trajectory of the mobilization of Catholic-inspired groups by pointing out some of the principal continuities and changes that we have discovered.

2 Esping-Andersen, *The Three Worlds of Welfare Capitalism*, 221.

The main continuity identified by this book is the long-standing mobilization of Catholic actors during the different phases of the development of the contemporary French welfare state. Catholics have always been present in French political life and they have always intervened in the public sphere by attempting to shape social legislation. Since the Vichy years, Catholic-inspired actors have been constantly active in debating, proposing, elaborating, implementing, advising on, and sometimes opposing social policy reforms. Catholic civil servants and politicians were involved in the elaboration of the social policies of the Vichy regime. In the early post-war period, the MRP made a decisive contribution to the establishment of a comprehensive system of social security.[3] After the demise of this party, Catholic ideals were taken up by the Gaullist movement[4]. Leftist Catholics also found a privileged space in the PS of François Mitterrand.[5]. Since the mid 1990s, the influence of Catholicism has become subtler, but nonetheless noticeable. Catholic values are widespread in contemporary French politics and society.[6] A consistent part of non-profit associations are inspired by Catholic social values,[7] and the mobilizations against same-sex marriage in 2012-2013 showed the strong capacity of conservative Catholic-inspired groups to sustain massive protest actions.[8] By demonstrating great adaptability to the changing social, political, and cultural circumstances, Catholic actors have always found a way to access the public sphere. One implication of this conclusion is that a crucial issue that current scholarship should address is not to understand whether Catholicism still has a role in public policy decisions, but how this role has changed over time. The observations presented in the various chapters are more telling because they are derived from the study of the impact of Catholic values in France, one of the most secular countries in Western Europe. In this sense, the French case may provide some insights into other countries that are characterized by a historically stronger role of political Catholicism and weaker constraints on the activism of religious-inspired groups in the public sphere.

The enduring presence of Catholics in the public domain contrasts with the paradigm of secularization and the idea of the privatization of religion in contemporary societies. Although the theories of secularization are composed of several and multifaceted arguments, their unifying principle is the claim that modernization goes hand in hand with secularization, and through a process of de-institutionalization religion has gradually shifted from the public to

3 Manow and Palier, 'A Conservative Welfare State Regime without Christian Democracy?', 158-162.
4 Goguel, *Chroniques électorales. 1*, 81.
5 Soulage, 'L'engagement politique des chrétiens de gauche, entre Parti socialiste, deuxième gauche et gauchisme', 425.
6 Hervieu-Léger, 'Sécularisation', 1153.
7 Schlegel, 'Conclusion', 586.
8 Béraud and Portier, *Métamorphoses catholiques.*

the private sphere. In other words, religious values have increasingly become a private affair that may influence personal life, but not public decisions. The research carried out for this book found that this argument does not have adequate empirical support. Though in contemporary Europe religion cannot structure collective life,[9] it still has a relevant factor in public debates and it may have some impact on collective decisions. Instead of rejecting the idea of the resilient influence of religious in secularized Western European societies, it would be more empirically and theoretically meaningful to understand the new public role of religious values and organizations in our secular times and the hybridization between religious and secular views in our secularized societies.[10] This book wants to contribute to this promising field of study.

The analysis reported in the various chapters shows that a large variety of Catholic-inspired social and political actors have constantly been engaged in supporting Catholic social ideals. Since the early 1940s, Catholic ideals have been defended by reactionary governments, Christian democratic parties, Catholic and Catholic-inspired labour unions, civil society organizations, and social movements.

The great internal pluralism of Catholicism has been accompanied by a gradual relocation of its activism that has shifted from the formal political sphere to civil society. In other words, the research for this book has led to the understanding that Catholics have promoted their social ideals less through their engagement with political parties and more through their involvement in voluntary associations and social movements. The thesis of a repositioning of religious activism from politics to civil society was explored, among others, by José Casanova's book *Public Religions in the Modern World*. Though this book is greatly indebted to Casanova's ideas, it made an effort to further elaborate them by investigating the impact of religious-inspired actors in the social policy domains. A first improvement made by this book to Casanova's thesis is the study of the role of Catholic-inspired groups instead of just the activism of the Church. A broader consideration of Catholicism would allow more insightful observations on the changing presence of religion in modern societies. A second improvement we made was the idea to go beyond the rather simplistic dichotomy between political society and civil society. The boundaries between institutionalized actors and politics and less institutionalized groups are becoming thinner in contemporary Western democracies.[11] Civil society organizations can exert a remarkable influence on political debates. Finally, a third improvement was the constant effort of our study to present a historical analysis that traced the development of the social mobilization of Catholic-inspired groups over a long period of time.

9 Gauchet, *Un monde désenchanté?*, 325-327.
10 Portier and Willaime, *La religion dans la France contemporaine*, 219.
11 Goldstone, 'Introduction'.

The shift from a politically-oriented to a socially-oriented mobilization of Catholic-inspired actors is more evident when their role in shaping social security is considered. For example, a cornerstone of Pétain's political project of a National Revolution was the ambition to provide Catholicism with the social role it had before the turmoil of the French Revolution and the militant secularization pursued during the Third Republic. This task had to be performed by political authorities and the state bureaucratic apparatus.

In the early years after the Liberation, the MRP became the main reference point of the national Catholic movement. Although the level of integration between the Catholic milieu and the MRP was far lower than in other European countries, notably Italy, and this party was unable to establish stable links with Catholic associations,[12] between 1944 and 1946, in those crucial years for the establishment of social security, the MRP had a pivotal role in French politics and French Catholicism. Senior leaders of Catholic associations and the labour unions were elected from the lists of the MRP, whose members considered politics as the main channel to shape society and to redefine its normative foundations.[13] Social legislation was the privileged instrument to realize this goal.

The final disbanding of the MRP in 1967 did not end the political engagement of Catholics. Some Catholic ideals were taken up by two major French political families: the Gaullist movement and democratic Socialism. However, the actual impact of Catholic values on social legislation was negligible. The demands of the social movements of the late 1960s for the modernization of social legislation, the gradual decline of the social basis of Catholicism, and the attention of right-wing and left-wing governments to the preservation of their power positions led them to disregard the Catholic ideals that inspired their political background in order to introduce policy reforms that could meet the prevailing social demands or the requests of pro-business elites. Indirectly, this provoked a decline in the Catholic imprint on the welfare state, most notably on family legislation, a traditional stronghold of Catholicism.

Since the 1960s there has been not only a proliferation of new Catholic movements,[14] but also a consolidation of Catholic-inspired associations engaged in providing social services. Voluntary groups have been increasingly involved in closer forms of collaboration with public authorities in the social policy sphere.[15] This new role has allowed them to exert a subtle influence on some social policy spheres by shaping the intellectual framework and the decisions of policy makers. Policy procedures and policy outcomes con-

12 Pasture, 'Multi-faceted Relations between Christian Trade Unions and Left Catholics in Europe', 243.
13 Manow and Palier, 'A Conservative Welfare State Regime without Christian Democracy?', 158-162; Mayeur, *Des partis catholiques à la démocratie chrétienne*, 167.
14 Hervieu-Léger, *Le pèlerin et le converti.*
15 Valasik, 'Church-state Relations in France in the Field of Welfare'.

sistent with Catholic social values have inspired French housing policies, as we pointed out in Chapter 6. Furthermore, the public trust that philanthropic organizations have been benefitting from, their capacity to give a voice to marginalized groups (e.g. immigrants, homeless, and poor families), and the mounting distrust of political institutions have provided them with a sort of informal political role, to the extent that we may wonder whether they may contribute to renovating the forms of political participation in our democracies.[16] However, Catholic-inspired associations have also originated a wave of social protests that opened ideological struggles and highly divisive public debates. The anti-gay marriage campaign in 2012-2013 was an example of that.

The shift of location of Catholic activism does not necessarily imply that these two kinds of mobilization may not coexist in the same period. What we indicated was a general historical trajectory, not a strict process of substitution. For example, in the post-war period, Catholic labour unions were important actors in the defence of Catholic-inspired values that were also promoted by the MRP. Nowadays, some French Catholic-minded politicians still intend to support Catholic anthropological ideals even if the focus of the Catholic mobilization is more located in the social sphere.

The simultaneous presence of civil-society-oriented and politically-centred engagement of Catholic-inspired groups may give rise to some tensions. For instance, most contemporary voluntary organizations tend to confer great importance on their autonomy vis-à-vis political institutions. Like all new social movements, the militants and leaders of the Catholic and Catholic-inspired organizations that we interviewed for this book consider the autonomy of their associations to be their central and defining value. This may lead to clashes with political authorities that sometimes tend to take over control of successful social programmes managed by voluntary groups.[17] Another telling example is provided by the social protests against gay marriage. Although the collective actions contributed to the political socialization of a new generation of French people, the leaders of the anti-gay marriage campaign made a great effort to reject any political affiliation, even with those politicians who were engaged in the parliamentary battle to oppose the legalization of same-sex marriage.[18]

The persistent inspiration provided by Catholic social doctrines to a large variety of actors is the second main continuity in the relationship between Catholicism and the welfare state that this book has recognized. The attention to human persons, the effort to alleviate poverty, the intention to provide

16 Barthélémy, *Associations*.

17 Valasik, 'Church-state Relations in France in the Field of Welfare', 142-144.

18 Jérôme Brunet, spokesperson for the Manif pour Tous and President of the association Appel des Professionnels de l'Enfance, 4 July 2014, personal interview, 11 February 2014, personal interview; Ludovine de La Rochère, President of the Manif pour Tous, 24 March 2014, personal interview.

stronger legal protection and more generous financial resources to families, particularly large families, and the defence of the anthropological principles of the natural law tradition on family and sexually-related matters are some of the most common and long-standing principles that inspired Catholic and Catholic-minded activists. On the other hand, this does not mean that all of these actors support the same policies and the same values. Contemporary political life is based on different interpretations of common principles.[19] What makes the social policy proposals advocated by Catholics different are dissimilar opinions on who the policies should support, under what circumstances, how, and why. We may argue that at an upper level of the scale of abstraction all Catholic-inspired groups promoted Catholic values. However, when the characteristics of their demands are considered in detail, at a lower level in the scale of abstraction, the kind of Catholicism that they support may change dramatically. This conclusion should not come as a surprise. From its origins, Catholic social teaching has been composed of a wide variety of principles. In the effort to be a 'third way' between Socialism and liberalism, social Catholicism integrated some ideas of democratic Socialism (e.g. its strong critique of capitalism and the need for greater social solidarity), liberalism (e.g. the defence of property rights), conservatism (e.g. the promotion of a patriarchal family model), authoritarianism (e.g. the mistrust of democracy), and so on.[20] Given the traditional vagueness of papal encyclicals, the core ideas of Catholicism have been reinterpreted in accordance with changing social, political, and intellectual contexts. Different Catholic actors have attempted to reformulate the social discourse of the Church and to reappropriate it on their own terms and, sometimes, in their own interests. For example, the family legislation of Vichy was inspired by a conservative, if not reactionary, Catholic moralism that promoted patriarchal familism. Financial help was given to the (male) head of the family and employment policies were inspired by gender discriminatory attitudes in order to encourage women to stay at home. After the Liberation, the family laws of the MRP rejected the anti-democratic attitudes of Pétain. However, they still shared with traditional Catholicism the idea of preserving the male breadwinner model that discouraged female employment. Nowadays these ideas also tend to be rejected by the great majority of Catholics, who no longer dispute the principle of equality of rights between men and women and are interested in promoting work-family reconciliation policies. In all these examples, Catholic and Catholic-inspired actors intended to support families, but the instruments and the strategies that they adopted changed dramatically.

Different interpretations of Catholic doctrines may coexist in the same historical period and they sometimes enter into conflict with each other. For

19 Mouffe, 'Democracy Revisited', 109.
20 Misner, 'Christian Democracy Social Policy', 69.

instance, in the late 1970s the traditionally conservative AFC asked for substantial financial support to encourage women to stay at home to look after their children, and it opposed the introduction of divorce, abortion, and contraceptive pills. In contrast, Catholic feminists gave strong support to the moral liberation of family legislation. In 2012-2013, the Church and several Catholic associations were mobilized against the legalization of same-sex marriage, but a large share of Catholics, including regularly practising Catholics, were in favour of full marriage and adoption rights to same-sex couples. In all these situations, Catholic and Catholic-inspired groups sustained antithetical positions without rejecting their faith.

This book has also noted that the mobilization of Catholic-inspired actors on social policy issues has been characterized by a gradual abandonment of grand social and political projects. Catholicism has lost, at least in part, its transformative ethos and it has become more concerned with strengthening the existing bonds of social solidarity threatened by increasing social inequalities and mounting individualism. While Pétain and post-war Christian democrats, with different means and dissimilar purposes, intended to impose important changes on the social order of their times, contemporary Catholic-inspired actors are far less ambitious. They do not want to establish a new society that bears the imprint of their ideals, but they would like to contribute to making the existing social order less unjust. The general decline of ideologies in the last decades of the twentieth century has also affected Catholicism, and it has undergone a process of narrowing down of its aims in comparison with those envisaged by the Catholic actors during the Second World War.

Another relevant change that occurred in the Catholic mobilizations over the past 80 years was a revision of the terminology used by Catholic actors whose values have been increasingly presented in non-religious terms. In the 1940s social policy reforms were still justified by the need to support Catholic ethical norms. The public statements by Marshal Pétain presented several examples of that. Since the 1950s, religious terms have almost disappeared from the vocabulary of Catholic-inspired actors. The structural differentiation between the religious sphere and other social spheres provoked by the process of secularization has deeply influenced the vocabulary of French Catholicism. The vast majority of voluntary organizations with a Catholic background tend to frame their public messages by placing greater emphasis on humanitarian, universalistic, and republican values instead of normative religious principles. The references to Catholic doctrines are rare, if not completely absent, in the public statements by the Secours Catholique and the FAP. Though the organizations involved in the anti-gay marriage campaign defended Catholic anthropological doctrines, they claimed that their mobilization was aimed at defending the universal principles of the Republic and social solidarity.[21] The use of secular terminology by Catholic-inspired actors is motivated by their attempt to give a broader resonance to their mobilizations. However, it is also the symptom of an intellectual crisis of religions that may need the support of non-religious ideals to strengthen their message to adapt it to contemporary secular societies.

A Way Ahead

This book has dealt with several topics that are the subjects of ongoing debate, such as the development of continental welfare states, the role played by values in public policies, the influence of religion in secular or post-secular societies, and so on. Two main scholarships were the constant reference for this study: the welfare state academic literature on Christian democracy and the comparative studies on secularization. At the conclusion of this book, it is appropriate to suggest some research hypotheses and questions that have arisen from our research and that should deserve further exploration.

Since the mid 1990s, the welfare state literature on Christian democracy has been deeply influenced by Kees Van Kersbergen's works.[22] Even though this book is greatly indebted to Van Kersbergen's studies, it has attempted to go beyond them. A first way to develop the existing scholarship on the impact of Catholicism on welfare states, we believe, should be the effort to individuate the large variety of Catholic-inspired actors that shape social legislation and to investigate their multiple and sometimes contrasting aims, strategies, resources, and forms of mobilization. In addition, we think it is important to investigate not only the complementarity, but also the degree of substitution between different social and political actors that inspired their activism around Catholic social values. For example, our historical analysis recognizes how the stronger role of political groups was often accompanied by the weaker mobilization of civil society associations, and the other way round. The policy domain is a competitive field that does not give the same opportunity for action to all the groups involved in it. The awareness of these multiple forms of institutional pressure from Catholic-inspired actors, which is missing in Van Kersbergen's theory of the Christian democratic welfare state, deserves to be further explored from a cross-national and historical comparative perspective, in order to have a more comprehensive understanding of the role played by Catholicism during the long-term development of Western European welfare

21 According to these associations the recognition of full marriage rights for same-sex couples will create social inequalities between children of married heterosexual couples and children adopted by same-sex parents.

22 Van Kersbergen, *Social Capitalism*; Van Kersbergen, 'The Christian democratic phoenix and modern un-secular politics'.

states. Even though some recent studies on the impact of values on the policy domain have demonstrated greater attention to the multifaceted mobilization of social and political actors,[23] the current sociological scholarship is still affected by a narrow historical perspective and it is still excessively attentive to the institutional influence of parties and labour unions. In other words, we think that we should broaden our analysis by enlarging the period and the actors taken into consideration to better understand the policy influence of religious values. This is what this book has attempted to do in relation to France.

We would also like to suggest to further studies to explore research fields in which the investigation of the role of religion and religious-inspired actors has been limited so far. This is particularly the case for the activism of religion-based groups in the community building process, especially in urban deprived areas and the capacity of religious organizations to promote autonomous social economic activities. In the empirical research that we carried out in France, we noticed several signs of this new role for faith-based or religious-inspired philanthropic associations that would require further investigation.

One of the main aims of the analyses in the previous chapters was to contribute to understanding the changing relationships between religion and social policies by going beyond the clichés presented by the paradigm of secularization. By comparing the historical periods taken into consideration, we recognized several signs that show the return to religion. Though this observation may seem counter-intuitive with reference to Catholicism in Western Europe, the empirical evidence in its support nonetheless seems striking. We thus consider it important to clarify the political and policy influence of the return to religion and how this phenomenon can coexist with the process of secularization.

The idea that secularization may bring back religion is not new. In the mid twentieth century, Protestant theology, and in particular the works of Paul Tillich[24] and the late Dietrich Bonhoeffer,[25] argued that the process of secularization was more an opportunity than a threat for religion. In his *Letters and Papers from Prisons*, Bonhoeffer argued that the secularization of the world is the emancipation of men. Human beings have become adult in the modern world and they may rediscover God without the temporally conditioned presuppositions of metaphysics and the regulations imposed by institutional churches.[26] This may lead people to stronger commitments to Christian ethical

23 Engeli, Green-Pedersen and Thorup Larsen, eds, *Morality Politics in Western Europe*; Knill, Adam and Hurka, eds, *On the Road to Permissiveness?*; Knill et al., eds, 'Religious tides'; Van Kersbergen and Manow, eds, *Religion, Class Coalitions and Welfare Regimes*; Van Oorschot, Opielka and Pfau-Effinger, eds, *Culture and Welfare State*.
24 Tillich, *The Courage to Be*.
25 Bonhoeffer, *Widerstand und ergebung*.
26 Ibid.

norms and to a liberation of their energies previously controlled by religious institutions. Even though these words were written by a man experiencing the extreme suffering of living in a Nazi concentration camp, they can be useful to understand the current situation of religion in several Western European countries. Although the phenomenon of the reaffirmation of religious values in secular countries has been acknowledged by some prominent social scholars,[27] the causes of the return to religion in the social policy domain are still awaiting the comprehensive analysis to which this book is making a small contribution. In relation to France, this book individuated four factors that may justify the new and stronger role for religious values in the social policy sphere.

First, the process of secularization has weakened the religious cleavage that has affected French political life for a long time and the early social policy developments.[28] The state does not perceive the weaker Catholic Church as a menace any more. Its declining authority over Catholic associations has given them more autonomy and it has confirmed in the public authorities the idea that faith-based organizations are less conditioned by clerical interests. As a consequence, religious-inspired groups are increasingly establishing stable forms of collaboration with secular powers, even in those public policy domains (e.g. education and social assistance) that in the past triggered intense political conflicts. Second, the disappearance of the MRP and the absence of any strong Catholic-inspired political party has not only further weakened the religious cleavage in France,[29] but it has also spread the ideological baggage of Christian democracy around French political society. Paradoxically, it seems that Christian democratic values are more diffused nowadays than in the past.[30] The recognition of the importance of the principle of subsidiarity, the greater administrative decentralization, and the acknowledgement of the relevant social role of faith-based associations are examples of that. These ideals may further contribute to the recognition of the important social role of Catholicism and to the reproduction of Catholic norms. Third, the process of relocation of Catholic activism from a politically-centred engagement to a socially-oriented mobilization has lessened the political controls on religious-inspired actors. The autonomy of several voluntary associations from the strict tutelage of political groups and administrative authorities allows them to better represent their ideals in the public sphere. Fourth, the further secularization of policy areas that are still shaped by the imprint of Catholic norms, such as family and bioethical policies, could intensify the sense of symbolic insecurity of advanced modernity and it may originate new

27 Beck, *Der eigene gott*, 40-46; Rémond, 'Un chapitre inachevé (1958-1990)', 395-402.

28 Morgan, *Working Mothers and the Welfare State*; Pedersen, *Family, Dependence, and the Origin of the Welfare State*.

29 Elgie, 'France', 127.

30 Pouthier, 'Émergence et ambiguïtés de la culture politique démocrate-chrétienne', 110.

social movements in defence of traditional anthropological norms inspired by Catholic doctrines.[31] Their appeal to universal values, their autonomy from political groups, and their independence from religious authorities may give ample resonance to their mobilizations. This is what happened, for example, with the social protests against same-sex marriage in 2012-2013. Though our findings suggest that secularization can bring back religion, the study of the influence of values in secular societies still requires further attention. We hope that this book can contribute to the scholarly field.

Concluding Remarks

This book does not intend to provide a final answer to the role played by religion in shaping welfare states, but rather it attempts to present an open-ended story of the influence of Catholicism and to spell out the changing characteristics of the mobilization of Catholic-inspired groups in social policy affairs. Given the breadth of the topic, not all the policy issues that provoked the mobilization of French Catholic and Catholic-inspired groups were studied. However, we believe that the representativeness of the cases discussed in the various chapters provided a reasonably accurate picture of the long-term trajectory of the institutional influence of Catholicism on social security.

We decided to study a country that represents a particularly challenging but, at the same time, intriguing and decisive case for understanding the changing role of Catholicism in the welfare state of secularized societies. Venturing into a difficult terrain and studying relatively unexplored fields may predispose the research to possible mistakes. However, we hope that this research will be evaluated on its effort to open up new research perspectives that may enrich the ongoing debate about the role of values in welfare policies in contemporary secular societies.

31 Hervieu-Léger, 'Sécularisation', 1153.

ABBREVIATIONS

AFC	Associations Familiales Catholiques
ACPM	Alliance pour les Chiffres de la Presse et des Médias
AN	Archives Nationales
CAF	Caisses d'Allocations Familiales
CFDT	Confédération Française Démocratique du Travail
CFTC	Confédération Française des Travailleurs Chrétiens
CGC	Confédération Générale des Cadres
CGT	Confédération Générale du Travail
CNAF	Caisse Nationale des Allocations Familiales
CNAFC	Confédération Nationales des Associations Familiales Catholiques
CNAMTS	Caisse Nationale de l'Assurance Maladie
CNAV	Caisse Nationale d'Assurance Vieillesse
CNPF	Conseil National du Patronat Français
DALO	Loi au Droit au Logement Opposable
DC	Democrazia Cristiana
FAP	Fondation Abbé Pierre
FN	Front National
FHEDLES	Femmes et Hommes, Égalité, Droits et Libertés dans les Églises et la Société
FO	Force Ouvrière
GDP	Gross Domestic Product
IFOP	Institut Français d'Opinion Publique
INED	Institut National d'Études Démogra-phiques
INSEE	Institut National de la Statistique et des Études Économiques
LGBT	Lesbian, Gay, Bisexual, Transgender
LR	Les Républicains
LOC	Ligue Ouvrière Chrétienne
MPF	Mouvement Populaire des Familles
MRP	Mouvement Républicain Populaire
OECD	Organisation for Economic Cooperation and Development
PaCS	Pacte Civil de Solidarité
PCF	Parti Communiste Française
PS	Parti Socialiste
PSU	Parti Socialiste Unifié
RN	Rassemblement National
RPF	Rassemblement du Peuple Français
RPR	Rassemblement pour la République
SRU	Loi Relatif à la Solidarité et au Renouvellement Urbains
SNEC	Syndicat National de l'Enseignement Chrétien
UDF	Union pour la Démocratie Française
UMP	Union pour un Mouvement Populaire
UNAF	Union Nationale des Associations Familiales

BIBLIOGRAPHY

Archives

Montreuil

Archives Institute CGT d'Histoire Sociale
- Fonds Comité Confédéral National (1945-1999)
- Fonds des Congrès (1946-1982)

Paris

Archives CFDT
- Fonds Gaston Tessier
- Fonds Paul Vignaux
- Fonds Protection Sociale Travail Emploi (1950-...)
- Fonds Publications Confédérales (1919- [...])
- Fonds Secrétariat Confédéral (1874-1988)
- Fonds Secrétariat Général (1944-1953)

Archives Électorals du Cevipof
- Fonds Election Présidentielle des 23 avril et 7 mai 1995
- Fonds Election Présidentielle des 21 avril et 5 mai 2002 et Élections Législatives des 9 et 16 juin 2002

Archives d'Histoire Contemporaine – Centre d'Histoire de Sciences Po
- Fonds Mayer Daniel and Cletta
- Fonds Groupe Parlementaire Socialiste
- Fonds Mouvement Républicain Populaire
- Fonds Parodi Alexandre
- Fonds Savary Alain

Archives Nationales
- Fonds Assemblées Nationales
- Fonds Bureau de la Famille (Direction de l'Action Sociale)
- Fonds Charte du Travail 1940-1944
- Fonds du Comité d'Histoire de la Deuxième Guerre Mondiale et Fonds Privés Relatifs à la Période 1939-1945
- Fonds Dautry Raoul
- Fonds État Français (1940-1944)
- Fonds Laroque Pierre
- Fonds Ministère de l'Intérieur (Bureau des Cultes)
- Fonds Privés du Domaine des Grands Corps de l'État
- Fonds Service des Affaires Sociales (Commissariat Général du Plan)

Centre d'Archives Socialistes
- Fonds Actions et Déclarations du PS (1971-1985)
- Fonds Transcription de Débats de Congrès/Conventions Nationales du PS (1971-1981)
- Fonds Transcription des Débats des 'Journées Portes Ouvertes' (1972-1973)

Administrative Reports

Agence Nationale pour la Rénovation Urbaine, Comité d'Évaluation et de Suivi de l'Agence Nationale pour la Rénovation Urbaine, and Agence de Recherche et d'Ingénierie Statistique et Qualitative. *La gouvernance de la rénovation urbaine à l'épreuve des territoires.* Paris: La Documentation française, 2014.

Assemblée Nationale. *Rapport fait au nom de la Mission d'information sur la question du port des signes religieux à l'école.* Paris: Assemblée Nationale, 2003.

Auroux, Jean. *Les droits des travailleurs. Rapport au Président de la République et au Premier ministre.* Paris: la Documentation française, 1981.

Comité Central des Allocations Familiales. *Rapports présentés à l'assemblée générale.* Paris: Édition sociale française, 1943.

Comité Central des Allocations Familiales. *Statistiques 1945 concernant l'activité des caisses de compensation et services particuliers d'allocations familiales.* Paris: Édition sociale française, 1945.

Commissariat Général du Plan. *Commissariat général du plan d'équipement et de la productivité.* Paris: La Documentation française, 1966.

Conseil Économique et Social. *Le bilan et les perspectives d'évolution du logement en France.* Paris: Direction des journaux officiels, 1989.

Cour des Comptes. *Fondation Abbé Pierre pour le logement des défavorisés.* Paris: La Documentation française, 2006.

Direction de l'Habitat et de la Construction. *Loger les Personnes Défavorisées: Une Politique Publique sous le Regard des Chercheurs.* Paris: La Documentation française, 1995.

France. *6e Plan de développement économique et social, 1971-1975.* Paris: Imprimerie des journaux officiels, 1971.

Haut Comité pour le Logement des Personnes Défavorisées. *8e Rapport. Vers un droit au logement opposable*, 2002. < http://www.hclpd.gouv.fr/IMG/pdf/rap_08_cle1e5d6e.pdf>. (16 December 2021).

Haut Comité pour le Logement des Personnes Défavorisées. *12e Rapport. Droit au logement opposable. Le temps de la décision?*, 2006. <http://www.hclpd.gouv.fr/IMG/pdf/12e_rapport_cle612ff9.pdf>. (16 December 2021).

Haut Conseil à l'Égalité entre les Femmes et les Hommes. *Rapport relatif à l'accès à l'IVG. Volet 1: Information sur l'avortement sur internet*, 2013. < https://haut-conseil-egalite.gouv.fr/IMG/pdf/hce-rapport_ivg_et_internet_20130912_version_adoptee-3.pdf>. (18 December 2021).

Haut Conseil à l'Égalité entre les Femmes et les Hommes. *Rapport relatif à l'accès à l'IVG. Volet 2: Accès à l'IVG dans les territoires*, 2013. < https://www.haut-conseil-egalite.gouv.fr/IMG/pdf/rapport_ivg_volet2_v10.pdf>. (18 December 2021).

Haut Conseil de la Population et de la Famille. *Vie professionnelle et vie familiale, de nouveaux équilibres à construire*. Paris: La Documentation française 1987.

Ministère des Droits de la Femme. *Les Femmes en France dans une société d'inégalités: Rapport au ministre des droits de la femme*. Paris: La Documentation française, 1982.

Ministère du Travail et de la Participation. *Maternité et travail. Rapport remis à Robert Boulin, Ministre du Travail et de la Participation, et à Nicole Pasquier, Secrétaire d'État (emploi féminin)*. Paris: Ministère du Travail et de la Participation, 1979.

Ministère du Travail et de la Sécurité Sociale. *Rapport sur l'application de la legislation sur les assurances sociales*. Paris: Imprimerie des journaux officiels, 1947.

Ministère du Travail et de la Sécurité Sociale. *Rapport sur l'application de la legislation sur les assurances sociales*. Paris: Imprimerie des journaux officiels, 1949.

Ministère du Travail et de la Sécurité Sociale. *Rapport sur l'application de la legislation sur les assurances sociales*. Paris: Imprimerie des journaux officiels, 1950.

Observatoire National de l'Économie Sociale et Solidaire. *Atlas commenté de l'économie sociale et solidaire*. Paris: CNCRES, Juris éditions, 2014.

Published Sources

Assemblée Nationale. *Projet de loi relatif à la solidarité et au renouvellement urbains*, 2000. <http://www.assemblee-nationale.fr/11/projets/pl2131.asp>. (20 November 2020).

Boisard, Pierre. 'Sécurité sociale et solidarité'. *Syndicalisme CFTC*, September-October, 1974, 16.

Bornard, Jean. 'Special 41° Congrès. Le rapport sur l'emploi'. *Syndicalisme CFTC*, January 1982, 10-11.

Conseil National de la Résistance. *Le programme d'action de la Résistance*, 1944. <http://museedelaresistanceenligne.org/media2839-Programme-daction-du-CNR>. (20 November 2020).

Council of Europe. *Women's Sexual and Reproductive Health and Rights in Europe*, 2017. <https://rm.coe.int/women-s-sexual-and-reproductive-health-and-rights-in-europe-issue-pape/168076dead>. (18 December 2021).

Direction des Études de l'UMP. *Contre la précarité, permettre à chacun d'être propriétaire*, 2006. <http://www.u-m-p.org/sites/default/files/fichiers_joints>. (5 October 2014).

Doutreligne, Patrick. *Rôle de plaidoyer des fondations et capacité financière ou statutaire à alerter les pouvoirs et l'opinion publics*. <https://www.centre-francais-fondations.org/cercles-themes/themes-1/fondations-gestionnaires-detablissements/ressources/compte-rendu-des-reunions-du-cercle/fdeg-abbe-pierre-role-de-plaidoyer-des-fondations.pdf >. (10 November 2020).

FAP. *L'état du mal logement en France*. Paris: FAP, 2012.

FAP. *L'état du mal logement en France*. Paris: FAP, 2013.

FAP. *L'état du mal logement en France*. Paris: FAP, 2014.

FAP. *L'état du Mal Logement en France*. Paris: FAP, 2015.

FAP. *Loi SRU pour le logement social. Le palmarès 2011 des communes*, 2011. <https://www.fondation-abbe-pierre.fr/sites/default/files/content-files/files/loi_sru_-_le_palmares_2011_des_communes.pdf >. (12 October 2020).

FAP. *Rapport du Commissaire aux comptes sur les comptes annuels*, 2018. <https://www.fondation-abbe-pierre.fr/documents/pdf/rapport_cac_certifie_conforme.pdf>. (11 October 2021).

Gay, Francisque. *Les démocrates d'inspiration chrétienne à l'épreuve du pouvoir*. Paris: Bloud et Gay, 1951.

Hollande, François. *Le changement c'est maintenant. Mes 60 engagements pour la France*, 2012. < https://www.vie-publique.fr/discours/184662-programme-electoral-de-m-francois-hollande-depute-ps-et-candidat-le >. (11 November 2020).

Lecourt, Robert 'Notre laïcité'. *L'Aube*, 16 May 1945, 1.

Lucas, Laurent. 'Le comité pleins feux sur les ordonnances. La situation génerale'. *Syndicalisme CFDT*, 7 October 1967, 3.

Maires pour l'Enfance. *Qui sommes-nous?*, 2013. <http://www.mairespourlenfance.fr/qui-sommes-nous>. (29 November 2022).

Manif pour Tous. *La Manif Pour Tous s'inquiète de la nomination de Manuel Valls*, 2014. <https://www.france-catholique.fr/La-Manif-Pour-Tous-s-inquiete-de-la-nomination-de-Manuel-Valls-au-poste-de.html>. (28 November 2022).

Manif pour Tous. *La Charte des signataires*, 2014 <http://www.chartedesmunicipales.fr>. (10 January 2015).

Manif pour Tous. *Charte des maires et des candidats aux élections municipales de 2014*. <https://94.citoyens.com/wp-content/blogs.dir/2/files/2014/03/charte-Manif-pour-tous.pdf>. (8 January 2015).

Manif pour Tous. *Our ethics*, 2013. <https://old-v3.lamanifpourtous.fr/c10-qui-sommes-nous/charte-des-actions-la-manif-pour-tous-6/>. (20 November 2022).

Mitterrand, François. *110 propositions pour la France*.<https://www.mitterrand.org/110-propositions-pour-la-france.html>. (18 January 2021).

Montaron, Georges. 'Mort du parti catholique'. *Témoignage Chrétien*, 21 September 1967.

Pétain, Philippe. 'La politique sociale de l'avenir'. *Revue Des Deux Mondes*, 59 (1940) 2, 113-117.

Pétain, Philippe. 'Comme le géant de la fable, la France retrouvera ses forces en reprenant contact avec la terre', *Le Figaro*, 24 August 1940.

Pétain, Philippe. 'La Révolution Nationale vise à restuarer les disciplines collective, fécondité de la famille, sens de la patrie qualité du travail', *Le Figaro*, 19 January 1941, 1.

Parti Socialiste. *Logement: «Je m'engage devant la Fondation Abbé Pierre et surtout devant les Français»*, 2012. < https://parti-socialiste-dreux.fr/communiquesdepre/index.html>. (11 October 2021)

Popolo della Libertá. *Carta dei valori*, 2014. < http://www.pdl.it/notizie/15346/carta-dei-valori>. (12 April 2020).

Salleron, Louis. *La Charte paysanne*. Le Mans: CEP, 1943.

Tessier, Gaston. 'Le syndicalisme chrétien devant les récents événements'. *Droit Social*, 4 (1941) 1, 35-40.

Tessier, Gaston. 'Les syndicats et la Charte du Travail', *La Croix*, 23 Décembre 1941, 1.

UMP. *La charte des valeurs*, 2012. <http://www.u-m-p.org/sites/default/files/fichiers_joints/pages/2012-10-19_-_ump_-_congres_-_charte_0.pdf> (20 April 2015).

Vignaux, Paul. *Traditionalisme et syndicalisme. Essai d'histoire sociale (1884-1941)*. New York: Éditions de la Maison Française, 1943.

Villain, Jean. *La Charte du Travail et l'organisation économique et sociale de la profession*. Paris: Éditions Spes, 1942.

Yaggvideo. *Najat Vallaud-Belkacem (PS)/Meeting LGBT pour l'Egalité*, 2012. <https://www.youtube.com/watch?v=cIntiOONoXk>. (10 September 2020).

Zirnheld, Jules. *Syndicalisme chrétien et corporatisme fasciste. Discours prononcé à Bordeaux, le 16 Décembre 1933*. Paris, Confédération Française des Travailleurs Chrétiens, 1933.

Zirnheld, Jules. 'Le rapport moral'. *Le Syndicalisme Chrétien: Organe mensuel de la C.F.T.C.*, 119 (1934), Juin-Juillet, 924-928.

Catholic documents

AFC. 'La mere de famille de jeunes enfants. Problèmes posés – difficultés à résoudre'. *Tâches familiales*, 129 (1975) May, 18-24.

AFC de Melun et sa Region. *Letter by Christian Jacob*, 2017. <https://www.afc-melun.org/elections-l%C3%A9gislatives-2017/2nd-tour/7704-4%C3%A8me-circonscription-cantons-de-provins-nangis-bray-sur-seine-donnemarie-dontilly-villiers-saint-georges-la-fert%C3%A9-gaucher-rebais-et-rozay-en-brie/christian-jacob-lr>. (30 November 2022).

Assemblée Générale de la CNAFC 'Motion sur la Polique Familiale'. *Tâches familiales*, 140 (1978) January, 33.

Benedict XVI. 2008. Address of His Holiness Benedict XVI to the Participants in the 14th Session of the Pontifical Academy of Social Sciences, 3 May 2008. <https://www.vatican.va/content/benedict-xvi/en/speeches/2008/may/documents/hf_ben-xvi_spe_20080503_social-sciences.html>. (10 May 2022).

Benedict XVI. *Caritas in Veritate*, 29 June 2009. <http://w2.vatican.va/content/benedict-xvi/en/encyclicals/documents/hf_ben-xvi_enc_20090629_caritas-in-veritate.html>. (10 October 2012).

CNAFC. 'Annex au rapport d'orientation. Propositions des Associationes Familiales Catholiques pour une authetique politique familiale'. *Tâches familiales*, 174 (1985) June, 30-34.

Commission Sociale de l'Épiscopat Français. *La sécurité sociale et ses valeurs*. Paris: Centurion, 1980.

Commission Sociale de l'Épiscopat Français. *Réhabiliter la politique*. Paris: Centurion and Éditions du Cerf, 1999.

Conférence Épiscopale Française. *Proposer la foi dans la société actuelle. Lettre aux Catholiques de France*. Paris: la Procure Missionnaire de l'Assomption, 1997.

Conférence Épiscopale Française. *Entre épreuves et renouveaux la passion de l'Évangile. Indifférence religieuse, visibilité de l'Église et évangelisation*. Paris: Bayard; Paris: Éditions du Cerf, Paris: Fleurus-Mame, 2010.

Congregation for the Doctrine of the Faith. *Persona Humana. Declaration on Certain Questions concerning Sexual Ehics*, 29 December 1975. <http://www.vatican.va/roman_curia/congregations/cfaith/documents/rc_con_cfaith_doc_19751229_persona-humana_en.html>. (10 May 2021).

Congregation for the Doctrine of the Faith. *Donum Vitae. Instruction on the Respect for Human Life in Its Origin and on the Dignity of Procreation. Replies to Certain Questions of the Day*, 22 February 1987. <https://www.vatican.va/roman_curia/congregations/cfaith/documents/rc_con_cfaith_doc_19870222_respect-for-human-life_en.html>. (12 December 2020).

Conseil Famille et Société. *Elargir le mariage aux personnes de même sexe? Ouvrons le débat!*, 28 September 2012. <http://www.eglise.catholique.fr/conference-des-eveques-de-france/textes-et-declarations/366187-elargir-le-mariage-aux-personnes-de-meme-sexe-ouvrons-le-debat-note-du-conseil-famille-et-societe>. (20 November 2020).

Conseil Pontifical pour la Famille. *Lexique des termes ambigus et controversés sur la famille, la vie et les questions éthiques*. Paris: Pierre Téqui, 2005.

Conseil Pontifical pour la Famille. *Gender. La controverse*. Paris: Pierre Téqui, 2011.

Feltin, Maurice. *Les syndicats et la Charte du travail. Lettre pastorale de Monseigneur Maurice Feltin*. Paris: Éditions du Bureau de la Propagande Ouvrière, 1942.

Godin, Henri and Daniel, Yvan. *La France, pays de mission?* Paris: Éditions de l'Abeille, 1943.

John Paul II. *Laborem Exercens*, 14 September 1981. <http://www.vatican.va/content/john-paul-ii/en/encyclicals/documents/hf_jp-ii_enc_14091981_laborem-exercens.html>. (14 February 2021).

John Paul II. *Apostolic Exhortation Familiaris Consortio*, 22 November 1981. <http://www.vatican.va/content/john-paul-ii/en/apost_exhortations/documents/hf_jp-ii_exh_19811122_familiaris-consortio.html>. (15 February 2021).

John Paul II. *Centesimus Annus*, 1 May 1991. <http://www.vatican.va/content/john-paul-ii/en/encyclicals/documents/hf_jp-ii_enc_01051991_centesimus-annus.html>. (18 February 2021).

Jean Paul II. *Evangelium Vitae*, 25 March 1995. <http://www.vatican.va/content/john-paul-ii/en/encyclicals/documents/hf_jp-ii_enc_25031995_evangelium-vitae.html> (11 January 2021).

Leo XIII. *Rerum Novarum*, 15 May 1891. <http://www.vatican.va/content/leo-xiii/en/encyclicals/documents/hf_l-xiii_enc_15051891_rerum-novarum.html>. (25 February 2021).

Pius XI. *Casti Connubii*, 31 December 1930. <http://www.vatican.va/content/pius-xi/fr/encyclicals/documents/hf_p-xi_enc_19301231_casti-connubii.html>. (10 February 2021).

Pius XI. *Quadragesimo Anno*, 15 May 1931. <http://www.vatican.va/content/pius-xi/en/encyclicals/documents/hf_p-xi_enc_19310515_quadragesimo-anno.html>. (28 February 2021).

Pius XII. *Questa grande vostra adunata. Women's duties in social and political life. Address of His Holiness Pope Pius XII to members of various Catholic women's associations, 21 October 1945*. <http://catholictradition.org/Encyclicals/questa1.htm>. (10 December 2021).

Pontier, Georges. *Délit d'entrave numérique à l'IVG: Lettre de Mgr Pontier au Président Hollande*, 22 November 2016. <http://eglise.catholique.fr/conference-des-eveques-de-france/textes-et-declarations/430718-lettre-de-mgr-pontier-president-hollande>. (1 December 2021).

Pontier, Georges. *Assemblée Plénière de Printemps 2017: Discours d'ouverture par Mgr Georges Pontier*, 28 March 2017. <http://eglise.catholique.fr/conference-des-eveques-de-france/textes-et-declarations/437022-assemblee-pleniere-de-printemps-2017-discours-douverture-mgr-georges-pontier>. (20 December 2021).

Secrétariat de la Conférence des Évêques de France. Déclaration du Conseil permanent. 'Le Pacte Civil de Solidarité (PACS): 'Une Loi Inutile et Dangereuse'. *La Documentation Catholique*, 2189 (1998), 845-846.

Semaines Sociales de France. *L'organisation corporative. Sommaire des leçons de la 27e Session des Semaines Sociales de France.* Lyon: Chronique Sociale de France, 1938.

Semaines Sociales de France *32e Session, 1946. Transformations sociales et libération de la personne.* Lyon: Chronique Sociale de France, 1946.

Vignon, Jérôme. *Conclusions de la session 2012 des Semaines Sociales de France*, 25 November 2012. <https://www.ssf-fr.org/articles/41672-conclusion-de-la-session-2012>. (20 December 2021).

Vingt-Trois, André. *Homélie du Cardinal André Vingt-Trois lors de la messe pour les responsables politiques et les parlamentaires*, 30 October 2012. <https://www.paris.catholique.fr/Homelie-du-Cardinal-Andre-Vingt,25088.html>. (5 December 2021).

Vingt-Trois, André. *Discours d'ouverture de l'Assemblée plénière de novembre 2012*, 3 November 2012. <https://eglise.catholique.fr/conference-des-eveques-de-france/textes-et-declarations/366131-discours-douverture-de-lassemblee-pleniere-de-novembre-2012/>. (10 October 2021).

Vingt-Trois, André. *Discours d'ouverture de l'Assemblée plénière d'avril 2013*, 16 April 2013.

<http://www.eglise.catholique.fr/conference-des-eveques-de-france/textes-et-declarations/365871-discours-douverture-de-lassemblee-pleniere-davril-2013/>. (18 October 2021).

Data Sources

ACPM. *Classements de presse payante.* <https://www.acpm.fr/ >. (20 November 2020).

CNAF. *Statistiques concernant l'action sociale.* Paris: CNAF, 1973.

CNAF. *Prestations familiales 2011. Statistiques nationales.* Paris: CNAF, 2013.

Comité Central des Allocations Familiales. *Statistiques concernant l'activité des caisses de compensation et services particuliers d'allocations familiales en 1943.* Paris: Édition Sociale Française, 1944.

Comité Central des Allocations Familiales. *Statistiques.* Paris: Édition Sociale Française, 1945.

Comité National Diaconat. *Statistiques sur la population des diacres permanents.* <https://diaconat.catholique.fr/le-diaconat-en-france/les-activites-du-cnd/statistiques-diaconat/statistiques-population-diacres-permanents/>. (20 October 2021).

Conférence des Évêques de France. *Guide 2013 de l'Eglise Catholique en France.* Paris: Bayard; Paris: Éditions du Cerf; Paris: Fleurus-Mame, 2013.

Conférence des Évêques de France. *Guide 2018 de l'Eglise Catholique en France.* Paris: Éditions du Cerf; Paris: Fleurus-Mame; Montrouge: Bayard, 2017.

Direction de la Statistique Générale. *Annuaire statistique abrégé.* Paris: Imprimerie Nationale, 1949.

Église Catholique en France. *Statistiques de l'Église Catholique en France.* <https://eglise.catholique.fr/guide-eglise-catholique-france/statistiques-de-leglise-catholique-france-monde/statistiques-de-leglise-catholique-france/ministres-ordonnes-religieux/>. (12 November 2019).

Enseignement Catholique. *Les chiffres clés de l'enseignement catholique, 2012-2013. Enseignement catholique actualités*, February-March, 2012.

Enseignement Catholique. *Les chiffres clés de l'enseignement catholique, 2013-2014. Enseignement catholique actualités*, February-March, 2013.

Enseignement Catholique. *Les chiffres clés de l'enseignement catholique, 2014-2015.* <https://enseignement-catholique.fr/wp-content/uploads/2018/01/dossier-eca-365.pdf>. (9 December 2021).

Enseignement Catholique. *Les chiffres clés de l'enseignement catholique, 2015-2016.* <https://enseignement-catholique.fr/wp-content/uploads/2018/01/dossier-eca-371.pdf>. (10 December 2021).

Enseignement Catholique. *Les chiffres clés de l'enseignement catholique, 2016-2017.* <https://enseignement-catholique.fr/wp-content/uploads/2018/01/dossier-eca-377.pdf>. (2 December 2021).

Enseignement Catholique. *Les chiffres clés de l'enseignement catholique, 2017-2018.* <https://enseignement-catholique.fr/wp-content/uploads/2018/01/dossier-eca-383.pdf>. (12 December 2021).

Enseignement Catholique. *Les chiffres clés de l'enseignement catholique, 2018-2019*. <https://enseignement-catholique.fr/wp-content/uploads/2019/03/chiffres_cles_2018_2019.pdf> (10 December 2021).

IFOP. *Les Français et les droits des couples homosexuels. Résultats détaillés janvier 2013*. <https://www.ifop.com/wp-content/uploads/2018/03/2127-1-study_file.pdf>. (2 March 2022).

IFOP. *Les Français et le mariage homosexuel. Résultats détaillés janvier 2013*. <https://www.ifop.com/wp-content/uploads/2018/03/2106-1-study_file.pdf>. (2 March 2022).

IFOP. *La position souhaitée de l'Église Catholique sur différents sujets. Résultats détaillés mars 2013*. <https://www.ifop.com/wp-content/uploads/2018/03/2177-1-study_file.pdf>. (20 December 2021).

IFOP. *Les Français et l'interruption volontaire de grossesse. Résultats détaillés 10 février 2014*. <https://www.ifop.com/wp-content/uploads/2018/03/2502-1-study_file.pdf> (12 January 2022).

IFOP. *Le vote des sympathisants de droite catholiques à la primaire de la droite et du centre. Novembre 2016*. <https://www.ifop.com/wp-content/uploads/2018/03/3568-1-study_file.pdf>. (8 January 2021).

IFOP. *Le vote des électorats confessionnels au 1er tour de l'élection présidentielle 23 avril 2017*. <https://www.ifop.com/wp-content/uploads/2018/03/3750-1-study_file.pdf>. (16 June 2021).

INSEE. *Enquête annuelle emploi*. Paris: INSEE, 1982.

INSEE. 'La Population active' in: INSEE, ed. *Données sociales*, Paris: INSEE, 26-32.

INSEE. *Trente ans de vie économique et sociale*. Paris: INSEE, 2014.

INSEE. *Convertisseur franc-euro*. < https://www.insee.fr/fr/information/2417794>. (18 January 2019).

INSEE. *Les indices et séries chronologiques*. <https://www.insee.fr/fr/information/2411675>. (18 January 2019).

INSEE. *Population*. <https://www.insee.fr/fr/information/2008354>. (18 March 2020).

INSEE. *Les conditions de logement en 2006*. <https://www.insee.fr/fr/statistiques/1912096>. (15 June 2020).

Ministère de l'Éducation Nationale, de l'Enseignement Supérieur, de la Recherche et de l'Innovation. *Les établissements d'enseignement supérieur privés*. <https://www.enseignement-sup-recherche.gouv.fr/cid49085/les-etablissements-d-enseignement-superieur-prives.html>. (16 December 2020).

Ministère de l'Intérieur, 2014. *Résultats des élections municipales 2014*. <http://www.interieur.gouv.fr/Elections/Les-resultats/Municipales/elecresult__MN2014/(path)/MN2014/index.html>. (20 January 2021).

OECD. *Social Expenditure: Detailed Data. OECD Social and Welfare Statistics* (database). <https://doi.org/10.1787/data-00167-en>. (14 March 2020).

Literature

Adam, Gérard. *La CFTC: 1940-1958. Histoire politique et idéologique*. Paris: Colin, 1964.

Adam, Gérard. 'De la C.F.T.C. à la C.F.D.T.'. *Revue française de science politique*, 15 (1965) 1, 87-103.

Afsa, Cédric and Buffeteau, Sophie. 'L'activité féminine en France: Quelles évolutions récentes, quelles tendances pour l'avenir?'. *Economie et statistique*, 398-399 (2006), 85-97.

Alber, Jens. *Vom Armenhaus sum wohlfahrtsstaat. Analysen zur entwicklung der sozialversicherung in Westeuropa*. Frankfurt: Campus Verlag, 1982.

Alber, Jens. 'A framework for the comparative study of social services'. *Journal of European Social Policy*, 5 (1995) 2, 131-149.

Aldridge, Alan E. *Religion in the Contemporary World. A Sociological Introduction*. Cambridge: Polity Press, 2013.

Almond, Gabriel A. 'The political ideas of Christian democracy'. *Journal of Politics*, 10 (1948) 4, 734-763.

Ambler, John S., 'Ideas, Interests and the French Welfare State' in: John S. Ambler, ed. *The French Welfare State. Surviving Social and Ideological Change*. New York: New York University Press, 1991, 1-31.

Amenta, Edwin. *When Movements Matter. The Townsend Plan and the Rise of Social Security*. Princeton: Princeton University Press, 2006.

Archambault, Edith. *The Nonprofit Sector in France*. Manchester: Manchester University Press, 1997.

Archambault, Edith. 'Les institutions sans but lucratif hier et aujourd'hui: Comparaison France-États-Unis'. *The Tocqueville review/La revue Tocqueville*, XXXII (2011) 2, 81-98.

Archambault, Edith. 'France: A late-comer to government–nonprofit partnership'. *Voluntas*, 26 (2015) 6, 2283-2310.

Armingeon, Klaus; Guthmann, Kai and Weisstanner, David. 'Choosing the path of austerity: How parties and policy coalitions influence welfare state retrenchment in periods of fiscal consolidation'. *West European Politics*, 39 (2016) 4, 628-647.

Atkin, Nicholas. *The French at War, 1934-1944*. Harlow: Longman, 2001.

Atkin, Nicholas and Tallett, Frank. *Priests, Prelates and People. A History of European Catholicism since 1750*. London: Tauris, 2003.

Audard, Catherine. *Qu'est-ce que le libéralisme? Éthique, politique, société*. Paris: Gallimard, 2009.

Azéma, Jean-Pierre and Wieviorka, Olivier. *Vichy, 1940-1944*. Paris: Perrin, 2004.

Bäckström, Anders and Davie, Grace. 'A Preliminary Conclusion. Gathering the Threads and Moving On' in: Anders Bäckström et al., eds. *Welfare and Religion in 21st Century Europe. Volume 1, Reconfiguring the Connections*. Farnham: Ashgate, 2010, 183-197.

Bäckström, Anders et al. eds. *Welfare and Religion in 21st Century Europe. Volume 1, Reconfiguring the Connections*. Farnham: Ashgate, 2010.

Balchin, Paul N. and Rhoden, Maureen. *Housing Policy. An Introduction*. London: Routledge, 2002.

Baldwin, Peter. *The Politics of Social Solidarity. Class Bases of the European Welfare State, 1875-1975*. Cambridge: Cambridge University Press, 1990.

Bardy, Gérard. *Charles le catholique. De Gaulle et l'Eglise*. Paris: Plon, 2011.

Barjot, Alain, ed. *La sécurite sociale, son histoire a travers les textes. Tome III, 1945-1981*. Paris: Association pour l'étude de l'histoire de la sécurité sociale, 1997.

Barjot, Frigide. *Confessions d'une catho branchée*. Paris: Plon, 2011.

Barjot, Frigide. *Touche pas à mon sexe! Contre le mariage gay*. Paris: Mordicus, 2012.

Barthélémy, Amandine, Keller, Sophie and Slitine, Romain. *Stratégie et financement des entreprises sociales et solidaires. Le grand livre*. Paris: Rue de l'Échiquier, 2014.

Barthélémy, Martine. *Associations. Un nouvel âge de la participation?* Paris: Presses de Sciences Po, 2000.

Baruch, Marc-Olivier. *Le régime de Vichy, 1940-1944*. Paris: Tallandier, 2017.

Baubérot, Jean. 'La laïcité française et ses mutations'. *Social Compass*, 45 (1998) 1, 175-187.

Baubérot, Jean. *Histoire de la laïcité en France*. Paris: Presses universitaires de France, 2013.

Baubérot, Jean. *La laïcité falsifiée*. Paris: La Découverte, 2014.

Baubérot, Jean. *Les sept laïcités françaises*. Paris: Éditions de la Maison des sciences de l'homme, 2015.

Baum, Gregory. *The Priority of Labor. A Commentary on Laborem Excercens, Encyclical Letter of Pope John Paul II*. New York: Paulist Press, 1982.

Beaumont, Justin and Dias, Candice. 'Faith-based organisations and urban social justice in the Netherlands'. *Tijdschrift voor economische en sociale geografie*, 99 (2008) 4, 382-392.

Bec, Colette. *La sécurité sociale. Une institution de la démocratie*. Paris: Gallimard, 2014.

Beck, Ulrich. *Der eigene gott: Von der friedensfähigkeit und dem gewaltpotential der religionen*. Frankfurt am Main: Verlag der Weltreligionen, 2008.

Becker, Howard S. 'Whose side are we on?' *Social Problems*, 14 (1967) 3, 239-247.

Béland, Daniel and Cox, Robert H., eds. *Ideas and Politics in Social Science Research*. Oxford: Oxford University Press, 2010.

Bell, David S. *Parties and Democracy in France. Parties under Presidentialism*. Aldershot: Ashgate, 2000.

Bellin, Eva. 'Faith in politics. New trends in the study of religion and politics'. *World Politics*, 60 (2008) 2, 315-347.

Béraud, Céline; Gugelot, Frédéric and Saint-Martin, Isabelle, eds. *Catholicisme en tensions*. Paris: Éditions de l'École des hautes études en sciences sociales, 2012.

Béraud, Céline. 'Un front commun des religions contre le mariage pour tous?' *Contemporary French Civilization*, 39 (2014) 3, 335-349.

Béraud, Céline. *Prêtres, diacres, laïcs. Révolution silencieuse dans le Catholicisme Français*. Paris: Presses universitaire de France, 2015.

Béraud, Céline and Portier, Philippe. *Métamorphoses catholiques. Acteurs, enjeux et mobilisations depuis le mariage pour tous*. Paris: Éditions de la Maison des sciences de l'homme, 2015.

Béraud, Céline and Portier, Philippe. '"Marriage pour tous. The Same-Sex Marriage Controversy in France"' in: Karel Dobbelaere and Alfonso Pérez-Agote, eds. *The Intimate. Polity and the Catholic Church. Laws about Life, Death and the Family in So-called Catholic Countries*. Leuven: Leuven University Press, 2015, 55-91.

Berger, Peter L. *The Sacred Canopy. Elements of a Sociological Theory of Religion*. London: Anchor Books, 1967.
Berger, Peter L. 'The Desecularization of the World: A Global Overview' in: Peter L. Berger, ed. *The Desecularization of the World. Resurgent Religion and World Politics*. Grand Rapids: William B. Eerdmans Publishing Company, 1999, 1-18.
Berger, Peter L. and Luckmann, Thomas. *The Social Construction of Reality. A Treatise in the Sociology of Knowledge*. Harmondsworth: Penguin, 1966.
Berger, Suzanne. 'Religious Transformations and the Future of Politics' in: Charles S. Maier, ed. *Changing Boundaries of the Political. Essays on the Evolving Boundaries Between the State and Society, Public and Private in Europe*. Cambridge: Cambridge University Press, 1994, 107-149.
Bergounioux, Alain. *Les socialistes*. Paris: Le cavalier bleu, 2009.
Berstein, Serge. 'Le programme présidentiel: Les 110 prepositions', in: Serge Berstein, Pierre Milza and Jean-Louis Bianco, eds. *Les années Mitterrand. Les années du changement*. Paris: Perrin, 2001, 77-90.
Berstein, Serge and Milza, Pierre. *Histoire de la France au XXe siècle. Vol. III, 1958 à nos jours*. Paris: Perrin, 2009.
Berstein, Serge and Winock, Michel, eds. *Fascisme français? La controverse*. Paris: CNRS éditions, 2014.
Berzano, Luigi. 'Research methodology between descriptive and hermeneutic interests'. *Annual Review of the Sociology of Religion*, 3 (2012) 1, 69-89.
Bethmont, Rémy and Gross, Martine, eds. *Homosexualité et traditions monothéistes. Vers la fin d'un antagonisme?* Genève: Labor et Fides, 2017.
Béthouart, Bruno. 'Le ministère du travail et de la sécurité sociale. Un monopole du M.R.P. de 1950 à 1962'. *Revue d'histoire moderne et contemporaine*, 43 (1996) 1, 67-105.
Béthouart, Bruno. 'Entry of the Catholics into the Republic: The Mouvement Républicain Populaire in France' in: Michael Gehler and Wolfran Kaiser, eds. *Christian Democracy in Europe since 1945*. London: Routledge, 2004, 74-87.
Béthouart, Bruno and Steck, Philippe. *Prestations familales. Une histoire française. Cahier d'histoire de la sécurité sociale n° 6*. Paris: Comité d'histoire de la sécurité sociale, 2012.
Beveridge, William H. *Social Insurance and Allied Services*. Report by Sir William Beveridge. London: HMSO, 1942.
Beyers, Jan; Eising, Rainer and Maloney, William. 'Researching interest group politics in Europe and elsewhere: Much we study, little we know?'. *West European Politics*, 31 (2008) 6, 1103-1128.
Bichot, Jacques. *Les politiques sociales en France au XXe siècle*. Paris: Colin, 1997.
Bigot, Régin and Hoibian, Sandra. 'Les Difficultés des français face au logement'. *Crédoc cahier de recherche*, 265 (2009) décembre. <http://www.credoc.fr/pdf/Rech/C265.pdf>. (10 November 2015).
Bobbio, Norberto. *Left and Right. The Significance of a Political Distinction*. Cambridge: Polity Press, 1996.
Bolzonar Fabio. 'A christian democratization of Italian politics. The new influence of Catholicism on Italian politics since the demise of the Democrazia Cristiana'. *Journal of Modern Italian Studies*, 21 (2016), 3, 445–463.
Bolzonar, Fabio. 'Dealing with a difficult past: Historical memories of the Vichy regime and fascism in the ideology of the Rassemblement National and the Lega'. *Journal of Contemporary European Studies*, 31 (2023) 2, 363-373.
Bolzonar, Fabio. 'Conservative Catholicism versus social Catholicism? Contrasting patterns in the political engagement of highly religious young Catholics in France and Italy'. *Sociology Compass*, 2023.
Bonhoeffer, Dietrich. *Widerstand und ergebung. Briefe und aufzeichnungen aus der haft*. Gütersloh: Kaiser, 1998.
Boninchi, Marc. *Vichy et l'ordre moral*. Paris: Presses universitaires de France, 2005.
Bonoli, Giuliano and Natali, David, eds. *The Politics of the New Welfare State*. Oxford, 2012.
Bordeaux, Michèle. *La victoire de la famille dans la France défaite. Vichy, 1940-1944*. Paris: Flammarion, 2002.
Boswell, Jonathan S.; McHugh, Francis P. and Verstraeten, Johan, eds. *Catholic Social Thought: Twilight or Renaissance?* Leuven: Leuven University Press, 2000.
Boudon, Raymond. 'Situation de la démocratie française'. *Commentaire*, 131 (2010) 3, 589-598.
Bourdieu, Pierre and de Saint Martin, Monique. 'La sainte famille. L'épiscopat français dans le champ du pouvoir'. *Actes de la recherche en sciences sociales*, 44-45 (1982) novembre, 2-53.
Boussard, Isabel. *Vichy & la Corporation paysanne*. Paris: Presses de la Fondation nationale des sciences politiques, 1980.

Branciard, Michel. *Syndicats et partis. Autonomie ou dépendance. Tome 1, 1879-1947*. Paris: Syros, 1982.

Braudel, Fernand. 'Histoire et sciences sociales: La longue durée'. *Réseaux*, 5 (1987) 27, 7-37.

Bréchon, Pierre. 'Religious Voting in a Secular France' in: David Broughton and Hans-Martien Ten Napel, eds. *Religion and Mass Electoral Behaviour in Europe*. London: Routledge, 2000, 97-117.

Bréchon, Pierre. *La France aux urnes. Soixante ans d'histoire électorale*. Paris: La Documentation française, 2009.

Bréchon, Pierre. 'La religion, le facteur le plus explicatif du vote!', *Le Figaro*, 07 May 2012.

Bréchon, Pierre. *Comment expliquer les opinions sur l'homosexualité?*, 2014. <https://halshs.archives-ouvertes.fr/halshs-01066140/document>. (10 December 2021).

Bréchon, Pierre, Duriez, Bruno and Ion, Jacques, eds. *Religion et action dans l'espace public*. Paris: L'Harmattan, 2000.

Brooke, Stephen. *Sexual Politics. Sexuality, Family Planning and the British Left from the 1880s to the Present Day*. Oxford: Oxford University Press, 2011.

Buisson-Fenet, Hélène. *Un sexe problématique. L'Église et l'homosexualité masculine en France (1971-2000)*. Paris: Presses de l'Université de Vincennes, 2004.

Bruce, Steve. *God is Dead. Secularization in the West*. Oxford: Blackwell, 2002.

Bruce, Steve. *Secularization. In Defence of an Unfashionable Theory*. Oxford: Oxford University Press, 2011.

Bruce, Steve. 'Secularization and its Consequences' in: Phil Zuckerman and John R. Shook, eds. *The Oxford Handbook of Secularism*. Oxford: Oxford University Press, 2017, 55-70.

Bruce, Steve. *Researching Religion. Why We Need Social Science*. Oxford: Oxford University Press, 2018.

Brustier, Gaël. *Le mai 68 conservateur. Que restera-t-il de la Manif pour tous?* Paris: Éditions du Cerf, 2014.

Cabanel, Patrick. *Les mots de la laïcité*. Toulouse: Presses universitaires du Mirail, 2004.

Cabanel, Patrick. *Entre religion and laïcité. La voie française*. Paris: Privat, 2007.

Cabanel, Patrick. *Le Protestantisme français. La belle histoire XVIe-XXIe siècle*. Nîmes: Alcide, 2017.

Cahill, Lisa S. 'Catholic Social Teaching' in: Craig Hovey and Elizabeth Phillips, eds. *The Cambridge Companion to Christian Political Theology*. Cambridge: Cambridge University Press, 2015, 67-87.

Camp, Richard L. *The Papal Ideology of Social Reform*. Leiden: Brill, 1969.

Capuano, Christophe. *Vichy et la famille. Réalités et faux-semblants d'une politique publique*. Rennes: Presses universitaires de Rennes, 2009.

Carbonnier, Jean. 'La religion, fondement du droit?'. *Droit et religion*, 38 (1993) 1, 17-21.

Casanova, José. *Public Religions in the Modern World*. Chicago: University of Chicago Press, 1994.

Castel, Robert. *La montée des incertitudes. Travail, protections, statut de l'individu*. Paris: Seuil, 2013.

Castles, Francis G. *The Social Democratic Image of Society. A Study of the Achievements and Origins of Scandinavian Social Democracy in Comparative Perspective*. London: Routledge and Kegan Paul, 1978.

Castles, Francis G. *The Future of the Welfare State. Crisis Myths and Crisis Realities*. Oxford: Oxford University Press, 2004.

Castles, Francis G. 'On religion and public policy: Does Catholicism make a difference?'. *European Journal of Political Research*, 25 (1994) 1, 19-40.

Ceccaldi, Dominique. *Histoire des prestations familiales en France*. Paris: Comité d'histoire de la sécurité sociale and Association pour l'étude de l'histoire de la Sécurité sociale, 2005.

Chamberlayne Prue; Cooper, Andrew; Freeman, Richard and Rustin Michael, eds. *Welfare and Culture in Europe. Towards a New Paradigm in Social Policy*. London: Jessica Kingsley 1999.

Chaves Mark. 'Secularization as declining religious authority'. *Social Forces*, 72 (1994) 3, 749-774.

Chesnais, Jean-Claude. 'La politique de la population française depuis 1914' in: Jacques Dupâquier, ed. *Histoire de la population française, Vol. 4. De 1914 à nos jours*. Paris: Presses universitaire de France, 1995, 181-231.

Chevandier, Christian. *L'hôpital dans la France du XXe siècle*. Paris: Perrin, 2009.

Cipriani, Roberto. *Diffused Religion. Beyond Secularization*. Cham: Palgrave Macmillan, 2017.

Clément, Jean-Louis. *Les évêques au temps de Vichy. Loyalisme sans inféodation. Les relations entre l'Église et l'état de 1940 à 1944*. Paris: Beauchesne, 1999.

Clément Jean-Louis. *La collaboration des évêques: 1920-1945*. Paris: Les indes savantes, 2011.

Clément, Jean-Louis. 'The birth of a myth: Maurras and the Vichy Regime'. *French History*, 17 (2003) 4, 440-454.

Clément, Jean-Louis. 'La hiérarchie catholique et les principes de la révolution nationale'. *Guerres mondiales et conflits contemporains*, 218 (2005) 2, 27-36.

Cointet, Michèle. *Le Conseil national de Vichy. Vie politique et réforme de l'État en régime autoritaire, 1940-1944*. Paris: Aux amateurs de livres, 1989.

Cointet, Michèle. *Vichy et le fascisme. Les hommes, les structures et les pouvoirs*. Bruxelles: Éditions complexe, 1991.

Cointet, Michèle. *L'Église sous Vichy: 1940-1945. La repentance en question*. Paris: Perrin, 1998.

Cointet, Michèle. *Nouvelle histoire de Vichy*. Paris: Fayard, 2011.

Conway, John S. *The Nazi Persecution of the Churches, 1933-1945*. New York: Basic Books, 1968.

Conway, Martin. *Catholic Politics in Europe, 1918-1945*. London: Routledge, 1997.

Cox, James L. *A Guide to the Phenomenology of Religion. Key Figures, Formative Influences and Subsequent Debates*. London: T. & T. International, 2006.

Cunningham, Ian and James, Philip, eds. *Voluntary Organizations and Public Service Delivery*. London: Routledge, 2011.

Cunningham, Lawrence S. *An Introduction to Catholicism*. Cambridge: Cambridge University Press, 2009.

Curran, Charles C. *Catholic Social Teaching and Pope Benedict XVI*. Washington: Georgetown University Press, 2014.

Curtis, Michael. *Three Against the Third Republic. Sorel, Barres and Maurras*. Westport: Greenwood Press, 1976.

Damamme, Dominique and Jobert, Bruno. 'Les paritarismes contre la démocratie sociale'. *Pouvoirs*, 94 (2000), Septembre, 87-102.

Dansette, Adrien. *Destin du Catholicisme français: 1926-1956*. Paris: Flammarion, 1957.

Dard, Olivier. 'Le corporatisme en France à l'époque contemporaine: Tentative de bilan historiographique et perspectives de recherches'. *Histoire, économie & société*, 35 (2016) 1, 45-57.

Dargent Claude, 'Les catholiques français et le Front national'. *Études*, 12 (2016), 19-30.

Dargent, Claude. 'Recul du Catholicisme, croissance des non-affiliés et des minorités religieuses' in: Pierre Bréchon, Frédéric Gonthier and Sandrine Astor, eds. *La France des valeurs. Quarante ans d'évolution*. Fontaine: Presses universitaires de Grenoble, 2019, 223-227.

Dargent Claude, 'Et Dieu dans tout ça?' in: Pierre Bréchon, Frédéric Gonthier and Sandrine Astor, eds. *La France des valeurs. quarante ans d'évolution*. Fontaine: Presses universitaires de Grenoble, 2019, 242-246.

Dargent, Claude. 'Assistance aux offices et prière' in: Pierre Bréchon, Frédéric Gonthier and Sandrine Astor, eds. *La France des valeurs. Quarante ans d'évolution*. Fontaine: Presses universitaires de Grenoble, 2019, 228-233.

Davie, Grace. *Religion in Britain since 1945. Believing without Belonging*. Oxford: Blackwell, 1994.

Davie, Grace. *The Sociology of Religion. A Critical Agenda*. London: SAGE, 2013.

Day, Abby. 'Propositions and performativity: Relocating belief to the social'. *Culture and Religion*, 11 (2010) 1, 9-30.

Deacon, Valerie. *The Extreme Right in the French Resistance. Members of the Cagoule and Corvignolles in the Second World War*. Baton Rouge: Louisiana State University Press, 2016.

De Felice, Renzo. *Mussolini il fascista. L'organizzazione dello stato fascista 1925-1929*. Einaudi: Torino, 2006.

De Gaulle, Charles. *Discours et messages, 1. Pendant la guerre, juin 1940-janvier 1946*. Paris: Plon, 1970.

Delbreil, Jean-Claude. 'The French Catholic Left and the Political Parties' in: Gerd-Rainer Horn and Emmanuel Gerard, eds. *Left Catholicism. Catholics and Society in Western Europe at the Point of Liberation, 1943-1955*. KADOC Studies 25. Leuven: Leuven University Press, 2001, 45-63.

Della Porta, Donatella and Diani, Mario. *Social Movements. An Introduction*. Oxford: Blackwell, 2006.

Descamps, Eugène. 'La CFTC-CFDT et la politique sociale du général de Gaulle et de ses gouvernments 1958-1968' in: Institut Charles de Gaulle, ed. *Approches de la philosophie politique du général de Gaulle à partir de sa pensée et de son action*. Paris: Cujas, 1983, 165-189.

Desmard, Laurent, Étienne, Raymond and Delahaye, Thierry, eds. *L'Abbé Pierre. Fondateur et rebelle*. Paris: Desclée de Brouwer, 2012.

De Singly, François. *Sociologie de la famille contemporaine*. Paris: Colin, 2017.

Diamanti, Ilvo and Ceccarini, Luigi. 'Catholics and politics after the Christian Democrats: The influential minority'. *Journal of Modern Italian Studies*, 12 (2007) 1, 37-59.

Dobbelaere, Karel. 'Towards an integrated perspective of the processes related to the descriptive concept of secularization'. *Sociology of Religion*, 60 (1999) 3, 229-247.

Dobbelaere, Karel. *Secularization. An Analysis at Three Levels*. Brussels: PIE-Peter Lang, 2002.

Dobbelaere, Karel. 'The Meaning and Scope of Secularization' in: Peter B. Clarke, ed. *The Oxford Handbook of the Sociology of Religion*. Oxford: Oxford University Press, 2009, 599-615.

Dobbelaere, Karel and Pérez Agote, Alfonso, eds. *The Intimate. Polity and the Catholic Church. Laws about Life, Death and the Family in So-called Catholic Countries*. Leuven: Leuven University Press, 2015.

Dobbelaere, Karel; Pérez Agote, Alfonso and Béraud, Céline. 'Comparative Synthesis' in Karel Dobbelaere and Alfonso Pérez-Agote, eds. *The Intimate. Polity and the Catholic Church. Laws about Life, Death and the Family in So-called Catholic Countries*. Leuven: Leuven University Press, 2015, 199-221.

Dobry, Michel, ed. *Le mythe de l'allergie française au fascisme*. Paris: Albin Michel, 2003.

Domenach, Jean-Marie. *Emmanuel Mounier*. Paris: Seuil, 2014.

Donegani, Jean-Marie. *La liberté de choisir. Pluralisme religieux et pluralisme politique dans le Catholicisme français contemporain*. Paris: Presses de la Fondation nationale des sciences politiques, 1993.

Dorr, Donal. *Option for the Poor. A Hundred Years of Vatican Social Teaching*. Dublin: Gill and Macmillan, 1992.

Driant, Jean-Claude. *Les politiques du logement en France*. Paris: La documentation française, 2009.

Dreyfus, François-Georges. *Histoire de la démocratie chrétienne en France*. Paris: Albin Michel, 1988.

Dreyfus, Michel et al. *Se protéger, être protégé. Une histoire des assurances sociales en France*. Rennes: Presses universitaires de Rennes, 2006.

Dupâquier, Jacques, ed. *Histoire de la population française 4. De 1914 à Nos Jours*. Paris: Presses universitaire de France, 1995.

Duquesne, Jacques. *Les Catholiques français sous l'Occupation*. Paris: Seuil, 1996.

Duthoit, Eugène M. 'Preface' in: Jules Lamoot. *La Charte du travail et la doctrine sociale de l'Église* Lille: S.I.L.I.C, 1943, 1-3.

Durand, Jean-Dominique. *L'Europe de la Démocratie chrétienne*. Bruxelles: Éditions complexe, 1995.

Duriez, Bruno. 'Left Wing Catholicism in France. From Catholic Action to the Political Left: The Mouvement Populaire des Familles' in: Gerd-Rainer Horn and Emmanuel Gerard, eds. *Left Catholicism, 1943-1955. Catholics and Society in Western Europe at the Point of Liberation*. KADOC Studies 25, Leuven: Leuven University Press, 2001, 64-90.

Duriez, Bruno et al. eds. *Les Catholiques dans la République, 1905-2005*. Paris, 2005.

Duroselle, Jean-Baptiste. *Les débuts du catholicisme social en France: 1822-1870*. Paris: Presses universitaires de France, 1951.

Duroselle, Jean-Baptiste and Mayeur, Jean-Marie. *Histoire du Catholicisme*. Paris: Presses universitaires de France, 1993.

Effosse, Sabine. *L'invention du logement aidé en France. L'immobilier au temps des trente glorieuses*. Paris: Comité pour L'histoire économique et financière de la France, 2003.

Elgie, Robert. 'France: Stacking the Deck' in: Michael Gallagher and Paul Mitchell, eds. *The Politics of Electoral Systems*. Oxford: Oxford University Press, 2005, 119-136.

Engeli, Isabelle; Green-Pedersen, Christoffer and Thorup Larsen, Lars, eds. *Morality Politics in Western Europe. Parties, Agendas and Policy Choices*. Basingstoke: Palgrave Macmillan 2012.

Esping-Andersen, Gøsta. *Politics Against Markets. The Social Democratic Road to Power*. Princeton: Princeton University Press, 1985.

Esping-Andersen, Gøsta. *The Three Worlds of Welfare Capitalism*. Cambridge: Polity Press, 1990.

Esping-Andersen, Gøsta. 'Welfare State without Work: The Impasse of Labour Shedding and Familialism in Continental European Social Policy' in: Gøsta Esping-Andersen, ed. *Welfare State in Transition. National Adaptations in Global Economies*. United Nations Research Institute for Social Development. London: SAGE, 1996, 66-87.

Esping-Andersen, Gøsta and Korpi, Walter. 'From poor relief to institutional welfare states: The development of Scandinavian social policy'. *International Journal of Sociology*, 16 (1986) 3-4, 39-74.

Essafi, Cédric A. and Buffeteau, Sophie. 'L'activité féminine en France: Quelles évolutions récentes, quelles tendances pour l'avenir?' *Économie et statistique*, (2006) 398-399, 85-97.

Fagnani, Jeanne. 'Continuities and Changes. Tensions and Ambiguities. Childcare and Preschool Policies in France' in: Karen Hagemann, Konrad H. Jarausch and Cristina, Allemann-Ghionda, eds. *Children, Families, and States. Time Policies of Childcare, Preschool, and Primary Education in Europe*. Oxford: Berghahn Books, 2011, 175-195.

Fahey, Tony and Norris, Michelle. 'Housing' in: Francis, G. Castles et al. eds. *The Oxford Handbook of the Welfare State*. Oxford: Oxford University Press, 2010, 479-493.

Fassin, Éric. *L'inversion de la question homosexuelle*. Paris: Éditions Amsterdam, 2008.

Ferhat, Ismail. 'Un chemin de Damas? Le Parti socialiste et les Chrétiens dans les années 1970'. *Chrétiens et sociétés*, 18 (2012), 165-184.

Ferrarotti, Franco. *La religione dissacrante. Coscienza e utopia nell'epoca della crisi*. Bologna: Edizioni Dehoniane, 2013.

Ferrera, Maurizio. *Le politiche sociali. L'Italia in prosettiva comparata*. Bologna: Il Mulino, 2006.

Ferrera, Maurizio. 'The 'southern model' of welfare in social Europe'. *Journal of European Social Policy*, 6 (1996) 1, 17-37.

Ferro, Marc. (With the participation of de Sampigny, Serge). *Pétain. Les leçons de l'histoire*. Paris: Tallandier, 2016.

Feuillet-Liger, Brigitte and Portier, Philippe, eds. *Droit étique et religion. De l'âge théologique à l'âge bioétique*. Bruxelles: Bruylant, 2011.

Feuillet-Liger, Brigitte and Portier, Philippe. 'Religion et bio-droit en France. Vers une post-sécularité juridique?' in: Brigitte Feuillet-Liger and Philippe Portier, eds. *Droit étique et religion. De l'âge théologique à l'âge bioétique*. Bruxelles: Bruylant, 343-376.

Fijalkow, Yankel. 'Le tiers secteur associatif dans la régulation de l'habitat en France: Une hypothèse géographique'. *L'information géographique*, 73 (2009) 2, 47-59.

Fillieule, Olivier and Tartakowsky, Danielle. *La Manifestation*. Paris: Presses de Sciences Po, 2013.

Fillon, François. *Faire*. Paris: Albin Michel, 2015.

Fink, Simon. 'Churches as societal veto players'. *West European Politics*, 32 (2009) 1: 77-96.

Fix, Birgit. *Religion und familienpolitik. Deutschland, Belgien, Österreich und die Niederlande im vergleich*. Opladen: Westdeutscher, 2001.

Flora, Peter and Alber, Jens. 'Modernization, Democratization, and the Development of the Welfare State' in: Peter Flora and Arnold J. Heidenheimer, eds. *The Development of Welfare States in Europe and America*. New Brunswick: Transaction, 2005, 37-80.

Flora, Peter and Heidenheimer, Arnold J. 'Introduction' in: Peter Flora and Arnold J. Heidenheimer, eds. *The Development of Welfare States in Europe and America*. New Brunswick: Transaction, 2005, 5-14.

Foret, François. *Religion and Politics in the European Union. The Secular Canopy*. Cambridge: Cambridge University Press, 2014.

Fouilloux, Étienne. *Les chrétiens français entre crise et libération: 1937-1947*. Paris: Seuil, 1997.

Fourquet, Jérôme. '*Les électorats confessionnels à la primaire de la droite: Des choix tranchés*'. *IFOP Focus*, 145 (2016), 1-11. <https://www.ifop.com/wp-content/uploads/2018/03/951-1-document_file.pdf>. (15 September 2021).

Fox, Jonathan. *An Introduction to Religion and Politics. Theory and Practice*. London: Routledge, 2018.

Galant, Henry C. *Histoire politique de la sécurité sociale française, 1945-1952*. Paris: Colin, 1955.

Gamson, William A. and Meyer, David S. 'Framing Political Opportunity' in: Doug McAdam, John D. McCarthy and Mayer N. Zald, eds. *Comparative Perspectives on Social Movements. Political Opportunities, Mobilizing Structures, and Cultural Framings*. Cambridge: Cambridge University Press, 1996, 275-290.

Garbagnoli, Sara. 'Italy as a Lighthouse. Anti-Gender Protests between the 'Anthropological Question' and National Identity' in: Roman Kuhar and Paternotte David, eds. *Anti-Gender Campaigns in Europe. Mobilizing Against Equality*. London: Rowman & Littlefield International, 2017, 151-173.

Garelli. Franco. *Religion Italian Style. Continuities and Changes in a Catholic Country*. Farnham: Ashgate, 2014.

Gauchet, Marcel. *La religion dans la démocratie. Parcours de la laïcité*. Paris: Gallimard, 2001.

Gauchet, Marcel. *Le désenchantement du monde. Une histoire politique de la religion*. Paris: Gallimard, 2005.

Gauchet, Marcel. *Un monde désenchanté?* Paris: Pocket, 2007.

Gauchet, Marcel. 'Laicitá e ruolo pubblico delle religioni. Postfazione all'edizione italiana de La religione nella democrazia', in: Marcel Gauchet, *La religione nella democrazia*. Bari: Edizioni dedalo, 2009, 143-150.

Gentile, Emilio. *Il fascismo in tre capitoli* Roma: Laterza, 2009.

Gerd-Rainer, Horn and Emmanuel Gerard, eds. *Left Catholicism. Catholics and Society in Western Europe at the Point of Liberation, 1943-1955*. KADOC Studies 25. Leuven: Leuven University Press, 2001.

Gill, Anthony. 'Religion and comparative politics'. *Annual Review of Political Science*, 4 (2001), 117-138.

Gilson, Étienne, ed. *The Church Speaks to the Modern World. The Social Teaching of Leo XIII*. New York: Image books, 1954.

Giugni, Marco G.; McAdam, Doug and Tilly, Charles, eds. *How Social Movements Matter.* Minneapolis: University of Minnesota Press, 1999.

Goguel, François. *Chroniques électorales. 1, La Quatrième République.* Paris: Presses de la Fondation nationale des sciences politiques, 1981.

Goguel, François. 'Christian Democracy in France' in: Mario Einaudi and François Goguel. *Christian Democracy in Italy and France.* Notre Dame: University of Notre Dame Press, 1952, 109-219.

Goldstone, Jack A. 'Introduction: Bridging Institutionalized and Noninstitutionalized Politics' in: Jack A. Glodstone, ed. *States, Parties, and Social Movements.* Cambridge: Cambridge University Press, 2003, 1-26.

Gorski, Philip S. and Altınordu, Ateş. 'After Secularization?'. *Annual Review of Sociology*, 34 (2008), 55-85.

Grenard, Fabrice; Le Bot, Florent and Perrin, Cédric. *Histoire économique de Vichy. L'état, les hommes, les entreprises.* Paris: Perrin, 2017.

Grew, Raymond. 'Suspended Bridges to Democracy. The Uncertain Origins of Christian Democracy in France and Italy' in: Thomas Kselman and Joseph A. Buttigieg, eds. *European Christian Democracy. Historical Legacies and Comparative Perspectives.* Notre Dame: University of Notre Dame Press, 2003, 11-42.

Grzymala-Busse, Anna M. *Nations Under God. How Churches Use Moral Authority to Influence Policy.* Princeton: Princeton University Press, 2015.

Grossman, Emiliano and Saurugger, Sabine. *Les groupes d'intérêt. Action collective et stratégies de représentation.* Paris: Colin, 2012.

Guadagno, Jill. 'Theories of the welfare state'. *Annual Review of Sociology,* 13 (1987), 109-128.

Haarscher, Guy. *La laïcité.* Paris: Presses universitaires de France, 2017.

Habermas, Jürgen. 'Religion in the public sphere'. *European Journal of Philosophy.* 14 (2006) 1, 1-25.

Habermas, Jürgen. *Entre naturalisme et religion. Les défis de la démocratie.* Paris: Gallimard, 2008.

Habermas, Jürgen. 'Notes on post-secular society'. *New Perspectives Quarterly*, 25 (2008) 4, 17-29.

Habermas, Jürgen. '"THE POLITICAL". The National Meaning of a Questionable Inheritance of Political Theology' in: Eduardo Mendieta and Jonathan Vanantwerpen, eds., *The Power of Religion in the Public Sphere.* New York: Columbia University Press, 2011, 15-33.

Haegel, Florence. *Les droites en fusion. Transformations de l'UMP.* Paris: Presses de la Fondation nationale des sciences politiques, 2012.

Halls, Wilfred D. 'Les Catholiques, l'intermède de Vichy, et la suite' in: Sarah Fishman et al., eds., *La France sous Vichy. Autour de Robert O. Paxton.* Bruxelles: Éditions complexe, 2004, 245-259.

Hamon, Hervé and Rotman, Patrick. *La Deuxième gauche. Histoire intellectuelle et politique de la CFDT.* Paris: Seuil, 2002.

Hatzfeld, Henri. *Du pauperisme a la sécurite sociale, 1850-1940. Essai sur les origines de la sécurite sociale en France.* Nancy: Presses universitaires de Nancy, 1989.

Heclo, Hugh. *Modern Social Politics in Britain and Sweden. From Relief to Income Maintenance.* New Haven: Yale University Press, 1974.

Heelas, Paul. *Spiritualities of Life. New Age Romanticism and Consumptive Capitalism.* London: Wiley-Blackwell, 2008.

Hemerijck. Anton. 'Two or Three Waves of Welfare State Transformation?' in: Nathalie Morel, Bruno Palier and Joakim Palme, eds. *Towards a Social Investment Welfare State? Ideas, Policies and Challenges.* Bristol: Policy Press, 2011, 33-60.

Hervieu-Léger, Danièle. *La religion en miettes ou la question des sectes.* Paris: Calmann-Lévy, 1999.

Hervieu-Léger, Danièle. *Le pèlerin et le converti. La religion en mouvement.* Paris: Flammarion, 2001.

Hervieu-Léger, Danièle. *Catholicisme, la fin d'un monde.* Paris: Bayard, 2003.

Hervieu-Léger, Danièle 'Bricolage vaut-il dissémination? Quelques réflexions sur l'opérationnalité sociologique d'une métaphore problématique'. *Social Compass*, 52 (2005) 3, 295-308.

Hervieu-Léger, Danièle (in collaboration with Champion, Françoise). *Vers un nouveau Christianisme? Introduction à la sociologie du Christianisme occidental.* Paris: Éditions du Cerf, 2008.

Hervieu-Léger, Danièle. 'Sécularisation' in: Régine Azria and Danièle Hervieu-Léger, eds. *Dictionnaire des faits religieux.* Paris: Presses universitaires de France, 2010, 1151-1158.

Hesse, Philippe-Jean. 'Les assurances sociales', in: Philippe-Jean Hesse and Jean-Pierre Le Crom, eds. *La Protection sociale sous le régime de Vichy.* Rennes: Presses universitaires de Rennes, 2001, 31-84.

Hesse, Philippe-Jean and Le Crom, Jean-Pierre, eds. *La protection sociale sous le régime de Vichy*. Rennes: Presses universitaires de Rennes, 2001.

Hesse, Philippe-Jean and Le Crom, Jean-Pierre, 'Conclusion' in: Philippe-Jean Hesse and Jean-Pierre Le Crom, eds., *La protection sociale sous le régime de Vichy*. Rennes: Presses universitaires de Rennes, 2001, 355-364.

Hilaire Yves-Marie. 'L'Influence de la Démocratie chrétienne dans la sphère de la religion, la morale et la culture en France' in: Emiel Lamberts, ed. *Christian Democracy in the European Union, 1945-1995. Proceedings of the Leuven Colloquium, 15-18 November 1995*. KADOC Studies 21. Leuven: Leuven University Press, 1997, 427-446.

Hoffman, Stanley. 'Aspects du régime de Vichy'. *Revue francaise de science politique*, 6 (1956) 1, 44-69.

Horn, Gerd-Rainer. *The Spirit of Vatican II. Western European Progressive Catholicism in the Long Sixties*. Oxford: Oxford University Press, 2015.

Hornsby-Smith, Michael P. 'The Catholic Church and Social Policy in Europe' in: Prue Chamberlayne et al., eds. *Welfare and Culture in Europe. Towards a New Paradigm in Social Policy*. London: Kingsley Publishers, 1999, 172-189.

Hornsby-Smith, Michael P. *An Introduction to Catholic Social Thought*. Cambridge: Cambridge University Press, 2006.

Huber, Evelyne and Stephens, John D. 'Welfare State and Production Regimes in the Era of Retrenchment' in: Paul Pierson, ed. *The New Politics of the Welfare State*. Oxford: Oxford University Press, 2001, 107-145.

Huber, Evelyne and Stephens, John D. *Development and Crisis of the Welfare State. Parties and Policies in Global Markets*. Chicago: Chicago University Press, 2001.

Huber, Evelyne, Ragin, Charles and Stephens, John D. 'Social democracy, Christian democracy, constitutional structure, and the welfare state'. *American Journal of Sociology*, 99 (1993) 3, 711-749.

Imbert, Jean. *Les hôpitaux en France*. Paris: Presses universitaires de France, 1996.

Inglehart, Ronald F. *Religion's Sudden Decline. What's Causing it, and What Comes Next?* Oxford: Oxford University Press, 2021.

Ion, Jacques. *S'Engager dans une société d'individus*. Paris: Colin, 2012.

Irving, Ronald E. M. *Christian Democracy in France*. London: Allen and Unwin, 1973.

Jabbari, Eric. *Pierre Laroque and the Welfare State in Post-war France*. Oxford: Oxford University Press, 2012.

Jackson, Julian. 'Vichy and Fascism' in: Arnold Edward J., ed. *The Development of the Radical Right in France. From Boulanger to Le Pen*. London: Palgrave Macmillan, 2000, 153–171.

Jennings, Éric T. 'Discours corporatiste, propagande nataliste, et contrôle social sous Vichy'. *Revue d'histoire moderne & contemporaine*, 49 (2002) 4, 101-131.

Jobert, Bruno and Muller, Pierre. *L'État en action. Politiques publiques et corporatismes*. Paris: Presses universitaires de France, 1987.

Joly, Laurent. *L'État contre les Juifs. Vichy, les Nazis et la persécution antisémite, 1940–1944*. Paris: Flammarion, 2020.

Jordan, Jason. (2016). 'Religion and inequality: The lasting impact of religious traditions and institutions on welfare state development'. *European Political Science Review*, 8 (2016) 1, 25-48.

Julliard, Jacques. 'Sur un fascisme imaginaire: Á propos d'un livre de Zeev Sternhell'. *Annales. Économie, sociétés, civilisations*, 39 (1984) 4, 849-861.

Julliard, Jacques. *Les gauches françaises. Histoire, politique et imaginaire, 1762-2012*. Paris: Flammarion, 2012.

Kahl, Sigrun. 'The religious roots of modern poverty policy: Catholic, Lutheran, and Reformed Protestant traditions compared'. *European Journal of Sociology*, 46 (2005) 1, 91-126.

Kalyvas, Stathis N. *The Rise of Christian Democracy in Europe*. Ithaca: Cornell University Press, 1996.

Kalyvas, Stathis N. 'Unsecular Politics and Religion Mobilization' in: Thomas Kselman and Joseph A. Buttigieg, eds. *European Christian Democracy. Historical Legacies and Comparative Perspectives*. Notre Dame: University of Notre Dame Press, 2003, 293-320.

Kalyvas, Stathis N. and Van Kersbergen, Kees. 'Christian democracy'. *Annual Review of Political Science*, 13 (2010), 183-209.

Kaufmann, Franz-Xaver. 'Les état providence européens dans leur rapport avec la famille' in: Jacques Commaille and François de Singly, eds. *La question familiale en Europe*. Paris: L'Harmattan, 1997, 121-136.

Kerschen, Nicole. 'L'influence du rapport Beveridge sur le plan français de sécurité sociale de 1945'. *Revue française de science politique*, 45 (1995) 4, 570-595.

Kim, Andrew. *An Introduction to Catholic Ethics since Vatican II.* Cambridge: Cambridge University Press, 2015.

Knill, Cristoph. 'The study of morality policy: Analytical implications from a public policy perspective'. *Journal of European Public Policy,* 20 (2013) 3, 309-317.

Knill, Cristoph; Adam, Christian, and Hurka, Steffen, eds. *On the Road to Permissiveness? Change and Covergence of Moral Regulation in Europe.* Oxford: Oxford University Press, 2015.

Knill, Cristoph; Preidel, Caroline and Nebel, Kerstin. 'Brake rather than barrier: The impact of the Catholic Church on morality policies in Western Europe'. *West European Politics,* 37 (2014) 5, 845-866.

Knill, Cristoph, et al. 'Religious tides: The time-variant effect of religion on morality policies', *Regulation & Governance,* 14 (2020) 2, 256-270.

Kocher-Marbœuf, Éric. *Le patricien et le général. Jean-Marcel Jeanneney et Charles de Gaulle, 1958-1969.* Paris: Comité pour l'histoire économique et financière de la France, 2003.

Korpi, Walter. *Working Class in Welfare Capitalism. Work, Unions and Politics in Sweden.* London: Routledge and Kegan Paul, 1978.

Korpi, Walter. *The Democratic Class Struggle.* London: Routledge & Kegan Paul, 1983.

Korpi, Walter. 'Un état-providence contesté et fragmenté. Le développment de la citoyenneté sociale en France. Comparaisons avec la Belgique, l'Allemagne, l'Italie et la Suède'. *Revue francaise de science politique,* 45 (1995) 4, 632-667.

Korpi, Walter. 'Power resources and employer-centered approaches in explanations of welfare states and varieties of capitalism. Protagonists, consenters, and antagonists'. *World Politics,* 58 (2006) 2, 167-206.

Kuhar, Roman. 'Playing with science: Sexual citizenship and the Roman Catholic Church counter- narratives in Slovenia and Croatia'. *Women's Studies International Forum,* 49 (2015), 84-92.

Kuhar, Roman and Paternotte, David, eds. *Anti-Gender Campaigns in Europe. Mobilizing against Equality.* London: Rowman & Littlefield, 2017.

Kuisel, Richard. *Capitalism and the State in Modern France. Renovation and Economic Management in the Twentieth Century.* Cambridge: Cambridge University Press, 1981.

Kuru, Ahmet T. 'Passive and assertive secularism: Historical conditions, ideological struggles, and state policies toward religion'. *World Politics,* 59 (2007) 4, 568-594

Lacroix, Jean. 'Les Catholiques et la politique'. *Esprit,* 13 (1945) 6, 70-78.

Landron, Olivier. *À la droite du Christ. Les Catholiques traditionnels en France depuis le Concile Vatican II, 1965-2015.* Paris: Éditions du Cerf, 2015.

Larkin, Maurice. *Religion, Politics and Preferment in France since 1890. La Belle Époque and Its Legacy.* Cambridge: Cambridge University Press, 1995.

Laroque, Michel, ed. *La sécurité sociale, son histoire à travers les textes. Tome VI, 1981-2005.* Paris: Association pour l'étude de l'histoire de la sécurité sociale, 2005.

Laroque, Pierre. 'Le plan française de sécurité sociale'. *Revue française du travail,* 1 (1946) 1, 9-20.

Laroque, Pierre. 'De l'assurance sociale à la sécurité sociale. L'experience française'. *Revue internationale de travail,* LVLL (1948) 6, 621-649.

Laroque, Pierre. 'La sécurité sociale dans l'économie française'. *Droit Social,* 11 (1948) 8: 306-309.

Laroque, Pierre. 'La sécurité sociale dans l'économie française'. *Droit Social,* 11 (1948) 9: 347-350.

Laroque, Pierre. *Au service de l'homme et du droit. Souvenirs et Réflexions.* Paris: Association pour l'étude de l'histoire de la sécurité sociale, 1993.

Launay, Michel. *Le syndicalisme chrétien en France: de 1885 à nos jours.* Paris: Desclée, 1984.

Le Bras, Gabriel. *Introduction à l'histoire de la pratique religieuse en France.* Paris: Presses universitaires de France, 1942.

Le Bras, Gabriel. Études de sociologie religieuse. Paris: Presses universitaires de France, 1955.

Le Bras, Hervé and Todd, Emmanuel. *Le mystère français.* Paris: Seuil, 2013.

Leclerc, Pierre, ed. *La sécurité sociale, son histoire à travers les textes. Tome II, 1870-1945.* Paris: Association pour l'étude de l'histoire de la sécurité sociale, 1996.

Le Crom, Jean-Pierre. *Syndicats, nous voilà! Vichy et le corporatisme.* Paris: Éditions de l'atelier, 1995.

Le Crom, Jean-Pierre. 'Trade Unions and Labour Law in France during the Second World War' In: Irene Stolzi, ed. *Unions and Labour-law between Dictatorships and Democracies in Mediterranean and Latin Europe of XX Century.* Milan: Giuffrè, 2019, 103-121.

Lee, Daniel. Pétain's Jewish Children. French Jewish Youth and the Vichy Regime, 1940-1942. Oxford: Oxford University Press, 2014.

Lee Downs, Laura. "And so we transform a people': Women's social action and the reconfiguration of politics on the right in France, 1934–1947', Past & Present, 225, (2014), 187–225.

Lenoir, Remi. 'L'effondrement des bases sociales du familialisme'. *Actes de la recherche en sciences sociales*, 57 (1985) 57-58, 69-88.

Lenoir, Remi. 'Family Policy in France since 1938' in: John S. Ambler, ed. *The French Welfare State. Surviving Social and Ideological Change*. New York: New York University Press, 1991, 144-186.

Lenoir, Remi. *Généalogie de la morale familiale*. Paris: Seuil, 2003.

Le Puill, Gérard and Le Puill, Stéphane. *La décennie des nouveaux pauvres*. Paris: Messidor/Éditions sociales, 1990.

Lequesne, Christian and Rivaud, Philippe. 'Les comités d'experts indépendants. L'expertise au service d'une démocratie supranationale?' *Revue française de science politique*, 51 (2001) 6, 867-880.

Letamendia, Pierre. *Le Mouvement républicain populaire. Histoire d'un grand parti français*. Paris: Beauchesne, 1995.

Le van-Lemesle, Lucette and Zancarini-Fournel, Michelle. 'Moderniser le travail. Temps de travail, conceptions de l'entreprise et lois sociales' in: Serge Berstein, Pierre Milza and Jean-Louis Bianco, eds. *Les années Mitterrand. Les années du changement, 1981-1984*. Paris: Perrin, 531-547.

Levillain, Philippe. 'La Pensée sociale du général de Gaulle Face à l'héritage du Catholicisme social' in: Robert Vandenbussche, Jean-François Sirinelli and Marc Sadoun, eds. *La politique sociale du général de Gaulle*. Lille: Publications de l'Institut de recherches historiques du septentrion, 1990, 41-50.

Lévy, Jean-Pierre and Fijalkow, Yankel. 'Les poliques du logement' in: Olivier Borraz and Virginie Guiraudon, eds. *Poliques publiques 2. Changer la société*. Paris: Presses de la Fondation nationale des sciences politiques, 2010, 113-138.

Levy, Jonah D. 'Vice into virtue? Progressive politics and welfare reform in continental Europe'. *Politics & Society*, 27 (1999) 2, 239-273.

Levy, Jonah D. 'France: Directing Adjustment?' in: Fritz W. Scharpf and Vivien A. Schmidt, eds. *Welfare and Work in the Open Economy. Volume II*. Oxford: Oxford University Press, 2003, 308-350.

Lipset, Seymour M. and Rokkan, Stein. *Party Systems and Voter Alignments: Cross-National Perspectives*. New York: Free Press, 1967.

Luckmann, Thomas. *The Invisible Religion. The Problem of Religion in Modern Society*. New York: Macmillan, 1967.

Luft, Aliza. 'Religion in Vichy France: How meso-level actors contribute to authoritarian legitimation'. *European Journal of Sociology*, 61 (2020) 1, 67-101.

Lustig, Andrew. 'Beginning of Life', in: Michael D. Palmer and Stanley M. Burgess, eds. *The Wiley-Blackwell Companion to Religion and Social Justice*. Oxford: Blackwell, 2012, 547-560.

Lynch, Julia. `Italy: A Christian Democratic or Clientelist Welfare State?` in: Kees Van Kersbergen and Philip Manow, eds. *Religion, Class Coalitions and Welfare Regimes*. Cambridge: Cambridge University Press, 2009, 91-118.

Madeley, John T. S. 'Religion and the Welfare State' in: Richard F. Tomasson, ed. *The Welfare State, 1883-1983*. Comparative Social Research 6. Greenwich and London: Jai Press, 1983, 43-49.

Manow, Philip. 'The "good, the bad and the ugly": Esping-Andersen's welfare state typology and the religious roots of the Western welfare state', *MPIfG working paper 04/3*, (2004). <https://www.econstor.eu/bitstream/10419/44286/1/644389354.pdf > (10 October 2021).

Manow, Philip and Palier, Bruno. 'A Conservative Welfare State Regime without Christian Democracy? The French État-providence, 1880-1960' in: Kees Van Kersbergen and Philip Manow, eds. *Religion, Class Coalitions and Welfare Regimes*. Cambridge: Cambridge University Press, 2009, 146-175.

Manow, Philip and Van Kersbergen, Kees. 'Religion and the Western Welfare State – The Theoretical Context' in: Kees Van Kersbergen and Philip Manow, eds. *Religion, Class Coalitions and Welfare Regimes*. Cambridge: Cambridge University Press, 2009, 4-37.

Manuel, Christopher P. and Glatzer, Miguel, eds. *Faith-based Organizations and Social Welfare. Associational Life and Religion in Contemporary Western Europe*. London: Palgrave Macmillan, 2019.

Maritain, Jacques. *Christianisme et démocratie*. New York: Éditions de la Maison française, 1943.

Martin, Claude. 'Les politiques de la famille' in: Olivier Borraz and Virginie Guiraudon, eds. *Poliques publiques. 2, Changer la société*. Paris: Presses de la Fondation nationale des sciences politiques, 2010, 31-56.

Martin, David. *A General Theory of Secularization*. Oxford: Blackwell, 1978.

Marzouki, Nadia; McDonnell, Duncan and Roy, Olivier, eds. *Saving the People. How Populist Hijack Religion*. London: Hurst & Co, 2016.

Mason, Timothy W. *Nazism, Fascism and the Working Class*. Cambridge: Cambridge University Press, 1996.

Mayeur, Jean-Marie. *Des partis catholiques à la démocratie chrétienne: XIXe-XXe siècles*. Paris: Colin, 1980.

Mayeur, Jean-Marie. 'Les démocrates d'inspiration chrétienne'. *Mélanges de l'Ecole française de Rome. Moyen-age, temps modernes*, 95 (1983) 2: 117-125.

Mayeur, Jean-Marie. *Catholicisme social et démocratie chrétienne. Principes romains, expériences françaises*. Paris: Éditions du Cerf, 1986.

Michel, Henri. *Les courants de pensée de la Résistance*. Paris: Presses universitaires de France, 1962.

Michelat, Guy. 'Ce que se dire Catholique veut dire. Les Facettes de l'appartenance au Catholicisme' in: Guy Michelat et al., eds. *Les Français sont-ils encore Catholiques?* Paris: Éditions du Cerf, 1991, 129-209.

Michelat, Guy and Dargent, Claude. 'Système symbolique catholique et comportements électoraux'. *Revue française de science politique*, 65 (2015) 1, 27-60.

Michelat, Guy; Potel, Julien and Sutter, Jacques. *L'Héritage chrétien en disgrâce*. Paris: L'Harmattan, 2003.

Michelat, Guy and Simon, Michel. *Classe, religion et comportement politique*. Paris: Presses de la Fondation nationale des sciences politiques, 1977.

Milza, Pierre. *Fascisme français. Passé et présent*. Paris: Flammarion, 1987.

Minonzio, Jérôme and Vallat Jean-Philippe. 'L'Union Nationale des Associations Familiales (UNAF) et les politiques familiales. Crises et transformations de la représentation des intérêts familiaux en France'. *Revue française de science politique*, 56 (2006) 2: 205-226.

Misner, Paul. *Social Catholicism in Europe. From the Onset of Industrialization to the First World War*. New York: Crossroad, 1991.

Misner, Paul. 'Christian Democracy Social Policy: Precedents for Third-Way Thinking' in: Thomas Kselman and Joseph A. Buttigieg, eds. *European Christian Democracy. Historical Legacies and Comparative Perspectives*. Notre Dame: University of Notre Dame Press, 2003, 68-92.

Morgan, Kimberley J. 'Forging the frontiers between state, church and family: Religious cleavages and the origins of early childhood education in France, Sweden, and Germany'. *Politics & Society*, 30 (2002) 1, 113-148.

Morgan, Kimberley J. 'The politics of mothers' employment: France in Comparative Perspective'. *World Politics*, 55 (2003) 2, 259-289.

Morgan, Kimberly J. *Working Mothers and the Welfare State*. Stanford: Stanford University Press, 2007.

Morgan, Kimberly J. 'The Religious Foundations of Work-Family Policies in Western Europe' in: Kees Van Kersbergen and Philip Manow, eds. *Religion, Class Coalitions and Welfare Regimes*. Cambridge: Cambridge University Press, 2009, 56-90.

Mouffe, Chantal. 'Democracy Revisited (in conversation with Chantal Mouffe)' in: Markus Miessen, ed. *The Nightmare of Participation. Crossbench Praxis as a Mode of Criticality*. New York: Sternberg, 2010, 105-159.

Mounier, Emmanuel. 'Tâches actuelles d'une pensée d'inspiration personnaliste'. *Esprit*, 16 (1948) 11, 679-708.

Mounier, Emmanuel. *Le Personnalisme*. Paris: Presses universitaires de France, 1951.

Mounier, Frédéric. *L'amour, le sexe et les Catholiques*. Paris: Centurion, 1994.

Mudde, Cas and Rovira Kaltwasser, Cristóbal. 'Populism', in Freeden Tower Sarget L. and Stears M. eds., *The Oxford Handbook of Political Ideologies*. Oxford: Oxford University Press, 2013, 493-512.

Nizey, Jean (with the collaboration of Chauvière, Michel). 'Le MPF à Vichy à travers les Conseils nationaux 1940-1943', in: Groupement pour la recherche sur les Mouvements familiaux, eds. *L'Action familiale ouvrière et la politique de Vichy. Monde ouvrier et la presse des mouvements familiaux populaires. Être femme, être militante au Mouvemnt populaire des familles*. Forest-sur-Marque: Groupement pour la recherche sur les Mouvements familiaux, 1985, 27-69.

Norris, Pippa and Inglehart, Ronald. *Sacred and Secular. Religion and Politics Worldwide*. Cambridge: Cambridge University Press, 2004.

O'Brien, David J. and Shannon, Thomas A. *Catholic Social Thought. Encyclicals and Documents from Pope Leo XIII to Pope Francis*. Maryknoll: Orbis Books, 2016.

Opielka, Michael. 'Christian Foundations of the Welfare State: Strong Cultural Values in Comparative Perspective' in: Wim van Oorschot, Michael Opielka and Birgit Pfau-Effinger, eds. *Culture and Welfare State. Values and Social Policy in Comparative Perspective*. Cheltenham: Edward Elgar, 2008, 89-114.

Outshoorn, Joyce. 'The Stability of Compromise' in: Marianne Githens and Dorothy McBride Stetson, eds. *Abortion Politics. Public Policy in Cross-Cultural Perspective*. London: Routledge, 1996, 145-164.

Ozzano, Luca and Giorgi, Alberta. *European Culture Wars and the Italian Case. Which Side Are You On?* London: Routledge, 2015.

Palier, Bruno. *Gouverner la sécurité sociale. Les réformes du système srançais de protection sociale depuis 1945*. Paris: Presses universitaires de France, 2005.

Palier, Bruno. 'Ordering Change: Understanding the 'Bismarckian' Welfare Reform Trajectory' in: Bruno Palier, ed. *A long Goodbye to Bismarck? The Politics of Welfare Reforms in Continental Europe*. Amsterdam: Amsterdam University Press, 2010, 19-44.

Parsons, Wayne D. *Public Policy. An Introduction to the Theory and Practice of Policy Analysis*. London: Edward Elgar, 1996.

Pasture, Patrick. 'The April 1944 *social pact* in Belgium and its significance for the post-war welfare state'. *Journal of Contemporary History*, 28 (1993) 4, 695-714.

Pasture, Patrick. *Histoire du syndicalisme chrétien international. La difficile recherche d'une troisième voie*. Paris: L'Harmattan, 1999.

Pasture, Patrick. 'Multi-faceted Relations between Christian Trade Unions and Left Catholics in Europe', in Gerd-Rainer Horn and Emmanuel Gerard, eds. *Left Catholicism, 1943-1955. Catholics and Society in Western Europe at the Point of Liberation*. KADOC Studies 25. Leuven: Leuven University Press, 2001, 228-246.

Pasture, Patrick. 'Syndicats et associations en France et en Europe, une interrogation sur les originalités françaises' in: Danielle Tartakowsky and Françoise Tétard, eds. *Syndicats et associations. Concurrence ou complémentarité?* Rennes: Presses universitaire de Rennes, 2006, 469-475.

Pasture, Patrick. 'Religion in Contemporary Europe. Contrasting Perceptions and Dynamics', *Archiv für sozialgeschichte*, 49 (2009), 319-350.

Pasture, Patrick. 'Christianity in a detraditionalising world: A historical-anthropological interpretation of the transformations in Europe since the 1950s'. *Kyrkohistorisk Årsskrift*, 110 (2010), 113-127.

Pasture, Patrick and Kenis, Leo. 'The Transformation of Christian Churches in Western Europe. An Introduction' in: Leo Kenis, Jaak Billiet and Patrick Pasture, eds. *The Transformation of the Christian Churches in Western Europe, 1945-2000*. KADOC Studies 6. Leuven: Leuven University Press, 2010, 7-19.

Paternotte, David; van der Dussen, Sophie and Piette, Valérie, eds. *Habemus gender! Déconstruction d'une riposte religieuse*. Bruxelles: Éditions de l'Université de Bruxelles, 2015.

Paxton, Robert O. *La France de Vichy, 1940-1944*. Paris: Seuil, 1997.

Pedersen, Susan. *Family, Dependence, and the Origins of the Welfare State. Britain and France, 1914-1945*. Cambridge: Cambridge University Press, 1993.

Pelletier, Denis. *Les Catholiques en France depuis 1985*. Paris: La Découverte, 1997.

Pelletier, Denis. *La crise catholique. Religion, société, politique en France (1968-1978)*. Paris: Payot, 2002.

Pelletier, Denis. 'Introduction. Les chrétiens de l'autre bord', in: Denis Pelletier and Jean-Louis Schlegel, eds. *À la gauche du Christ. Les chrétiens de gauche en France de 1945 à nos jours*. Paris: Seuil, 2012, 7-14.

Pelletier, Denis. 'Les évêques de France et la République de l'intime -1968-2005' in: Céline Béraud, Frédéric Gugelot and Isabelle Saint-Martin, eds. *Catholicisme en tensions*. Paris: Éditions de l'École des hautes études en sciences sociales, 2012, 179-189.

Pelletier, Denis and Schlegel, Jean-Louis, eds. *À la gauche du Christ. Les chrétiens de gauche en France de 1945 à nos jours*. Paris: Seuil, 2012.

Peschanski, Denis. *Vichy 1940-1944. Contrôle et exclusion*. Bruxelles: Éditions complexe, 1997.

Petitfils, Jean-Christian. *Le gaullisme*. Paris: Presses universitaires de France, 1994.

Pierson, Paul. 'The new politics of the welfare state'. *World Politics*, 48 (1996) 2, 143-179.

Pierson, Paul. 'Irresistible forces, immovable objects: Post-industrial welfare states confront permanent austerity'. *Journal of European Public Policy*, 5 (1998) 4, 539-560.

Pierson, Paul, ed. *The New Politics of the Welfare State*. Oxford: Oxford University Press, 2001.

Piketty, Thomas and Zucman, Gabriel. 'Capital is back: Wealth-income ratios in rich countries 1700-2010'. *The Quarterly Journal of Economics*, 129 (2014) 3, 1255-1310.

Pollard, John F. 'Corporatism and Political Catholicism: The Impact of Catholic Corporatism in Inter-war Europe' in: Antonio Costa Pinto, ed. *Corporatism and Fascism: The Corporatist Wave in Europe*. London: Routledge, 2017, 42-59.

Pollard, John F. 'Fascism and Catholicism' in: Richard J. B. Bosworth, ed. *The Oxford Handbook of Fascism*. Oxford: Oxford University Press, 2010, 166-184.

Portier, Philippe. 'Le général de Gaulle et le Catholicisme. Pour une autre interprétation de la pensée gaullienne'. *Revue historique*, 602 (1997) 1, 533-562.

Portier, Philippe. *État et les religions en France. Une sociologie historique de la laïcité*. Rennes: Presses universitaires de Rennes, 2016.

Portier, Philippe. 'Norme démocratique et loi naturelle dans le Catholicisme contemporain. Retour sur la mobilisation contre le «mariage pour tous»'. *Société, droit et religion*, 1 (2016) 6, 39-54.

Portier, Philippe. *Un siècle de construction sociale. Une histoire de la Confédération française des travailleurs chrétiens*. Paris: Flammarion, 2019.

Portier, Philippe and Willaime, Jean-Paul. *La religion dans la France contemporaine: Entre sécularisation et recomposition*. Paris: Armand Colin, 2021.

Poucet, Bruno. *L'enseignement privé en France*. Paris: Presses universitaires de France, 2012.

Poulat, Èmile. *Une Église ébranlée. Changement, conflit et continuité, de Pie XII à Jean-Paul II*. Tournai: Casterman, 1980.

Poulat, Èmile. *Liberté, laïcité. La guerre des deux France et le principe de la modernité*. Paris: Éditions du Cerf/Cujas, 1988.

Poulat, Èmile. *L'ère postchrétienne. Un monde sorti de dieu*. Paris: Flammarion, 1994.

Poulat, Èmile. *Où va le Christianisme? À l'aube du IIIe millénaire*. Paris: Plon, 1996.

Poulat, Émile. *Aux carrefours stratégiques de l'Église de France xxe siècle*. Paris: Berg International, 2009.

Poulat, Émile. *Notre laïcité! Ou les religions dans l'espace public*. Paris: Desclée de Brouwer, 2014.

Pouthier, Jean-Luc. 'Émergence et ambiguïtés de la culture politique démocrate-chrétienne' in: Serge Berstein, ed. *Les cultures politiques en France*. Paris: Seuil, 303-334.

Raison du Cleuziou, Yann. *Une contre-révolution catholique. Aux origines de La Manif pour Tous*. Paris: Seuil, 2019.

Ranci, Costanzo. *Il volontariato. Volti della solidarietá*. Bologna: Il Mulino, 2006.

Rathbone, Keith. 'Athletes for France or athletes for the church: Conflict between sports officials and Catholic sportsmen during the Vichy regime (1940-1944)'. *French History*, 33 (2019) 1, 88-109.

Reisebrodt, Martin. 'Religion in the modern world: Between secularization and resurgence', *Max Weber Lecture Series 1*, (2014). <https://cadmus.eui.eu/bitstream/handle/1814/29698/MWP_LS_2014_01_Riesebrodt.pdf?sequence=1&isAllowed=y>. (11 June 2020).

Rémond, René. *Les crises du Catholicisme en France dans les années trente*. Paris: Seuil, 1979.

Rémond, René. *Les droites en France*. Paris: Aubier Montaigne, 1982.

Rémond, René. 'Introduction' in: Robert Vandenbussche; Jean-François, Sirinelli and Marc, Sadoun, eds. *La politique sociale du général de Gaulle*. Lille: Publications de l'Institut de recherches historiques du septentrion, 1990, 7-12.

Rémond, René. *Le Catholicisme français et la société politique. Écrits de circonstance, 1947-1991*. Paris: Les Éditions de l'Atelier, 1995.

Rémond, René. *Religion et société en Europe. Essai sur la sécularisation des sociétés européennes aux XIXe et XXe siècles, 1789-1998*. Paris: Seuil, 2001.

Rémond, René. *Les droites aujourd'hui*. Paris: Seuil, 2007.

Rémond, René, 'Un chapitre inachevé (1958-1990)' in: René Rémond, ed. *Histoire de la France religieuse. Tome 4. Société sécularisée et renouveaux religieux (xxe siècle)*. Paris: Seuil, 1992. 347-459.

Riboud, Michelle. 'An analysis of women's labor force participation in France: Cross-section estimates and time-series evidence'. *Journal of Labor Economics*, 3(1985) 1, S177-S200.

Rimlinger, Gaston V. *Welfare Policy and Industrialization in Europe, America and Russia*. New York: John Wiley and Sons, 1971.

Roméro, Jean-Luc. *Homopoliticus. 'Comme ils disent': 2013, le mariage pour tous?* Paris: EGL-La Cerisaie, 2012.

Rosanvallon, Pierre. 'L'identité CFDT'. *Esprit*, 40 (1980) 4, 9-14.

Rosanvallon, Pierre. *La nouvelle question sociale. Repenser l'état-providence*. Paris: Seuil, 1998.

Rosanvallon, Pierre. *La contre-démocratie. La politique à l'âge de la défiance*. Paris: Points, 2014.

Rouilleault, Henri. *Où va la démocratie sociale?* Paris: Éditions de l'atelier, 2010.

Roussellier, Nicolas, 'Un pouvoir présidentiel encombré de sa force' in: Olivier Duhamel et al., eds. *La Ve République démystifiée*. Paris: Presses de la Fondation nationale des sciences politiques, 2019, 11-35.

Saresella, Daniela. *Cattolici a sinistra. Dal modernismo ai giorni nostri*. Roma: Laterza, 2011.

Sarkozy, Nicolas. *La République, les religions, l'espérance. Entretiens avec Thibaud Collin et Philippe Verdin*. Paris: Éditions du Cerf, 2004.

Sartori, Giovanni. 'Comparing and miscomparing'. *Journal of Theoretical Politics*, 3 (1991) 3, 243-257.

Saudejaud, Carole. *Le syndicalisme chrétien sous l'Occupation*. Paris: Perrin, 1999.

Sauvy, Alfred. *La vie économique des Français de 1939 à 1945*. Paris: Flammarion, 1978.

Scharpf, Fritz W. and Schmidt, Vivien A., eds. *Welfare and Work in the Open Economy. Volume II*. Oxford: Oxford University Press, 2003.

Schlegel, Jean-Louis. 'Conclusion. Les Leçons d'une Histoire' in: Denis Pelletier and Jean-Louis Schlegel, eds. *À la gauche du Christ. Les chrétiens de gauche en France de 1945 à nos jours*. Paris: Seuil, 2012, 577-587.

Schmid, Josef. 'Two steps forward – one step back? Some critical comments on F. G. Castles' "On religion and public policy: Does Catholicism make a difference?"'. *European Journal of Political Research*, 30 (1996) 1, 103-109.

Scott, John. *A Matter of Record. Documentary Sources in Social Research*. Cambridge: Polity Press in association with Blackwell, 1991.

Seeleib-Kaiser, Martin; van Dyk, Silke and Roggenkamp, Martin. *Party Politics and Social Welfare. Comparing Christian and Social Democracy in Austria, Germany and the Netherlands*. Cheltenham: Edward Elgar, 2008.

Sirinelli, Jean-François. *La Ve République*. Paris: Presses universitaires de France, 2018.

Slama, Alain-Gérard. 'Vichy était-il fasciste?' *Vingtième siècle. Revue d'histoire*, 11 (1986) 11, 41-54.

Smith, Timothy B. *Creating the Welfare State in France, 1880-1940*. Montreal: Mc Gill-Queen's University Press, 2003.

Smith, Timothy B. *France in Crisis. Welfare, Inequality and Globalization since 1980*. Cambridge: Cambridge University Press, 2004.

Smith, Timothy B. 'The Two World Wars and Social Policy in France' in: Herbert Obinger, Klaus Petersen and Peter Starke, eds. *Warfare and Welfare. Military Conflict and Welfare State Development in Western Countries*. Oxford: Oxford University Press, 2018, 127-148.

Soucy, Robert. *French Fascism. The Second Wave, 1933-1939*. New Haven: Yale University Press, 1995.

Soulage, Vincent. 'L'engagement politique des chrétiens de gauche, entre Parti socialiste, deuxième gauche et gauchisme' in: Denis Pelletier and Jean-Louis Schlegel, eds. *À la gauche du Christ. Les chrétiens de gauche en France de 1945 à nos jours*. Paris: Seuil, 2012, 425-455.

Stake, Robert E. 'Case Studies' in: Norman K. Denzim and Yvonna S. Lincoln, eds. *Strategies of Qualitative Inquiry*. London: SAGE, 1998, 86-109.

Stark, Rodney. 'Europe's receptivity to new religious movements: Round two'. *Journal for the Scientific Study of Religion*, 32 (1993) 4, 389-397.

Stark, Rodney. 'Secularization, R.I.P.'. *Sociology of Religion*, 60 (1999) 3, 249-273.

Steck, Philippe. 'Les prestations familiales' in: Michel Laroque, ed. *La sécurité sociale, Son histoire à travers les textes. Tome VI, 1981-2005*. Paris: Association pour l'étude de l'histoire de la sécurité sociale, 2005, 137-189.

Steck, Philippe. 'Partie II. Histoire de 1967-2009' in: Bruno Béthouart and Philippe Steck, eds. *Prestations familales: Une histoire française. Cahier d'histoire de la sécurité sociale n° 6*. Paris: Comité d'histoire de la sécurité sociale, 2012, 175-256.

Stark, Rodney and Finke, Roger. *Acts of Faith. Explaining the Human Side of Religion*. Berkeley: University of California Press, 2000.

Stephens, John D. *The Transition from Capitalism to Socialism*. London: Macmillan, 1979.

Sternhell, Zeev. *Ni droit ni gauche. L'idéologie fasciste en France*. Paris: Gallimard, 2012.

Swidler, Ann. 'Culture in action: Symbols and strategies'. *American Sociological Review*, 51 (1986) 2, 273-286.

Swidler, Ann. 'Foreword' in: Max Weber, *The Sociology of Religion*. Boston: Beacon, 1993, ix-xvii.

Tarrow, Sidney G. *Power in Movement. Social Movements and Contentious Politics*. Cambridge: Cambridge University Press, 2011.

Tartakowsky, Danielle. *Les Droites et la rue. Histoire d'une ambivalence de 1880 à nos jours*. Paris: La Découverte, 2013.

Taylor, Charles. *A Secular Age*. Cambridge: Belknap Press of Harvard University Press, 2007.

Taylor-Goody, Peter. *The Double Crisis of the Welfare State and What We Can Do About It*. London: Palgrave MacMilliam, 2013.

Tchernonog, Viviane et al. *Le paysage associatif français. Mesures et évolutions*. Paris: Dalloz, 2013.

Therborn Göran. 'Another way of taking religion seriously. Comment on Francis G. Castles'. *European Journal of Political Research*, 26 (1994) 1, 103-110.

Therborn, Göran. 'Ambiguous Ideals and Problematic Outcomes. Democracy, Civil Society, Human Rights, and Social Justice' in: Zacher Hans F., ed. *Democracy Reality and Responsibility. The Proceedings of the Sixth Plenary Session of the Pontifical Academy of Social Sciences 23-26 February 2000*. Vatican City: The Pontifical Academy of Social Sciences, 2001, 121-156.

Therborn, Göran. *Between Sex and Power. Family in the World, 1900-2000*. London: Routledge, 2004.

Théry, Irène. *Le démariage. justice et vie privée*. Paris: Odile Jacob, 2001.

Théry, Irène, ed. *Mariage de même sexe et filiation*. Paris: Éditions de l'École des hautes études en sciences sociales, 2013.

Tiberj, Vincent; Bernard, D. and Mayer Nonna. 'Un choix, des logiques multiples. Préférences politiques, espace des possibles et votes en 2012'. *Revue française de science politique*, 63 (2013) 2, 249-279.

Tillich, Paul. *The Courage to Be*. New Haven: Yale University Press, 2014.

Titmuss, Richard M. *Social Policy. An Introduction*. London: Allen and Unwin, 1974.

Toft, Monica D.; Philpott, Daniel and Shah, Timothy S. *God's Century. Resurgent Religion and Global Politics*. New York: Norton & Company, 2011.

Touraine, Alain. 'Face à l'exclusion'. *Esprit*, 169 (1991) 2, 7-13.

Tschannen, Olivier. *Les théories de la sécularisation*. Genève: Droz, 1992.

Ullman, Claire F. *The Welfare State's Other Crisis. Explaining the New Partnership Between Nonprofit Organizations and the State in France*. Bloomington: Indiana University Press, 1998.

Valat, Bruno. *Histoire de la sécurité sociale, 1945-1967. L'État, l'institution et la santé*. Paris: Économica, 2001.

Valat, Bruno and Laroque, Michel. 'La démocratie sociale dans la gestion de la Sécurité sociale de 1945 à 1994'. *Vie sociale*, 10, (2015) 2, 89-107.

Valasik, Corinne. 'Church-State Relations in France in the Field of Welfare: A Hidden Complementarity' in: Anders Bäckström et al., eds. *Welfare and Religion in 21st Century Europe. Volume 1, Reconfiguring the Connections*. Farnham: Ashgate, 2010, 129-145.

Van Kersbergen, Kees. *Social Capitalism. A Study of Christian Democracy and the Welfare State*. London: Routledge, 1995.

Van Kersbergen, Kees. 'The Christian democratic phoenix and modern un-secular politics'. *Party Politics*, 14 (2008) 3, 259-279.

Van Kersbergen, Kees and Manow Philip, eds. *Religion, Class Coalitions and Welfare Regimes*. Cambridge: Cambridge University Press, 2009.

Van Oorschot, Wim; Opielka, Micheal and Pfau-Effinger, Birgit, eds. *Culture and Welfare State. Values and Social Policy in Comparative Perspective*. Cheltenham: Edward Elgar, 2008.

Vaussard, Maurice. *Histoire de la démocratie chrétienne. France, Belgique, Italie*. Paris: Seuil, 1956.

Verloo, Mieke. 'Gender knowledge, and opposition to the feminist project: Extreme-right populist parties in the Netherlands'. *Politics and Governance*, 6 (2018) 3, 20-30.

Vergez-Chaignon, Bénédicte. *Pétain*. Paris: Perrin, 2018.

Vichard, Philippe. 'La loi hospitalière du 21 décembre 1941: Origines, conséquences'. *Histoire des sciences médicales*, XLI (2007) 1, 61-70.

Voicu, Malina. 'Religion and gender across Europe'. *Social Compass*, 56 (2009) 2, 144-162.

Walder, Andrew G. 'Political sociology and social movements'. *Annual Review of Sociology*, 35 (2009) 1, 393-412.

Warner, Carolyn M. *Confessions of an Interest Group. The Catholic Church and Political Parties in Europe*. Princeton: Princeton University Press, 2000.

Weber, Max. *The Sociology of Religion*. Boston: Beacon Press, 1993.

Wilensky, Harold L. 'Leftism, Catholicism and Democratic Comporatism: The Role of Political Parties in Recent State Development' in: Peter Flora and Arnold J. Heidenheimer, eds. *The Development of Welfare States in Europe and America*. New Brunswick: Transaction, 1981, 345-382.

Willaime, Jean-Paul. *Le retour du religieux dans la sphère publique. Vers une laïcité de reconnaissance et de dialogue*. Lyon: Éditions Olivétan, 2008.

Wilson, Bryan R. *Religion in Secular Society. A Sociological Comment*. London: C. A. Watts and Co. Ltd., 1966.

Winock, Michel. *La droite. Hier et aujourd'hui*. Paris: Perrin, 2012.

Winock, Michel. *François Mitterrand*. Paris: Gallimard, 2016.

Winock, Michel. *La France républicaine. Histoire politique XIXe-XXIe siècle*. Paris: Robert Laffont, 2017.

Yin, Robert K. *Case Study Research. Design and Method*. London: SAGE, 2013.

Yip, Andrew K-T. and Page, S-J. *Sexuality and Religious Identities*. Farnham: Ashgate, 2013.

Websites

Communauté de l'Emmanuel. *Qui sommes nous? La Communauté de l'Emmanuel en bref.* <https://emmanuel.info/qui-sommes-nous/>. (10 September 2020).

Emmaüs International. The History of the Emmaüs Movement. <https://www.emmaus-international.org/en/who-are-we/2014-12-03-10-21-24/history-emmaus-movement.html#:~:text=Since%201949%2C%20the%20Emmaus%20movement,of%20those%20without%20a%20voice%E2%80%9D.> (11 January 2022).

Survivants. Notre chance de vivre. <https://les-survivants.com/notre-chance-de-vivre/> (11 January 2022).

Interviews

Archambault Edith, Emeritus Professor Université Paris 1 Panthéon-Sorbonne and Deputy President of the Association pour le Developpement des Données sur l'Economie Sociale, 26 January 2014.

Ariño Philippe, writer and spokesperson of the Manif pour Tous, 25 January 2014.

Austin Michael J, Milton and Florence Krenz Mack Distinguished Professor of Nonprofit Management, School of Social Welfare, University of California Berkeley, 10 March 2010.

Baujard Monique, former Director of the Service National Famille et Société of the Conférence des Évêques de France, 23 July 2014.

Bergounioux Alain, historian and President of the Office Universitaire de Recherche Socialiste, 10 July 2014.

Brunet Jérôme, spokesperson for the Manif pour Tous and President of the association Appel des Professionnels de l'Enfance, 11 February 2014 and 4 July 2014.

Chanu Pierre-Yves, CGT Confederal Advisor on Social Security and President of the Plaftorme Résponsabilité Sociétal des Entreprises, 17 July 2014.

Colin Yves, Director of Communication of FAP, 18 December 2013.

Crépin Annie, Historian and Deputy President of FHEDLES, 19 March 2014.

Delargilliere Anne, volunteer for Secours Catholique 11th arrondissement Paris, 8 October 2013.

De la Rochère Ludovine, President of the Manif pour Tous, 24 March 2014.

Delaume-Myard Jean-Pier, writer and spokesperson for the Manif pour Tous, 24 March 2014.

Favier Anthony, historian and activist of the FHEDLES and David & Jonathan, 19 March 2014.

Gambart Alain, Episcopal Vicar Pastoral de la Santé Paris, 20 November 2012.

Gaymard Hervé, former Secretary of State for Health and Social Security and Minister of Economy, Finance and Industry, 11 November 2011.

Giuglaris Alexandre, researcher at the Direction des Études of the UMP, 18 November 2011.

Kapel Laurent, volunteer of the Secours Catholique 18th arrondissement and Responsible for the thérapie communautaire intégrative, 4 March 2014.

Landete Laurent, former President Communauté de l'Emmanuel, 25 January 2014.

Morel Bruno, Director General of Emmaüs Solidarité, 11 February 2013.

Neiertz Nicolas, Co-president of David & Jonathan (Christian LGBT Movement), 14 January 2014.

Orsoni Annie, Head of the Secours Catholique-Caritas 11th arrondissement of Paris, 21 February 2013.

Porteret Vincent, Delegate General of the Confédération Nationale des Associations Familiales Catholiques, 22 September 2013.

Pruvost Fabrice, researcher at the Institut d'Histoire Sociale of the CGT and member of the CGT, 17 July 2014.

Robert Christophe, Delegate General of the FAP, 18 December 2013.

Roméro Jean-Luc, PS politician and LGBT activist, 12 July 2013.

Toniolo Jean, Deputy Mayor of Homécourt and LGBT activist, 17 December 2012, personal interview.

Vignon Jérôme, former President of the Semaines Sociales de France and President of the Observatoire National de la Pauvreté et de l'Exclusion Sociale, 8 January 2012.

Around forty interviews with participants at the national protest marches against the Taubira Bill in Paris on 13 January 2013 and 24 March 2014. Most of the people that we interviewed preferred to remain anonymous.

Around fifteen interviews with participants at the national march in support of the Taubira Bill in Paris on 17 December 2012.

INDEX OF PERSONS

COLOPHON

FINAL EDITING
Luc Vints

LAY-OUT
Alexis Vermeylen

KADOC
Documentation and Research Center on Religion, Culture and Society
Vlamingenstraat 39
B - 3000 Leuven
www.kadoc.kuleuven.be

Leuven University Press
Minderbroedersstraat 4
B - 3000 Leuven
www.lup.be

23W38860/ T1/ 9789462703889